FREE BOOKS

www.*forgottenbooks*.org

You can read literally <u>thousands</u> of books
for free at www.forgottenbooks.org

(please support us by visiting our web site)

Forgotten Books takes the uppermost care to preserve the entire content of the original book. However, this book has been generated from a scan of the original, and as such we cannot guarantee that it is free from errors or contains the full content of the original. But we try our best!

Truth may seem, but cannot be:
Beauty brag, but 'tis not she;
Truth and beauty buried be.

To this urn let those repair
That are either true or fair;
For these dead birds sigh a prayer.

Bacon

THE LIFE

OF

MAXIMILIEN ROBESPIERRE;

WITH EXTRACTS

FROM HIS

UNPUBLISHED CORRESPONDENCE.

BY G. H. LEWES,

AUTHOR OF "THE BIOGRAPHICAL HISTORY OF PHILOSOPHY," ETC. ETC.

"Cet homme ira loin, car il croit tout ce qu'il dit."—MIRABEAU.

PHILADELPHIA:
CAREY AND HART, PUBLISHERS.
1849.

DEDICATORY PREFACE

SWYNFEN JERVIS, ESQ.

My Dear Sir,

I wish to inscribe your name on this work, not only as a slight tribute of respect and affection, but also because, as your friend Catullus says on a similar occasion:—

"Tu solebas
Meas esse aliquid putare nugas."

And as, with all this good-will, I shall have no more fastidious critic than yourself, to you I may offer the explanations which custom insists upon in prefaces.

There has hitherto been no biography of Robespierre. Notices in Biographical Dictionaries and in Histories of the French Revolution, are the only records of a career which has left so deep an impression upon men's minds. It seemed, therefore, desirable on many accounts, that the materials for a more complete understanding of this remarkable man, scattered through numerous and not easily accessible volumes, should be brought together, and something like a connected view of his career—his opinions—and his acts be given to the public. The Revolution of February, 1848, by once more bringing Robespierre's name and doctrines into alarming prominence, suggested this undertaking; the time which has since elapsed, will show that it has been executed in no unseemly haste.

PREFACE.

The sources from which it has been compiled are as follows:—

I. "Mémoires de Charlotte Robespierre sur ses Deux Frères." Published by Dapormerage, in 1835. (Upon the authenticity of which the *Quarterly Review*, Sept. 1835, should be consulted.)

II. "Mémoires authentiques de Maximilien Robespierre." 2 vols. Paris, 1830.

This pretended autobiography is the production of M. Charles Reybaud—the husband of the charming novelist—and although a scarcely disguised fabrication, contains some authentic biographical materials. It is, however, incomplete, going no further than Sept. 1791.

III. "Papiers Inédits trouvés chez Robespierre." Published by Courtois, with a virulent report.

IV. Montjoie: "Histoire de la conjuration de Robespierre:" one of the many libels published about the "Tyrant."

V. Des Essarts: "Crimes de Robespierre." Ditto.

VI. Vilate: "Causes secrètes de la Rev. du 9 au 10 Thermidor."

Ditto: "Des Mystères de la Mère de Deux Devoiles."

VII. "Biographie Universelle," and "Biographie des Contemporains."

VIII. "The Revolutionary Memoires" (Camille Desmoulins, Mirabeau, Ferrières, Barère, Mad. Roland, Garat, Louvet, Weber, Benseuval, &c.). Published in the collection of Berville et Barrière.

IX. Carlyle, Alison, Thiers, Mignet, Louis Blanc, and Michelet: Histories of the French Revolution.

X. Lamartine: "Histoire des Girondins."

XI. The "Ancien Moniteur."

XII. The long and invaluable "Histoire Parlementaire de la Rev. Franç." By Buckey and Roux.

XIII. "Quarterly Review, Sept. 1835:" An article on Robespierre, written from the Quarterly point of view, but written by one celebrated for his minute and ample knowledge of the period.

In the "British and Foreign Review, July, 1844," there was a vigorous defence of Robespierre, by a writer who had taken great pains to master the subject; but the article contained no new facts.

XIV. MSS. Letters of Robespierre, placed at my disposal by the kindness of my friend M. Louis Blanc.

I have been thus particular in enumerating the sources, because they are rarely mentioned at the bottom of the pages, where to have mentioned them on every occasion would have been needlessly tiresome.

It is only necessary to allude to that tissue of folly and slander which, under the title of the "History of Robespierre, Personal and Political," was published anonymously in London, 1794. I have taken nothing from it but one sample of the slanders.

Before this work was quite completed, I met with the first volume (all published) of a work by Mr. Bronterre O'Brien, the Chartist. The title-page runs thus:—"The Life and Character of Maximilien Robespierre; proving by Facts and Arguments that that much-calumniated Person was one of the greatest of Men and most enlightened of Reformers that ever existed in the World." It would scarcely be becoming in me to pass an opinion on the composition of this work, but I feel bound to quote one typical passage illustrative of the idolatry with which Robespierre is regarded in some quarters:—"The more virtuous," Mr. O'Brien says, "the more magnanimous, the more god-like (!) I prove Robespierre's conduct to have been, the greater will be the horror in which his memory will be held by the upper and the middle classes."

So much for the biographical materials which were accessible to me. There is still a point, however, on which I must be as explicit as possible; viz. the extent of obligation to the works of Louis Blanc, Michelet, and Lamartine. To have cited chapter and verse for every statement or detail drawn from these works would have been to disfigure the page and annoy the reader by useless iteration of the same words. Be it understood, therefore, that in the historical and biographical matter of this volume I have mainly followed the three authors just named, very often using their own language in adopting their views and statements, and completing or modifying what I found there by the facts and details gathered from the other sources previously named. The very popularity of these works exonerates me from any suspicion of a desire to pass off their matter as my own; while, by the course I have adopted, the narrative is made at once briefer and more continuous than if I had balanced authority against authority, and discussed the correctness of contending statements. I will not stop to discuss the question whether such a plan, which would be indefensible in a history, be or be not justifiable in biography. I have only to say that such has been the plan upon which the present work has been mainly compiled.

The care which Lamartine has bestowed upon Robespierre exceeds that of all previous writers, and no one coming after him can hope to add much to those portions of Robespierre's life, traced in "L'Histoire des Girondins." I have ventured to interpret differently some of the facts, and silently to correct some of the errors; but the basis of all the latter portion of Robespierre's Life is taken from Lamartine. Occasionally, also, I have adopted his abridgments of Robespierre's speeches; in these cases they are printed in smaller type.

In a word, my dear sir, you must not criticise this as a work of art, nor as a work of historical pretensions, but simply what it professes to be—a marshaling together of widely-scattered details, so selected as to present a view of the separate phases in the career of a remarkable man, and thus furnishing the data upon which a judgment of him may be formed. Everything known about him is here collected; all his opinions are stated, and the pith and substance of almost all his published speeches translated.

Whatever your judgment—be it approval or be it condemnation—be it whatever may be the interest or the yawns with which you read it,

    Believe me, my dear Sir,
     Very sincerely yours,
      G. H. LEWES.

CONTENTS.

CHAPTER I.

Introduction 13

CHAPTER II.

Birth of Robespierre—His family—Is left an orphan—Protected by the clergy—Anecdotes of his childhood—College friends and studies—Scholastic success—Commences study of the law—State of France—Frivolous occupations of the aristocracy—Skepticism of the epoch 16

CHAPTER III.

The Philosophy of Rousseau 26

CHAPTER IV.

Robespierre returns to Arras — His sister — Mistakes about his obscurity—His first important pleading—The case of M. Vissery's lightning conductor—Robespierre as a poet—Amusing letter—Robespierre at five-and twenty—Les Rosatis—Specimens of his poetry—Academy of Arras—His éloge de Gresset—His first love . . 41

CHAPTER V.

Robespierre named member of the Criminal Court—Resigns, from opposition to capital punishment—"L'Affaire du Collier"—Convocation of the notables—States General—The press loud for liberty—Robespierre's memoir on reform—Opposes his benefactor, the bishop—His pleading Dupond's cause—Writes against "lettres de cachet"—Address to the king—Letter about Canary birds—Chosen as deputy. 55

CONTENTS.

PAGE

CHAPTER VI.

Causes of the Revolution—The Tiers-Etat—Opening of the States-General—Description of Robespierre's appearance—Loyalty of the deputies—Struggle between the court and the Tiers-Etat—Robespierre makes his first motion—Received in silent disdain . . . 63

CHAPTER VII.

Distress of the country—Robespierre bids the clergy sacrifice their superfluities—The "Jeu de Paume"—Attitude of the court—Mirabeau and Robespierre—Troubles of Paris—The Palais Royal: scene in, reported by Desmoulins—The cockade—Apathy of the court—Fall of the Bastille 74

CHAPTER VIII.

Agitation of Paris—Kings learn no lessons from experience—"Not a revolt, a revolution"—The King comes over to the Assembly—New hopes!—Creation of a national guard: Lafayette General—Bailly, Mayor of Paris 87

CHAPTER IX.

Robespierre's energetic protest against the reaction—Horrors commencing: massacres and burnings—Labors of the Assembly—The counter-revolution—Declaration of Rights of Man, compared with that of 1848—Robespierre on the veto—His republicanism becomes avowed—Two of Robespierre's letters—Agitation in Paris respecting the veto—The famine—The insurrection of women . . 93

CHAPTER X.

The Assembly transferred to Paris—The Jacobin Club—Murder of François—Robespierre opposes martial law—Speaks on the distribution of church property—His style of eloquence—Speech on the right of voting—Defends the rights of Jews and comedians—Dr. Guillotin on the penal code—His machine—The King declares himself the friend of the Constitution 109

CHAPTER XI.

Robespierre a rising man—Chateaubriand's description of him—Ridiculed by the deputies—Letters and verses addressed to him—Defends the people—Tribune of the people—Was Robespierre honest?—The federation of mankind: fete of July—The Ca Ira!—The emigration—Robespierre in private—The Jacobin Club: his ascendency there—Speeches in favor of the clergy—The "incorruptible"—The Cordelier's Club 118

CHAPTER XII.

Robespierre's activity in the Assembly—Letter to Camille Desmoulins—Defends the Jews—Elected Secretary of the Assembly and "Juge de District"—Defends Camille—Struggles against Mirabeau—Speaks on the right of the people to choose the form of government—Robespierre challenged by royalists—Oath demanded from the clergy 133

CHAPTER XIII.

Marriage of Camille Desmoulins—The King meditating flight—Robespierre's royalism—The Club des Femmes—Robespierre's speech on the right of emigrating—Death of Mirabeau . . . 142

CHAPTER XIV.

Robespierre's growing importance—Proposes the exclusion of the deputies from the coming Assembly—Speeches on the national guard, capital punishment, and on juries—His philanthropy—Appointed public accuser—Flight of the King—Robespierre's speech on that subject—The captive King—Riot in the Champ de Mars—Cowardice of Robespierre—Termination of the Assembly's labors—Robespierre defends the people and the right of universal suffrage—The King accepts the Constitution—What had the Constituent Assembly effected? 154

CHAPTER XV.

The Legislative Assembly—Robespierre retires to Arras—His reception there—Anecdotes—Returns to Paris—Some account of his private life—His betrothed Eléonore—His amability in society—Anecdote—His friends—Personal traits—Was he a man of no talent?—His power—His eloquence—Madame Roland . . . 179

CONTENTS.

CHAPTER XV*.

Emigration of the nobles—The coalition—Patriots urgent for war: opposed by Robespierre—Quarrel between him and the Girondins—Accused of ambition, and of aspiring to a dictatorship—Robespierre avows his belief in a Providence—His Defenseur de la Constitution—Condemns the bonnet rouge—The mob enter the Tuileries; Louis puts on the bonnet rouge—Robespierre's attack on Lafayette—Arrival of the Marseillais—Plan of their attack—The 10th of August . 194

CHAPTER XVI.

Robespierre after the 10th of August—His flattery of the mob—Appointed President of the Revolutionary Tribunal, but resigns—The Septembrizers: did Robespierre participate in these massacres?—Visit of St. Just to Robespierre on the night of the 2d of September—Robespierre's denial of any participation: his impudent hypocrisy—He is again accused of aspiring to the dictatorship—Marat defends him—Louvet's attack—Robespierre's reply—His Lettres à ses Commettans—His feeling towards the clergy and defence of their interests 212

CHAPTER XVII.

The captive king—Robespierre demands that the king be tried—The trial—The execution—Robespierre's reflections on this deed—His self-glorification—Verses against him 231

CHAPTER XVIII.

Dissension between the Gironde and the Mountain—The date of Robespierre's election into the Revolutionary Tribunal—Meeting of Robespierre and Danton—Robespierre's doctrines—Accusation and triumph of Marat—Robespierre openly attacks the Girondins—Fall of the Gironde—Charlotte Corday: Assassination of Marat—Garat's interview with Robespierre to save the Girondins—Robespierre elected into the Comité de Salut Public—Interview with Danton, whom he promises to defend: his defence—Robespierre as a minister 242

CHAPTER XIX.

Robespierre's task as minister—The Terror—Trial of Marie Antoinette—Trial of the Girondins—The Feast of Reason—Robespierre's

CONTENTS.

PAGE

opposition to it—His reports on the Principles of Government and on Political Morality—His desire for the cessation of the Revolution—His share in the bloodshed exaggerated—Hébert—Robespierre's struggle against the Anarchists—Defence of Danton and Camille—Fall of Hébert—Danton threatened—Robespierre's hypocrisy—Fall of Danton and Camille 259

CHAPTER XX.

The Comité—Robespierre at the height of power—Speaks against the Atheists—Attempt to assassinate him—Festival of the Supreme Being, and Robespierre's discourse—Robespierre weary of the Terror—The law of the 22d Prairial—Robespierre's cowardice—His struggle against his enemies—Catherine Théot—Charlotte Robespierre's letter to Maximilien 277

CHAPTER XXI.

Conspiracy of the Thermidorians—Robespierre's discourse against them—The struggle—His arrest—The closing scene—His execution . 301

CONCLUSION 326

THE LIFE OF ROBESPIERRE.

CHAPTER I.

Introduction.

Le roi règne et ne gouverne pas: such is the strange political formula of the nineteenth century: a formula that would have justly astonished the thinking men of former generations. Is it not a striking evidence of the make-shift philosophy, to which this *transition-age* is condemned, that a *powerless* chief power should be tacitly accepted by the mass, and openly advocated by their teachers, as the one safeguard against anarchy and misrule? Our *faith* in royalty has expired: in its place Expediency suggests the constitutional fiction of a king who reigns but does not govern!

That Royalty was once accepted as of divine origin can be no secret to any reader; and yet so little trace of the faith now exists in Europe, that it sounds blasphemous in our ears, when we are told of a Bossuet urging a Louis XIV. to use his power boldly, "for kings are gods and their power is divine." The French Revolution was only the bursting of a long-gathering storm which was to sweep away that and many other prejudices. The outbreak of that storm was accelerated by the faults of princes and nobles, though no virtue on their side could have done more than delay the crisis.

Louis XIV. *was* a king, and the nation bowed to him. His

stateliness and polished courtesy; his ready wit and graceful bearing; his theatrical sentiments, not without a certain grandeur; his *kingliness*, in a word, or such *simulacrum* of it as passed for kingliness, raised him on so high a pedestal, that we cannot wonder if the nation worshiped him. True it is that he drained the resources of France by ruinous wars; but France rejoiced, for he ministered to that master-passion of her heart—glory. Deep, indeed, were the wounds he inflicted on her prosperity; but the wounds were hidden under laurels, and she was proud. The lustre of his reign has not yet passed away; they style him still *le grand monarque*. He was the last of the Romans.

The Regent Orleans succeeded: what could France worship in him? If kingship means leadership, in what was he the leader? In disgraceful orgies! He was the king of *petits soupers*.

To him succeeded Louis XV., by clamorous France entitled "Well-beloved." At this time, France had ceased to believe in her nobility and in her clergy, but she believed in her king; and what a king! His history is the rapid degradation of the faith in royalty: the "Well-beloved" lived to become the "Well-abhorred" of his people; lived, to have it believed of him that he took baths of human blood! lived, to become the King of the Parc-aux-Cerfs. His reign should be written by a Suetonius.

Indolent in all affairs of state, he was active only in sensual pleasures. His very mistresses typify the degrees of degradation: he began with duchesses to end with peasant-girls. All his predecessors had their mistresses, and France was contented that it should be so. But they preserved even in libertinage a certain respect for appearances. Louis XV. was altogether shameless. The Duchesse de Chateauroux was succeeded by Madame d'Etioles, afterwards Madame de Pompadour; and she, in turn, gave place to a common courtesan, picked up from gaming-houses,—a woman whose empire was in her reckless cynicism and daring licentiousness. A husband—Jean du Barri—was found willing "for a consideration" to lend her his name; and now, the courtesan being thus transformed into a married woman, the king was enabled to possess her without outraging *propriety*—"la morale," as Léon Gozlan sarcastically remarks, "recevait une pleine satisfaction."*

Yet, so conservative is man by nature, so tenaciously does he cling to any faith, long after it has become a mere formula, that even a Regent Orleans and a Louis XV. opened not his eyes to the fact that kings were men, and might be very incompetent, disreputable men. There was still a halo of divinity round the name of king, and when Louis XVI. ascended the throne, he seated himself on the throne of the people's hearts. He was young, good, uncontaminated; he was neither philosopher nor roué; and his queen was lovely and imperial.

Born in happier times, Louis XVI. would have been an excellent King Log. No better man could better have realized our modern constitutional fiction of a king. Unhappily for him and his people, the times needed a ruler: a Cromwell, a Frederick, a Napoleon. The disruption of society was at hand: the great social fabric, reared during centuries, was tottering to the base. No single hand could save it; weak hands could only accelerate its fall by their bungling.

The storm burst. From among the turbulent spirits of that epoch three men issued into something like sovereignty: Mirabeau—Robespierre—Napoleon.

Mirabeau was the genius of the Revolution.

Robespierre strove to be its king, and to rule it by metaphysical philosophy.

Napoleon was the soldier of the Revolution, and closed it by a despotism.

It is the Life of him, who in his heart believed the gospel proclaimed by the Revolution to be the real gospel of Christianity, and who vainly endeavored to arrest anarchy, and to shape society into order by means of his convictions, that I now desire to place impartially before the reader: a picture of political fanaticism worthy of more than a careless glance, or a contemptuous sneer.

---

* See the admirable article on Madame du Barri: *Revue des Deux Mondes*, tome 20, p. 798.

CHAPTER II.

Birth of Robespierre—His family—Is left an orphan—Protected by the clergy—Anecdotes of his childhood—College friends and studies—Scholastic success—Commences study of the law—State of France—Frivolous occupations of the aristocracy—Skepticism of the epoch.

TYPICAL of the uncertainty and obscurity which envelop the early years of his history is the fact, that the very date of Robespierre's birth has hitherto been erroneously given by all biographers. The certificate of his birth has only quite recently been discovered by M. Degeorge of Arras. From it we learn that it was in the year 1758, in the dismal town of Arras, the capital of the Comté d'Artois, that FRANÇOIS-MAXIMILIEN-JOSEPH-ISIDORE DE ROBESPIERRE was ushered into this breathing world, upon whose stage he was to play so strange a part.

The epoch was an important one. While Robespierre was still at his mother's breast, Voltaire retired to Ferney, there to live "en grand seigneur," and write revolutionary works; and the Minister of Finance placed before the king a statement of affairs, *as accurately as he was able to ascertain them!* This statement showed a deficit of 217,214,114 francs. He proposed to remedy it by a tax upon the wealthier classes; a proposition which was met by so vehement an outcry, that it was, perforce, abandoned. These two words indicate the anarchy of that epoch: Voltaire and the *Deficit!*

Strange uncertainty exists about Maximilien's family. On the one hand it is said, that he was of Irish origin; that his grandfather was devoted to the cause of the Pretender, whom he accompanied into France, and there finally settled in Arras, as an advocate. This is the generally received account; but Michelet has discovered a document, relating to one of the Robespierres, as early as the year 1600; and he says:—" They had been, from father to son, notaries, at Carvin, near Lille. They are supposed to have come over from Ireland. Their ancestors perhaps formed, in the sixteenth century, a portion of those numerous Irish colonies, which came over to people the monasteries and seminaries on the coast, when they received from the Jesuits a sound education, of wranglers and cavilers. In the eighteenth century, the Robespierres sought for a wider field: one branch of the family remained near Carvin, the other settled at Arras."

Many conjectures have been formed respecting the origin of Robespierre's name, which is certainly not Irish. Assuming that the family was Irish, it appears to me very obvious that the name must have been Robert Spiers: the pronunciation of Spiers, in French, being *spierre*.

There is also a tradition of Robespierre being a nephew of Damiens, the assassin of Louis XV., but this I believe to have been only the offspring of the hatred which Robespierre subsequently inspired; his enemies wished to blacken even his genealogy. In reference to this, I may quote the following doggerel verses, which I stumbled on in my researches into his origin:—

> "Continue Jean F—— de mener ta conduite
> Ce Robespierre
> Qui descend de Damien
> Tient de son père,
> Et n'est qu'un franc vaurien,
> A la galère
> Il ramera fort bien."

This much, however, is certain; that his father was a successful advocate at Arras, where he married Marie Josephine Carreau, the daughter of a brewer. She died young, leaving the widower with four children, the eldest of whom was Maximilien.

During the eighteenth century, the lodges of Freemasonry were turned into powerful secret societies, wherein men not only learned revolutionary doctrines, but boldly conspired against all existing dynasties. M. Louis Blanc has written a graphic chapter on this subject, in his History of the Revolution. Arras was not without its lodges; and one of them, called *L'Ecosse Jacobite*, was founded by Charles Edward, the young pretender, in 1744, who confided the presidency of it to his old adherent, Robespierre's father. So that Maximilien may be said to have sprung from a family of conspirators.

The next glimpse we get of the father, shows him in a questionable light. He has made a precipitous retreat from Arras: so precipitous that—doubtless in the mere confusion of hurry—he has forgotten to settle some outstanding debts, and forgotten to provide for the maintenance of his children. The fact of the retreat is certain; but different explanations are given. Charlotte Robespierre, in Laponneraye's "Memoir," says, that it was grief at his wife's death which obliged him to seek in travel the recovery of his health. She says he visited England, Germany, and America, kept a school at Cologne, returned to Arras, and tried to resume his profession; but, unable to withstand the painful associations which that place forced upon him, he again abandoned it, resumed his wanderings, and died at Munich, worn out by grief and fatigue.

I confess I have some suspicion of this uxorious sensibility in an advocate and a Frenchman; and, all things considered, I think the painful associations of Arras much more likely to have had reference to some "unsettled bills." Men *do* fly from creditors; but they seldom leave their native town, their profession, and their children, from grief at the loss of a wife.

Thus, at the age of ten or eleven, Maximilien found himself, as it were, at the head of his family; the guardian of his brother and two sisters. He had been one of the best pupils at the College of Arras, and the bishop was easily induced to confer upon him what is called "a purse," at the College of Louis le Grand.*

Robespierre had this in common with most scholars and poets of his time—that they were unable to dispense with lordly protection. Beaumarchais was first protected by the princesses; Mably, by the Cardinal de Tencin; Chamfort, by the Prince de

---

* In England we call it "being placed on the foundation."

Condé; Malouet, by Madame Adelaïde; Laclos, by Madame de Genlis; Brissot, by the Duke of Orleans; Vergniaud was brought up under the protection of Turgot and Dupoty; Marat was protected, though late in life, by the Count de Artois; and Camille Desmoulins, by the Chapter of Laon.

Little Maximilien was an agreeable boy, I presume, or the bishop would hardly have exerted himself thus in his favor. To think of Robespierre as a child, to realize to one's self an image of him lisping,—toddling about,—with yearnings for sweetmeats,—beating his sisters,—now smiles, now tears—the pride and torment of his *Bonne*, is not easy; yet such a child he certainly was: and I have turned over endless dusty volumes in the hope of getting at some authentic evidence of the fact,—some traits of childhood, some light anecdotes preserved by citizens of Arras, and significantly quoted when the child became famous. In vain. Not a trace can be found. His life was so obscure, until it became so glaring; and then people had other things to speak and write about.

Even his sister Charlotte can tell us nothing about him, unless we are to except that anecdote which she quotes when indignantly repelling the slanders of certain writers, who declared that Robespierre's "ferocious disposition exhibited itself in infancy, by beheading pigeons and sparrows:" an anecdote to the effect that she one night left a pigeon belonging to Maximilien in the garden, where it perished in a storm; on hearing of the tragic event, he burst into tears, overwhelmed her with reproaches for her carelessness, and vowed never again to trust her with any more of his dear pigeons.

It was in the year 1770 that he first came to Paris. He had brought with him a letter of recommendation to M. de la Roche, a canon of Notre Dame, who took him under his protection, and to whom he became excessively attached. Unfortunately, M. de la Roche died shortly after, and at the same time Maximilien learned the death of his youngest and best loved sister.

He began his studies gaily and resolutely. College was a new scene to him, and he had not left behind at Arras a mother's tenderness or the delights of a home, for which to weep. Poor though he was, at college he stood on an equality with the rest; and amongst his companions were some to whom he attached himself. One of them, in the same condition as himself, was Camille Desmoulins, destined to become famous for his light wit, his dexterous argument, and unflinching patriotism. Ugly, vulgar-looking, and ridiculed for his stutter, he was prompt, reckless, and ardent: a dare-devil boy, whose character (in its very opposition to his own) must have attracted Robespierre. There, also, was Fréron, the well-known People's Orator, son of that Fréron whom Voltaire has impaled upon his sarcasms, and rendered immortal by his hatred. There, also, were Duport Dutertre, Lebrun, and Suleau. In the same class as Robespierre there was, also, a fierce, vehement, bold, and generous boy, with loud voice, and scarred face:—his name was Danton.

"Within those high and dismal walls of Louis le Grand, blackened by the shadow of the Jesuits, and in those deep courts, where the sun so seldom shines, little Maximilien would walk alone, not much sympathizing with the noisy youths about him." He had little of the boy's vivacity; his bilious, melancholy temperament, no less than his condition in life, made him fonder of study than of play, doubtless to the no small contempt of his companions.

His studies were, as is usual at colleges, principally directed to Greece and Rome, and so ardently did he pursue them, so completely did he accept the spirit of antiquity, as reproduced by the professor, that M. Hérivaux, his master, named him "the Roman." The great events of Roman history, the austere morality of Sparta, the glorious deeds of ancient heroes, inflamed his youthful imagination as they have inflamed thousands of others. But whereas *our* young Epaminondases mostly curb their exaltation by copying invoices, or weighing out pounds of molasses, *this* youth was called upon to consolidate a republic, conceived according to that spirit of antiquity, which spirit, by the way, was as like that of antiquity as rhetoric is like truth.

Instruction was fruitful in his soul. Pictures of the ancient forum with tribunes of the people—of the deliberations of a great nation—of patriotism absorbing all other feelings, and sacrificing dearest interests, dearest affections, to the stern decrees of law, or to the sterner necessities of the country;—these constantly filled his mind. He learned to love the ferocious Romans, he learned to regard as heroism the sacrifice of humanity to an idea.

Not only did he imbue himself with this rhetorical spirit of antiquity so as to gain the applause of professors; but in the more technical portion of his studies he also gained honorable distinction. His name we find cited in the *Concours* of the university in 1772, 1774, and 1775; where, by the way, his name is uniformly written *de* Robespierre. It was not till the suppression of titles had rendered the *de* "suspect," that Robespierre's name was shorn of that noble particle.

For eight years did Maximilien pursue his studies. On quitting the university, he himself called upon the Cardinal de Rohan, who was then the Abbé de Saint Waast, to beg as a favor, that the *purse*, which had been given to him, should now be transferred to his brother Augustin. The cardinal prince, with a true Frenchman's courtesy and grace, not only accorded the favor, but said, "*Il s'estimait heureux de faire à Louis le Grand un nouveau cadeau.*" Maximilien then began his studies in Jurisprudence, at *L'Ecole de Droit*. His college exercises had given him phrases, which sounded like ideas. His education as an advocate was now to give him something of that readiness of speech, that power of debate, and that spirit of analysis and subtle distinction, which form the public speaker. Many have wondered, and many have deplored, that there should have been so great a proportion of lawyers among the national assembly. But surely nothing was more natural than that the deputies should be men accustomed to all the tactics of debate,—men, in short, who could *speak*. In a free country like ours, all men have some knowledge of government, most men have some powers of public speaking, "unaccustomed as they are;" but even with us, lawyers form a large portion of the representation of the country. They are trained speakers; and, except in moments of enthusiasm, oratory is an acquisition, quite as much as an inspiration. M. Ferrières, a man of some eminence at the bar, received Maximilien gratuitously as a pupil; and under his instruction the technicalities of the profession were soon mastered.

He led a life of honorable poverty, seclusion, and study; the life that is led by thousands of young men both in England and in France. He occupied a small apartment *au cinquième* in the Rue St. Jacques. His slender means admitted of but very little of that dissipation with which young law students seek relief from their wearisome studies.

Jurisprudence did not, however, wholly occupy him. He was at Paris, in the midst of its pleasures, its frivolities, its debates. Too poor to enjoy many of these delights, of a disposition naturally reserved and unsocial, he had little to interrupt his studies, so that, when not attending lectures or bending over digests, he was walking along the quays or down the shady, dusty avenues of the Tuileries, meditating on the destinies of mankind, and striving, with the help of Rousseau and others, to solve the vexed problems which then agitated Europe.

He was in Paris; yet not in its giddy vortex, not among its brilliant courtiers, not moving amid the rustling hoops of its court, nor adding to the elegant frivolity of its *salons*. He was in its dark and narrow streets, amidst its misery and squalid rags. He fought no duels, sparkled at no suppers, was the hero of no *bonnes fortunes*. He was near enough to the court and the salons to know what passed there; far enough removed from them to feel some hatred at the distinction. He could see that the Great were only the Privileged, and had no real title to be an aristocracy. Any common observer might have seen that; but the serious, unfriended Robespierre saw it with terrible distinctness.

Aristocracy had indeed fallen more completely than even kingship. If the nobles ever were the foremost, topmost men, they long had ceased to be so. A more finished grace of deportment; a more thorough comprehension of the futilities and elegancies of luxurious idleness; and perhaps a more perfect code of duelling, might be conceded to them. If life were as gay and frivolous a thing as Paris seemed to believe, if its interests were none other than the ingenious caprices of otiose magnificence,—then indeed these were the topmost men, and formed a veritable Aristocracy.

But the brilliant fête was drawing to a close; and while the beams of morning made the rouged and fatigued cheeks of the giddy dancers look somewhat ghastly, there was heard the distant tramp of an advancing army, which told them that a conflict was at hand. Some heard it, and with reckless indifference danced on, exclaiming, like Madame de Pompadour, "*Après nous le déluge!*" Others resolutely shut their ears, and would *not* hear it.

Since the last days of the Roman Empire no such spectacle had been exhibited by society as that exhibited by France during the eighteenth century. To look at it from afar, as seen in books, how gay and brilliant it appears. What wit, what eloquence! What charming futilities, what amiable society! What laughter, what amusement! If man's life were but a genteel comedy, acted before well-fed, well-bred, well-dressed audiences, this was a scene to draw forth all our plaudits. A secretary of state at eighteen (M. de Maurepas) decides state questions with a *bon mot*. A miserable negro page, Du Barri's favorite, is thought fitted to become the governor of a royal château. Storms lower on the horizon: they are met with epigrams! Dandy abbés make their lacqueys repeat the breviary for them, and having *thus* discharged the duties of their office, set themselves with all seriousness to turning couplets, and to gaining the reputation of gallantry. Women of the highest rank go to hear mass; but take with them, under guise of a prayer-book, some of those witty licentious novels, which are to be compared only to the *Satyricon* of Petronius.

These charming women "violated all the common duties of life, and gave very pleasant little suppers."* They had effaced the negative from the seventh commandment, and made marriage, as the witty Sophie Arnould felicitously defined it, "the sacrament of adultery."

The treasury was drained to enrich favorites, and to supply splendid fêtes. "Sometimes," says Louis Blanc, "there were cavaliers emulous of the *preux de Charlemagne*, who, in sumptuous gardens, under trees upon which were suspended shields and lances, feigned a magic sleep, till the queen appearing, deigned to break the spell. Sometimes, after reading of the loves of deer, these cavaliers took it into their heads to transform themselves into stags, and to hide themselves, clothed in skins, in the thickest part of the shady park. In the days when the nobility had manly passions, they amused themselves with tournaments which counterfeited war; now it was dancers who, mingling with the nobles, wore the colors of their ladies in fêtes counterfeiting tournaments!"

What could France think of her aristocracy, while the highest people in the realm were objects of contempt? Her Queen, the lovely Marie Antoinette, whom France had welcomed with such rapture and such pride, what figure did she make in this dissolute court? Did she set an august example of virtue, and of regal grandeur? Could hopes be formed of her? Alas, no! Young, ardent, quick-blooded, fond of pleasure, reckless as to means, careless of appearances, she was no longer the queen to whom a gallant Brissac, pointing to a jubilant crowd, could say "Behold! they are so many lovers!" She had become the object of hatred. She had been imprudent, perhaps worse; and princely libellers had circulated atrocious charges against her. She had forgotten herself so far as to appear at the *Bal de l' Opéra*. She had worn a heron's plume, which Lauzun had taken from his hat to give her. It was said that, dancing with Dillon, and thinking herself out of hearing, she had told him to feel how her heart beat; to which the king sternly replied, "Monsieur Dillon will take your word for it, madame!" This, and more was said of her; and an irritated nation eagerly credited the odious reports, which transformed their young queen into a Messalina. That she was libeled, no one now pretends to doubt; but *then* those libels were almost universally accredited.

And the king? His great occupation was clock-making! His brothers were less innocently employed. The one devoting himself to intrigue, a shameless libeler, and daring conspirator; and the other flaunting at *Bals masqués*.

Thus were the great names of France illustrious only in the annals of debauchery or folly; and the people asked themselves, Are these our rulers? The few exceptions to the general degradation only make the degradation more patent. Nobles, heretofore so proud, were now ambitious of repairing their ruined fortunes by marrying the daughters of opulent financiers. The courts of justice were scandalized by trials for robbery, in which noblemen figured as criminals. Not only had they lost their self-respect, but they had also lost the respect of the nation.

Seriousness, and serious topics, were by no means banished; they were only transformed into *agréments*. Philosophy was rouged, and wore a hoop. It found ready admission into all salons. Ruddy lips propounded momentous problems; delicate fingers turned over dusty folios. The "high argument" of God's existence and man's destiny—the phenomena of nature, the deepest and most inscrutable of questions, were discussed over the supper table, where *bon mots* and champagne sparkled as brightly as the eyes of the questioners. No subject was too arid for these *savantasses* (to use Mademoiselle de Launay's admirable expression); mathematics did not rebut them; political economy was charming; and even financial reports were read as eagerly as romances. And amidst this chaos of witticisms, paradoxes, and discussions, colonels were seated, occupied with embroidery, or with *parfilage;* noblemen made love to other noblemen's wives; while a scented abbé

"Fait le procès au Dieu qui le nourrit."*

Society never exhibited greater contrasts, nor greater anarchy; old creeds and ancient traditions were crumbling away; and amidst the intellectual orgies of the epoch, the most antagonistic elements had full play. D'Alembert, Lalande, Lagrange, Buffon, and Lavoisier, were jostled by Cagliostro, Mesmer, Saint Martin, and Weishaupt: the exact sciences had rivals in the wildest chimeras and quackeries. Atheists proclaimed, with all the fervor of conviction, their faith in the eternal progress of humanity; skeptics, who assailed Christianity with all the powers of mockery and logic, were the declared apostles of the three fundamental principles of Christianity: the principles of charity, fraternity, and equality. Voltaire attacked all sacred institutions, devoting himself to *écraser l'infame*. Montesquieu examined, with no reverent spirit, the laws of every species of established government. Rousseau went deeper still, and struck at the root of all society by a production as daring as it was well-timed, the "Discours sur l'Inégalité."

The Philosophy of Rousseau.

THE spirit which animated the Revolution was the spirit of Rousseau. From the Declaration of the Rights of Man to the formation of the Constitution in 1793, there is no important act in which the influence of the Genevese philosopher is not discernible. But beyond this Rousseau has special interest for us here, as the acknowledged teacher of Robespierre, who, of all his disciples, adhered most rigidly to his principles, and gave him the most unflinching application.

Rightly to understand Robespierre, it is first indispensable that we should understand Rousseau. I shall be fulfilling, therefore, the first object of this Biography in devoting a few pages to the political writings of the author of the "Social Contract."

The gaiety, frivolity, wit, and elegance of France, so charming to those who lived in the salons, formed as it were but the graceful vine which clustered over a volcano about to burst; or rather, let me say, it was the rouge, which, on a sallow, sunken cheek, simulated the ruddy glow of health. Lying deep down in the heart of society there was profound seriousness: the sadness of misery, of want, of slavery clanking its chains, of free thought struggling for empire. This seriousness was about to find utterance. The most careless observer could not fail to perceive the heavy thunderclouds which darkened the horizon of this sunny sky. The court and the salons were not France; they occupied the foremost place upon the stage, but another actor was about to appear before whom they would shrink into insignificance; that actor was the People.

The people became the fashion. Philanthropy was *de bon ton*. The philosophers speculated about the people; the *littérateurs* declaimed about them. Courtiers played at being peasants. A village was constructed at Trianon; village fêtes were given at royal farms by royal peasants. Idylls were *à la mode*. Florian, Gessner, and *Paul et Virginie* were the flowers of this peasant literature. As in our own day we see some aristocratic writers joining with the most democratic in the senseless laudation of that grandiose abstraction — "The People," — so in unhappy France the warmest eulogists of the starved, uneducated, uncared-for masses, were those who profited by their subjection. Restless, unbelieving, sick at heart of the existing state of things, they played at being peasants and poetised the people!

Among the philosophic nobles, there were some who quitted their *talons rouges* to wear thick shoes; and relinquished their costume to put on that of the bourgeoisie. It was very dangerous work playing thus with their dignities when those dignities were already tottering!

Few were in earnest, because few had convictions. At length a man arose in whom pretence grew into seriousness, paradoxes ripened into convictions: that man was Rousseau. The *Contrat Social* was the Bible of the Revolution. From it orators drew their principles, their political aphorisms, their political language. As a metaphysician, and as a rhetorician, his influence was incalculable. He was the man of his epoch, and therefore was he powerful. He united the elegance and eloquence of the philosophers and *littérateurs* to the sadness and seriousness of the people.

In his strange career we see him uneasily moving amidst the salons of Paris dressed in his Armenian robes, creating a sensation amongst the Wits and Poets, the Dilettanti and Beauties; "among them, but not of them;" and then, sick of his uneasy position, brusquely breaking away from all society; turning misanthrope; disdaining all the elegancies of life; and endeavoring in solitude to find that peace among plants, which man had denied him.* A similar course is observable in his writings; he commences with a frivolous paradox to end with an extravagant conviction.

The mixture of pretence and reality in Rousseau; of wilful folly, and of glorious truth; of despicable baseness, and of noble qualities, makes up the mystery and piquant charm of his character. "He was," as Carlyle finely says, "a lonely man, his life a long soliloquy." In that soliloquy may be read the heights and depths of human nature. His ideas were often noble, grand, and tender; his acts degraded. He taught mothers by his eloquence to nurse their children, and threw his own children into the Foundling Hospital. His sensibility led him to sympathize with whatever was beautiful; his weakness and selfishness suggested acts which have left ineffaceable stains upon his memory. He was one of that class of men whose practice springs not from their precepts; in whom the unclouded intellect discerns and honors truth, while the will is too miserably weak to act the truth. He has had his acrid antagonists, and his eloquent defenders. Are not both right—both wrong? It is possible to draw, and truly draw, a fearful picture of one-half of this man, but such a one-sided view will never obtain general acceptance; for many will deeply sympathize with what was noble in him, and impartial men will always proclaim it.

Few read his works. That marvellous book, "The Confes-

---

* "Vous attendrez un homme de lettres, un beau diseur," he writes to a Russian Count who offered to place his country house at his disposal, "et vous n'auriez qu'un bon homme, bien simple, que son goût et ses malheurs ont rendu fort solitaire, et qui pour amusement herborise toute la journée, trouve à commercer avec les plantes cette paix si douce à son cœur que lui ont refusée les humains."

sions," will never indeed cease to find readers; but while "Emile" and "La Nouvelle Héloïse" from time to time tempt the adventurous, lured by celebrated titles, I do not believe that one student in fifty ever looks into the "Discourse on the Inequality of Conditions," or the "Social Contract." But as these were his great revolutionary works, it is to them that I must here direct attention.

The period which elapses between 1745 and 1764 is at once the most disastrous, and in some respects the most remarkable, in the history of France. No period offers such striking contrasts. On the one hand, France, beaten in every quarter of the globe, loses her colonies, her marine, and even her honor; on the other hand, she collects together at Paris a brilliant band of writers, whose ideas are destined to become the guiding lights of Europe. Among these, Rousseau holds a foremost rank.

In the year 1750, the academy of Dijon proposed, as the subject of its Prize Essay, this question: "*Has the establishment of Science and Literature contributed to purify Society?*"

It was an absurd question. Absurd, because as literature is itself the *expression* of society, which it in turn *reacts upon*, you cannot separate the two, and determine either the influence of literature upon society, or what society would have been had there been no literature: in other words, what society would have been, had it not been society; for society is a *complex* condition, of which literature is a vital element. In rude ballads as in wealthy libraries, literature is an agent inseparable from civilization. You might as well speculate on what a man's constitution would be without a liver, as on what the constitution of society would be without literature. In this question, however, the metaphysicians of the eighteenth century saw no absurdity. Rousseau determined to answer it.

"One day walking with Diderot, at Vincennes, talking on the proposed question, 'Which side do you take?' I asked him (it is Diderot who speaks). He replied, 'The affirmative.' 'That,' said I, 'is the *pons asinorum:* all the mediocre talents will take that route, and you can only utter commonplaces. Take the other side, and you will find it an open field, rich and fruitful, for eloquence and philosophy.' 'You are right,' said he, after a few moments' reflection; 'I will follow your advice.'"*

It was as a paradox which would startle, rather than as a truth which might be commonplace, that Rousseau first threw down the gauntlet against civilization, proclaiming the superiority of ignorance, and the greatness of savage life. There was something piquant in the idea. He confesses as much in the first page, where he asked himself, "How shall I dare to blame the sciences, in the presence of one of the most learned bodies of Europe? or praise ignorance before a celebrated Academy?" But the result is more piquant still: this Academy absolutely awarded the prize to the audacious eulogist of ignorance! After this we cannot wonder if a paradox, which an Academy could crown, should produce an immense sensation in a frivolous society startled by the novelty, and allured by the eloquence of the Discourse. There was an air of serious conviction about Rousseau. A close and pressing logic, bold and sweeping dogmatism, and a masterly style, if they failed to convince, at least left readers in an embarrassment from whence there was no escape. No one was persuaded, yet no one could refute him. Replies abounded; even a king condescended to step into the arena; but Rousseau's antagonists did not see the absurdity of the question, and could not, therefore, see the πρῶτον ψεῦδος of his answer.

Rousseau's position is this: Science, Art, and Literature are the produce and producers of all the vices of civilization. Man in a state of unlettered simplicity is healthy, brave, and virtuous. He loses these qualities in society. "The ebb and flow of the ocean have not been more regularly subjected to the course of the planet which illumes the night, than the fate of morals and probity to the progress of science and art." This aphorism is universally accepted; and Rousseau's tactic consists in boldly, and without qualification, applying it in the sense *contrary* to that accepted by mankind. He thus continues: "We have seen virtue disap-

---

* Marmontel, "Mémoires," p. 283, ed. Barrière.

pear, according as the light of the sciences has risen upon our horizon, and the same phenomenon has been observed in all times, and in all countries." This position, so authoritatively assumed, domineers over the whole argument. He subsequently supports it by a magnificent audacity; he gives to every science a *vice* as its origin! "Astronomy is born from superstition; Eloquence from ambition, from hate, from flattery, from falsehood; Geometry from avarice (!) Physics from a vain curiosity; all—including Morality itself—from human pride."

No sane man could seriously maintain such arguments, although this was not the first time they had found utterance. St. Aubain, in a now forgotten work, called "*Traité de l' Opinion*," which Rousseau had studied in his youth, advanced most of the objections to be found in this *Discours*. In fact, skepticism had infested every department of human inquiry; until at last men began to doubt whether *all* inquiry were not useless. Rousseau's paradox, therefore, although suggested by Diderot, was the legitimate product of the epoch, and hence its success.

Not merely as a protest against the science and literature of the age did this *Discours* startle France; there were tones in it of a higher strain. There were sentences of serious application. Philosophers were on thrones, were at court, were caressed in *salons*. Princes prided themselves on their patronage of literature. Rousseau, instead of swelling the list of eulogists who proclaimed such liberality as the great virtue of an enlightened monarch, boldly declared this patronage was adroit tyranny.

Extravagant as the leading idea of this Discourse unquestionably is, it was surpassed in his next work. Men are prone to believe in their own lies when they find others credulous; and the idea which Rousseau took up as a paradox to display his ingenuity, produced so great a sensation that he began to believe he had discovered a truth. He had accidentally lighted upon a mine; and now dug vigorously onwards in search of the ore. His own unhappy life, his own unsociable temper, his consciousness of genius, and irritated self-love all fitted him for the task of declaiming against unjust social distinctions; and while thus indulging in his vengeance, he was earning his laurels. He spat upon the society wherein he felt his false position; and the world applauded that indulgence of his wrath!

The Academy of Dijon having gained celebrity by its foolish programme, grew bolder, and proposed this momentous question: *What is the origin of the inequality among men, and is it sanctioned by the law of nature?* Rousseau's famous *Discours* did not obtain the prize; but it created a greater sensation than any prize-essay ever written. It is the paradox of the first *Discours*, but more seriously meditated, more powerfully stated. It is less of a caprice, and more of a conviction. It is a sombre, vehement protest against civilization; a protest in favor of the poor against the rich, of the oppressed and degraded Many against the polished vicious Few. This very seriousness, I suppose, prevented the prize being awarded to the *Discours*. Certain it is, that it alarmed the ingenious, frivolous society of France, and that its full success was not obtained till some years later, when the times had grown more serious.

"*L'homme qui médite est un animal dépravé.*" That is the keystone of the arch; and it is nothing more than the aphoristic formula of his first Discours. He admits that inequalities, physical as well as mental, exist, but these inequalities he attributes to the corrosive influence of civilization, with its luxuries, its subtleties, and its vices. In a state of nature, men's bodies being equally exercised, become equally vigorous, and the healthy body forms the healthy mind. He paints in glowing colors the ideal state of savage life, when men without language, except a few expressive sounds such as animals employ to articulate their wants, wandering amidst boundless forests, chasing their game, reposing under trees, unperverted by the illimitable desires and unsatisfied passions of civilized men, knowing none of the subtleties of affection, taking a wife to satisfy a passing desire, and heedless of his offspring; brave, simple, truthful, and free.

Not with blinded eyesight poring over miserable books!

This is what man *was;* and what he *is*, you are called upon to compare with that primeval state.*

So far it is only another statement of his former idea; but as he proceeds, the dangerous consequences, rigorously deduced from it, appear. Men were born equal. Equal in health, in strength, in virtue, in property. The earth belonged to all, and to none. Society began with the spoliation of the many, in favor of the few: it, and its laws, are the consecration of that spoliation.

"The first man who, having enclosed a piece of land, took it into his head to say, '*This is mine,*' and found people simple enough to believe him, was the real founder of civil society. What crimes, what battles, what murders, and what horrible miseries, would he have spared the human race, who should have torn down the fence, and exclaimed, '*Beware how you listen to this impostor; you're lost if you forget that the fruits belong to all, and the earth to no one!*' "†

This bold attack upon the very nature of property so startled the age, that even Voltaire called it the philosophy of a blackguard who counseled the poor to plunder the rich. It was passing beyond the limits of permissible paradox, and was becoming alarming. Rousseau was serious. He met the objection naturally made, that a man, having built a wall by his own labor, was entitled to its benefit, by asking, " Who gave you the right to build it? How can you pretend to be repaid for a labor we, the masses, never imposed upon you? The unanimous consent of the whole human race was necessary before you could appropriate from the

---

* "On n'a jamais employé tant d'esprit à vouloir nous rendre bêtes," wrote Voltaire to him on the receipt of this discourse; and he continues, in his delicate strain of irony: " il prend envie de marcher à quatre pattes, quand on lit votre ouvrage: cependant, comme il y a plus de soixante ans que j'en ai perdu l'habitude, je sens malheureusement qu'il m'est impossible de la reprendre."

† From this we see that Proudhon's definition of property being theft, is only an energetic expression of Rousseau's idea. Yet what an uproar it created but the other day!

common funds, more than was necessary for your own subsistence. You are rich! but we suffer. Your wealth is our poverty. In vain you appeal to laws. What are laws but the adroit selfishness of men who framed maxims for the preservation of their possessions? Property is a spoliation; laws may secure, but they cannot justify it."

This is no longer a mere audacious paradox; it is an unhappy error. It is not a caprice of speculative ingenuity; it is a vigorously deduced conclusion. It has not only logical consistency, but is strengthened by popular feeling. It is a doctrine which will fructify in Revolutions! To those who are in misery and want, it comes like a revelation of truth, responding to their sense of social injustice. To those who roll in wealth it comes like a spectre to scare them from their possessions: a spectre *they* cannot exorcise. It is a doctrine, it is a conviction, and is backed by millions, stung by a sense of injustice! Attempt not to answer it with phrases about "sacred rights of property," "security of order," "well-being of the state," and so forth; it tells you plainly that these rights are *unsacred*, and that *this* well-being of a state is the pampered indulgence of a few, wrung from the sufferings of millions!

That bold idea once thrown upon the world, the world "will not willingly let die." France suffered from it. We in our wealthy England also suffer from it. In thousands of heads and hearts it works, forming the basis of a political gospel. Those who most revolt against it, find it difficult to answer. It never will be answered so long as social science continues in the hands of metaphysicians. Happily their reign is drawing to a close!

In a former work, after due recognition of the services which metaphysical speculation has afforded to the development of opinion, I have endeavored to show the incompetence of Metaphysics to solve its own problems, and have historically exhibited the gradual decline it has undergone, till it has now almost universally fallen into discredit. But the metaphysical *method* still remains. It still lingers on the outskirts of the sciences; while in the sciences of man and of society it is almost the universal method. That method may be characterized in a sentence: it is the method whereby, instead of *examining the thing before us* to find out its properties, we studiously examine *the idea of that thing as it exists in our own minds.*

In the sciences another method is pursued. A man wishing to know the structure and organic processes of plants, examines plants, and not his *idea* of a plant; but wishing to know the nature of mind, he is not content, as in the former instance, with the observation of phenomena, and from that observation deducing the laws which regulate them, but must, forsooth, despise that as " materialism," and straightway occupy himself with the " idea."

In Rousseau we see this vicious method leading to vicious consequences. Instead of examining society as a natural growth— as the sum total of man's nature, developed through an infinite variety of circumstances—he straightway eliminates all the phenomena before him, and reduces society to its abstract idea; arriving at a period when society was *not*, he there discovers certain metaphysical Rights and Conventions; and these he proclaims to be the eternal principles of things; these he proclaims to be the great truths upon which social science must be based. As well might the botanist disregard all present phenomena, and, eliminating the various influences of air, earth, and water, arrive at the abstract idea of a flower, and tell us *that* is the flower!

When Charles Bonnet objected to Rousseau's system, that society was the natural product of man's faculties, the inevitable result of his constitution,* Rousseau replied, " Yes, in the same

---

* The argument is as old as Aristotle. It was reproduced by Cicero, in his " Treatise on a Republic." Who can help regretting that one of the many *lacunæ* in that interesting work should occur precisely at this point? All that has been rescued I cite here : " Populus autem non omnis hominum cœtus quoque modo congregatus, sed cœtus multitudinis juris consensu et utilitatis communione sociatus. Ejus autem prima causa coeundi est non tam imbecillitas quàm naturalis quædam hominum quasi congregatio: non est enim singulare nec solivagum genus hoc ; sed ita generatum, ut ne in omnium quidem rerum affluentiâ." . . . . Lib. i. c. xxv.

way as old age and decrepitude are natural to man, the inevitable results of his constitution; and arts, laws, and governments are as necessary to people as crutches to old men. All the difference is, that old age results naturally and solely from the human constitution; whereas society is not immediately derived from man's faculties, but also from certain external circumstances."* Neither Rousseau, nor his adversaries, saw that he was stepping out of the question, and that his political philosophy was constructed on a radically false basis.

But this metaphysical method was in high favor at that period; and Rousseau's success is owing as much to it as to his eloquence. It has been well said of him, "*il a plus de logique que de raison;*" which is an epigrammatic way of saying, that he reasoned closely upon loose premises—a true description of a metaphysician, and —will the reader pardon the *rapprochement?*—has often been given as the definition of a madman.

At last he produced "Le Contrat Social" (1762), and this, as the consummation of his metaphysical speculation, became the text-book of the Revolution. Here all trace of paradox has disappeared, and he seems thoroughly in earnest. In proof of this earnestness let not the important modification of his two leading ideas be forgotten. He no longer regards society as necessarily corrupt, nor indeed as inferior to a savage life. In the chapter *De l'Etat civil*, he says, the passage from savage to civilized life produces a remarkable change in the substitution of justice to instinct, and giving to man's actions a morality they wanted before. "C'est alors seulement que la voix du devoir, succédant à l'impulsion physique, et le droit à l'appétit, l'homme qui jusque-là n'avait regardé que lui-même, se voit forcé d'agir sur d'autres principes, et de consulter sa raison avant d'écouter ses penchans." And he concludes by a panegyric on intelligence, as developed by civilization, adding, that if abuses did not sometimes degrade him lower than his primitive condition, man ought incessantly to bless the happy occasion "qui d'un animal stupide et borné, fit un être in-

---

* Lettre de J. J. Rousseau à M. Philopolis, p. 344.

telligent et un homme." Here he has come round to the opinion of Lucretius, whose picture of savage life he formerly borrowed, omitting the important reserves which that great poet made—such for instance as—

> Et frutices inter condebant squalida membra,
> Verbera ventorum vitare imbresque coacti.
> *Nec commune bonum poterant spectare, nec ullis*
> *Moribus inter se scibant, nec legibus uti.*

Equally important is his modification of the theory of property. It is no longer a spoliation, but the right of the first occupant, and to this right he annexes three conditions,—1st. That the land be not already occupied; 2d. That a man occupies only so much as is necessary for his subsistence; 3d. That possession be taken, not by an idle ceremony, but by labor and cultivation—the only signs of proprietorship, which, in default of legal titles, ought to be respected.

With regard to the fundamental idea of this work, viz.: that *society* is a contract by which the members consent to abide—a contract made by all for the good of all—it is the most powerful revolutionary dogma ever put forward. It has the great merits of distinctness, and apparent certainty. Capable of being understood by the most ignorant, it seems to carry with it the irresistible force of an axiom. It is a striking example of the metaphysical method employed in politics. Let us examine it.

That society exists by the consent of its members is so far true, that if all men *chose* to separate from their fellows, and live like birds and beasts of prey, they certainly *could* do so. In this sense there is a sort of tacit contract which forms the basis of society. But I need scarcely say, that, in point of fact, this contract is altogether illusory; no one's consent was ever *asked* or *given*. The contract is not a reality, but an hypothesis. As M. de Barante appositely remarks, "C'est ainsi qu'en géométrie on dit qu'un solide est engendré par le mouvement d'un plan." He adds, "The definition is geometrically correct, but it has no relation whatever to the conditions of the existence of a solid body. The geometrician is enabled to imagine it; but its existence is altogether independent of his definition. In the same way society is, in the abstract, the result of the consent of all its members; in reality, it results from the fact of many men congregating in one portion of the earth, settling there, having children, a government, and certain customs. No geometrician ever attempted to create a solid in accordance with the terms of his definition; but it is possible to inspire men with the idea of being able to break or to renew a social contract; and with this idea empires are overturned."*

To show the absurdity of this hypothesis of a social contract, we have only to refer to a despotism. In a despotic country, society exists only by the same tacit consent of its members; since if they chose to withdraw their consent, and revolt, the despotism must cease. But to draw from such a premise the conclusion, that *despotism was a social contract made by all for the good of all*, however it might satisfy a Hobbes, would scarcely be accepted by any one else. The truth is, men are very much like sheep: gregarious by nature, willing to follow any leader, to obey any one bold enough to assume the command; their consent is never asked; they are ordered, and obey. Force has always been King. Mights have been rights.

If we throw aside this abstract and metaphysical method of inquiry, and follow the march of history, we shall see at once, that, so far from there having been a social contract (in which each individual member consented to forego certain privileges for the security of the whole fabric of society), this recognition of every individual member and his rights has been a growing tendency—the great development of the law of progress—the greatest fact in history. Whether we date the origin of society from a family, or from the aggregation of tribes, in each case we see a few leading men, and a mass of obedient followers dependent on their captains. In the ancient republics it was only the few who were free, who were real participators in the legislation. Athens and

---

* Tableau de la Littérature Française du XVIII. Siècle, p. 175.

Sparta were but aristocracies. It appeared necessary to the wisest of the Greeks that the masses should blindly obey the behests of the few. Slaves were *necessary* to society. They are weak and ignorant, and therefore are they slaves.* 'The strong *deserved* the power, and took it. Might was right. So clearly did Aristotle see this, that he finely says, he is a slave who *can* belong to another:—ἔστι γὰρ φύσει δοῦλος, ὁ δυνάμενος ἄλλου εἶναι·

Slavery itself, horrible as it may appear, was a step in advance towards civilization. Instead of slaughtering their captives, victorious tribes converted them to *use;* they made their captives slaves. Servage succeeded slavery. Servage became abolished. The growing necessities of the times, and the widening of social views, gradually enfranchised serfs, and proclaimed at last the Rights of Man. Before the eighteenth century, although the rights of every individual member of the state were not formally *denied*, they were not distinctly recognized. Even now in our nineteenth century they are only distinctly recognized by the democratic party.

To talk of a social contract in face of an historical survey is preposterous. The time *will* come when society will be a contract; when government will be made by all for the good of all; but Rousseau should have placed his ideal in the future, instead of in the past. It was thus Plato framed his "Utopia," though he looked back upon a golden age when society was perfect. But his golden age was not an age of ignorance; it was the age when men were ruled by superior beings, by guardian demons, by intelligences. The ideal of all politicians is to restore this age, which can be done in some degree, by the creation of just laws,

---

* Aristotle, De Polit. lib. i. c. iii. He calls a slave κτῆμά τι; and speaks of the necessity no less than the utility of slaves. He further says that Nature herself has made the distinction among men: some are born to command, others as mere beasts of burden to obey: τὰ μὲν ἰσχυρὰ πρὸς τὴν ἀναγκαίαν χρῆσιν· τὰ δὲ ὀρθὰ καὶ ἄχρηστα πρὸς τὰς τοιαύτας ἐργασίας, ἀλλὰ χρήσιμα πρὸς πολιτικὸν βίον. With his usual boldness and sagacity, however, he adds, that sometimes freemen have the souls of slaves, and slaves the nature of freemen.

which, emanating from the universal reason of mankind, will take the place of those departed guardians.*

Whatever may be the value of Rousseau's doctrine as a philosophical solution of the great problem, its potency as a revolutionary instrument, and its fitness for the age which produced it, are incontestable.

It was a political transformation of the dogma of man's fall; and made civilization the instrument of degeneration. By this it led to the conviction of the necessity for an entire renovation of society. Civilization, it said, tends to an increased development of the inequality of mankind. But men are born equal; and they should preserve their birthright by resisting that pernicious tendency.

Absolute equality—the most disorganizing of all doctrines—was proclaimed as the basis of the new scheme of society. We must do Rousseau the justice to say, that he did not warrant all the extravagances of this doctrine. On the contrary, he sometimes speaks with great moderation, as in this passage:—

"By equality, we must *not understand that the degrees of power and wealth are to be absolutely the same;* but that power should be purified from all violence, and should be exercised only in strict accordance with the laws; and that in wealth no citizen should be rich enough to purchase another citizen, nor poor enough to be forced to sell himself. If you wish to make the State durable, you must neither allow *opulence* nor *want*."†

Before closing this chapter let me not omit to mention Rousseau's religious fervor, as another trait he has in common with his disciple Robespierre. Amidst the almost universal skepticism of the epoch, Rousseau's religious convictions were eloquent, though heterodox. He had not only religious belief, he had religious intolerance; and in his "Contrat Social" he lays it down as an axiom, that a legislator may banish from the State any one who

---

* See the splendid passage *De Legibus*, iv., p. 349—50, ed. Bekker.

† Contrat Social, liv. ii., c. xi. Plato lays down a similar rule in the 4th Book of his Republic.

refuses to accept the religion of the State; and that any one accepting the religion of the State, and acting as if he did not believe in its dogmas, should *be put to death!* for he has committed the greatest of crimes, he has lied in the face of Law: "que si quelqu'un après avoir reconnu ces dogmes, se conduit comme ne les croyant pas, qu'il soit pu de mort: il a commis le plus grand des crimes; il a menti devant les lois!"

We may now resume our narrative. This digression will save many digressions and many explanations in future chapters; for we now know the doctrine which Robespierre accepted—we know the ideal which he held before his aspirations.

CHAPTER IV.

Robespierre returns to Arras—His sister—Mistakes about his obscurity—His first important pleading—The case of M. Vissery's lightning conductor—Robespierre as a poet—Amusing letter—Robespierre at five-and-twenty—Les Rosatis—Specimens of his poetry—Academy of Arras—His éloge de Gresset—His first love.

His term of study completed, we are told by M. Laponneraye that Robespierre was admitted to the bar of the parliament of Paris. The *Quarterly Review* doubts this, asserting that his name is not on the official list. Be this as it may, he never attempted to practice in Paris, but returned to his native town, hoping on the remains of his father's *clientelle* to found a lucrative practice. He brought back with him a reputation as a *Lauréat* of Louis le Grand, which, in so small a town as Arras, was not without importance. It aided him in his laborious struggle for existence. Respected by the citizens for his probity and disinterestedness, also for a certain air of seriousness, Maximilien worked resolutely on, and obtained some practice.

Coincident with his return was the arrival of his eldest sister, Charlotte, from the convent where she had been placed by the worthy bishop; and now, her education completed, she undertook the charge of housekeeping for Maximilien and his younger brother, Augustin. Arras was a great ecclesiastical, political, and juridical centre; a city of provincial states and upper tribunals, abounding with business and law-suits. In no place did the nobility and clergy hold their sway more despotically. There were especially two princes, or rather two kings of Arras, the bishop, and the powerful abbot of Saint Waast, to whom about one-third of the city belonged. The bishop had preserved the seigniorial right of appointing judges to the criminal tribunal. Even at the present day his enormous palace buries the half of Arras in its shadow. Damp and dismal streets, with expressive names, Rue du Conseil, Rue des Rapporteurs, &c., reminding one of a chancery life, wind about the walls of its palace.* In the dismal and solitary Rue des Rapporteurs stood Robespierre's house; but we have scarcely any glimpse of what passed within it.

That Robespierre was not then a marked man, among cotemporary Frenchmen, may be readily acknowledged; but it is quite erroneous to assert that he was altogether obscure in Arras. The difference between the provinces and the capital is enormous; and many a lawyer of great provincial celebrity is never heard of beyond the *barrière* of his native town.

So early as 1783, I find Maximilien called upon to defend an important cause. The recent discoveries of Franklin had been adopted in France; and even in the province of Artois a rich landed proprietor, M. de Vissery de Boisvallé, had erected a lightning conductor on his property, much to the scandal of the worthy citizens. "What!" said they, "shall we rend the lightning from the hand of God? Shall man presume to intercept the wrath of the Deity. If God wills to destroy houses or farms, it is his will and pleasure —man's duty is to submit. These lightning conductors are but the impious thoughts of Deistical philosophy! Away with them!"

Thus reasoned these obese and stupid citizens of Arras. Nay, more; they not only reasoned, they threatened the demolition of the conductor. They applied to the Echevins of St. Omer, to order its removal; and the municipal authorities, equally bigoted, yielded to their request. M. de Vissery was not so easily to be conquered: he determined to try the cause; and selected Robespierre as his advocate. Robespierre's practice was in the upper council, a court of appeal having an extensive jurisdiction. He pleaded several times before the council, and obtained not only the compliments of his judges, but what is more rare, those of his brethren of the bar. This, however, was the first important cause he had received. He began by publishing an essay on the subject, in which the question was treated both legally and scientifically. The pamphlet made some little noise, and when the trial came on (31st of May, 1783) he was triumphant.

Let us turn awhile from these pleadings, to view him in another character, namely, in that of an academician and poet. A smile will doubtless curl the lips of the reader, as the sacred name of poet is heard in conjunction with the "sea-green Incorruptible." Yet if we look closer, we shall find, not indeed "the vision and the faculty divine," but that which many worthy people mistake for it, namely, a certain literary ambition, and a faculty for turning verses, which, if not good, have the negative merit of not being worse than those commonly produced. Had the young ladies of Arras indulged in albums, Robespierre's flourish would no doubt have graced them all. In default of albums, there was something still more imposing: a poetical society called "Les Rosatis," which numbered among its members magistrates, lawyers, judges, priests, and noodles of every *nuance*. It was a society very similar to those so abundant in Italy. The members met, listened in politest agony to the recitation of each other's verses—and conferred crowns of roses on their illustrious victors. Robespierre, as the *lauréat* of Louis le Grand, and as a young gentleman with the "accomplishment of verse," was of course admitted into this society; and I know few things much more curious than that picture of Maximilien-Isidore-Joseph, with a garland of roses round his head, and a scroll of bad verses in his hand, reciting, with true French emphasis, and theatrical gesture, those same verses to his fellow poets. Two or three specimens of his poetry must be given.

CHANSON.

O dieux! que vois-je, mes amis?
    Un crime trop notoire
Du nom charmant des Rosatis
    Va donc flétrir la gloire!
      O malheur affreux!
      O scandale honteux!
    J'ose le dire à peine,
      Pour vous j'en rougis,
      Pour moi j'en gémis,
    Ma coupe n'est pas pleine.

Eh! vite donc, emplissez-la
    De ce jus salutaire,
Ou du dieu qui nous le donna
    Redoutez la colère;
      Oui dans sa fureur,
      Son thyrse vengeur
    S'en va briser mon verre.
      Bacchus, de là-haut,
      A tous buveurs d'eau
    Lance un regard sévère.

Sa main sur leurs fronts nébuleux,
    Et sur leur face blême,
En caractères odieux,
    Grava cet anathème.
      Voyez leur maintien,
      Leur triste entretien,
    Leur démarche timide:
      Tout leur air dit bien,
      Que, comme le mien,
    Leur verre est souvent vide.

O mes amis, tout buveur d'eau,
    Et vous pouvez m'en croire,

THE LIFE OF ROBESPIERRE.

Dans tous les temps ne fut qu'un sot,
    J'en atteste l'histoire.
       Ce sage effronté,
       Cynique vanté,
    Me paraît bien stupide.
       Oh le beau plaisir
       D'aller se tapir
    Au fond d'un tonneau vide!

Encore s'il eût été plein,
    Quel sort digne d'envie!
Alors dans quel plaisir divine
    Aurait coulé sa vie!
       Il aurait eu droit
       De braver d'un roi
    Tout le faste inutile.
       Au plus beau palais
       Je préférerais
    Un si charmant asile.

Quand l'escadron audacieux
    Des enfants de la terre
Jusque dans le séjour des dieux
    Osa porter la guerre,
       Bacchus, rassurant
       Jupiter tremblant,
    Décida la victoire;
       Tous les dieux à jeun
       Tremblaient en commun,
    Lui seul avoit su boire.

Il fallait voir, dans ce grand jour,
    Le puissant dieu des treilles,
Tranquille, vidant tour à tour
    Et lançant des bouteilles;
       A coups de flacons,
       Renversant les monts
    Sur les fils de la terre:
       Ces traits, dans la main
       Du buveur divin,
    Remplaçaient le tonnerre.

THE LIFE OF ROBESPIERRE.

Vous dont il reçut le serment
   Pour de si justes causes,
C'est à son pouvoir bienfaisant
   Que vous devez vos roses;
     C'est lui qui forma
     Leur tendre incarnat,
   L'aventure est notoire;
     J'entendis Momus
     Un jour à Venus
   Rappeler cette histoire.

La rose était pâle jadis,
   Et moins chère à Zéphire,
A la vive blancheur des lis
   Elle cédait l'empire;
     Mais un jour Bacchus,
     Au sein de Vénus,
   Prend la fille de Flore;
     La plongeant soudain
     Dans des flots de vin,
   De pourpre il la colore.

On prétend qu'au sein de Cypris
   Deux, trois gouttes coulèrent,
Et que dès-lors parmi des lis
   Deux roses se formèrent;
     Grâce à ses couleurs,
     La rose, des fleurs
   Désormais fut la reine;
     Cypris, dans les cieux,
     Du plus froid des dieux
   Devint la souveraine.

Amis, de ce discours usé
   Concluons qu'il faut boire;
Avec le bon ami Ruzé
   Qui n'aimerait à boire?
     A l'ami Carnot,
     A l'aimable Cot,
   A l'instant je veux boire:
     A vous, chère Fosseux,
     Au groupe joyeux,
   Je veux encore boire.

One would but have slightly relished listening to the recitation of such verses as the above; but here is a madrigal which is somewhat better:—

> Crois-moi, jeune et belle Ophélie,
> Quoi qu'en dise le monde, et malgré ton miroir,
> Contente d'être belle et de n'en rien savoir,
> Garde toujours ta modestie;
> Sur le pouvoir de tes appas
> Demeure toujours alarmée:
> Tu n'en seras que mieux aimée
> Si tu crains de ne l'être pas.

And here is the first stanza of a song which is really not without merit:—

> *Remercimens à Messieurs de la Société des Rosatis.*
>
> *Air*—"Resiste moi, belle Aspasie."
>
> Je vois l'épine avec la rose
> Dans les bouquets que vous m'offrez;
> Et lorsque vous me célébrez,
> Vos vers découragent ma prose.
> Tout qu'on me dit de charmant,
> Messieurs, a droit de me confondre—
> La rose est votre compliment,
> L'épine est la loi d'y répondre!

Strange as the figure of Robespierre as a poet may appear, it is on the whole less opposed to the current notions of him, than the one presented by his Letters, which exhibit him in his unstudied character. Among the rare fragments preserved of this singular being, are some letters, hitherto unpublished, which M. Louis Blanc very handsomely placed at my service; though my publication of them will forestall his own. They are written with a carelessness of orthography and grammar not unusual in French correspondence:—"auteur" is always spelled "autheur" —"alarmé" is written "allarmé"—"une vaste *pleine*" (for *plaine*); subjunctives are employed for indicatives, and singular tenses follow plural nouns; and we sometimes stumble on such a phrase as "empressement pour nous voir." The tone of *badinage* which runs through the following letter—the minuteness of the details recalling Gil Blas—the animal spirits and expansiveness of the feelings—render it, when we consider who was the writer, one of the most curious and suggestive letters we have ever met with.

"Carvins, June 12, 1783.

"Sir,

"There is no such thing as pleasure unless it be shared among friends. I am about to give you a sketch, therefore, of what I have enjoyed these last few days.

"Don't expect a book of travels! For several years the public has been so prodigiously overstocked with that kind of work, that it may well be satiated with them now. I can conceive an author who has made a journey of five leagues, celebrating it in prose and verse; and yet what is that adventurous enterprise compared with the one I have executed? I have not only traveled five leagues, I have traveled six; and *such* leagues, that the opinion of the inhabitants of this country would go to prove that they were equal to seven ordinary leagues. And, nevertheless, I will not tell you a single word respecting my journey; I regret it, for your sake; you lose much. It would have offered you some adventures which would have been infinitely interesting: those of Ulysses and Telemachus were nothing by their side.

"We started at five in the morning. Our car quitted the gates of the city at precisely the same moment as the chariot of the sun sprang from the bosom of the ocean. It was adorned with a cloth of brilliant white, one portion of which floated, breathed on by the zephyrs. It was thus we passed the *aubette des Commis*[*] in triumph. As you may suppose, I did not fail to cast my eyes on them. I wished to ascertain whether these Arguses would not give the lie to their ancient reputation; and, animated with a noble emulation, I dared to ambition the glory of vanquishing

---

[*] Most probably the guard-house of the *Octroi*.

them in politeness, if that was possible. I leant over the side of our car, and taking off the new hat which covered my head, I saluted them with my most graceful smile. I reckoned on a proper return. Would you believe it? These clerks, motionless as the god Terminus at the entrance of their cabin, regarded me fixedly without returning my salute. I have always had an infinite self-love; that mark of contempt cut me to the quick; and for the rest of the day my temper was unbearable.

"Meanwhile our coursers bore us onwards with a rapidity which the imagination can scarcely conceive. It seemed as if they wished to emulate the fleetness of the coursers of the sun who flew over our heads; in the same bold spirit as that which dictated my chivalrous *assaut de politesse* with the clerks at the Meaulens Gate. With one bound they cleared the Faubourg St. Catherine; a second bound carried us to the square at Sens. We stayed a short time in that town. I profited by the delay to examine the beauties it presents to the curiosity of the traveler. While the rest were breakfasting I ascended the hill upon which the Calvary is placed. From that point my eyes wandered forth with a mingled sentiment of sadness and exultation, upon the vast plain where Condé, at twenty, gained that famous victory over the Spaniards which saved France.

"But an object interesting for other reasons next absorbed my attention—the Hotel de Ville. It is remarkable neither for its greatness nor its magnificence; but it has not the less claim upon my attention—it does not the less inspire me with lively interest. This modest edifice, said I, meditatively, is the sanctuary where the hunchback T . . . ., with his blonde wig, holding the balance of Themis in his hand, formerly weighed with great impartiality the claims of his co-citizens. Minister of Justice and the favorite of Esculapius, he passed a sentence and then wrote a prescription. The criminal and the patient were equally terrified by his presence; and this great man, by virtue of his double office, was in possession of the most extensive power that man ever exercised over his fellow-citizens.

"In my enthusiasm I could not rest until I had penetrated

within the walls of this Hôtel de Ville. I wanted to see the *salle d'audience;* I wanted to see the tribunal of the *Echevins.* I ransack the town to find the porter. He comes; he opens; I rush into the salle. Seized with a holy awe I fall on my knees in this august temple, and kiss with transport the seat which was formerly pressed by the rump of the great T . . . . It was thus that Alexander knelt at the tomb of Achilles, and that Cæsar paid his homage to the monument which contained the ashes of the conqueror of Asia!

" We remounted our conveyance. Scarcely had I comfortably settled myself on a bundle of straw when Carvins rose into view. At the sight of this happy spot we all burst forth into a shout of joy, comparable to that which burst from the Trojans escaped from the disasters of *Ilos* (*sic* in MS.) when they perceived the shores of Italy. The inhabitants of this village gave us a welcome which was an ample compensation for the indifference of the clerks at the Meaulens gate. Citizens of every class manifested their enthusiasm for us. The cobbler arrested his awl, about to pierce a sole, that he might contemplate us at leisure; the barber abandoned a half-shaved chin, and rushed out before us, razor in hand; the huswife, to satisfy her curiosity, braved the perils of a burnt tart; I actually saw three gossips break off in the midst of an animated conversation to rush to the window. In short, we tasted during our passage—which was, alas! too brief—that satisfaction, so flattering to our self-love, of seeing a numerous people occupied with us. How pleasant it is to travel! I said to myself. It is said with great truth that one is never a prophet in one's own land. At the gates of your own town you are despised; six leagues beyond it you are a personage worthy of public curiosity.

" I was occupied with these wise reflections when we arrived at the house which was the end of our voyage. I will not attempt to depict the transports of tenderness which broke forth in our embraces. It was a spectacle to have drawn tears from your eyes. In history I know but of one scene of the kind to compare with it. When Eneas, after the fall of Troy, lands in Epirus with his fleet, and there meets with Helenus and Andromache, whom destiny had placed upon the throne of Pyrrhus, it is said their meeting was most affecting. I have no doubt Eneas had an excellent heart. Helenus, the best Trojan in the world, and Andromache, the amiable widow of Hector, shed many tears and sighed many sighs on this occasion. I am willing to believe that their transports were not inferior to ours; but after Eneas, Helenus, Andromache, and us, you must let the curtain fall (*il faut tirer l'échelle*).

"Since our arrival, all our time has been occupied with pleasures. Ever since last Saturday I have been eating tarts. Destiny has willed that my bed should be placed in a room which is the dépôt of the pastry. That was exposing me to the temptation of eating tarts all night! But I reflected that it was noble to subdue one's passions, and I slept therefore, though in the midst of these seductive objects. It is true I made up during the day for this long abstinence."

[Robespierre's enthusiasm here breaks forth into verse, and for a moment I cease to translate.]

"Je te rends grace, ô toi qui d'une main habile,
Façonnant le premier une pâte docile,
Presentas aux mortels ce mets delicieux.
Mais ont-ils reconnu ce bienfait precieux ?
De tes divins talens consacrant la mémoire,
Leur zèle a-t-il dressé des autels à ta gloire ?
Cent peuples, prodiguant leur encens et leurs vœux,
Ont rempli l'univers de temples et de dieux :
Ils ont tous oublié ce sublime génie,
Qui pour eux sur la terre apporta l'ambroisie ;
La tarte en leurs festins domine avec honneur,
Mais daignent-ils songer à son premier autheur !

"Of all the traits of ingratitude which the human race has been guilty of towards its benefactors, that is the one which has always most revolted me. It is for the Artesians to expiate it; seeing that the opinion of all Europe pronounces that they know the value of the tart better than every other people. Their glory calls upon them to build a temple to its inventor. I will confess to you, between ourselves, that I have drawn up a project to that effect, which I propose presenting to the Artesian States. I count upon the powerful support of the clergy.

"But to eat tarts is nothing; one must eat them in good company. I have enjoyed that advantage. Yesterday I received the greatest honor to which I could ever aspire. I dined with three lieutenants and the son of a *bailli*. The whole magistrature of the neighboring villages was assembled at our table. In the centre of this senate shone monsieur the lieutenant of Carvins, like Calypso amidst her nymphs. Ah! if you could have seen with what affability he conversed with the rest of the company, as if he were an ordinary mortal; with what indulgence he approved of the champagne which was poured out for him; with what a satisfied air he seemed to smile at the reflection of his image in the glass! I saw all that; yes I . . , and yet observe how hard it is to content the heart of man! All my desires are not yet satisfied. I am preparing to return to Arras; and I hope to find greater pleasure in seeing you than even in all that above described! We shall meet with the same satisfaction as Ulysses and Telemachus after twenty years of absence. I shall have no difficulty in reconciling myself to the loss of my *baillis* and lieutenants. (However seductive a lieutenant may be, believe me, madame, he can never enter into comparison with you. His countenance, even when champagne has tinged it with a soft carnation, does not present the charm which Nature alone has given to yours; and the company of all the *baillis* of the universe never can compensate for your agreeable conversation.)

"I remain, with the sincerest expression of friendship, sir, your very humble and very obedient servant,

"DE ROBESPIERRE."

Robespierre was five-and-twenty when he wrote that letter. In it we may read what he was at that age. Its playfulness and expansiveness, its lively record of trifles in the language of one ambitious of literary fame, its classical allusions constantly dropping from his pen, and its attempts at sarcasm, more complimentary to his disposition than to his wit, are curious traits. The oftener I read over this letter, the more vivid the contrast stands out between the gloomy, concentrated, pedantic, fanatic of after days, and the gossiping playful youth, giving a mock heroic description of a journey of eighteen miles, writing a tirade about pastry and improvising verses on the inventor of tarts. This lively letter shows us how much the spirit of an age and the great events in which men co-operate, affect the bias of their characters. Without a revolution to foster and call forth the stern fanaticism which grew out of his overweening pride, Robespierre would doubtless have been a mere provincial advocate with a taste for literature. He would have been a thoroughly "respectable" citizen, and a thoroughly insignificant writer.

Literature occupied much of his attention. Besides "Les Rosatis," Arras boasted of an academy, similar to those of the other provinces of France, and which still flourishes in mild mediocrity. Robespierre, who, as I said, was rather a lion in Arras, was early made a member of this academy (15th of November, 1783).

In the next year, I find him ambitious of still higher academic success. Not content with reading papers at his own academy, he throws himself into the arena, and hopes to obtain the public prize! The celebrity obtained by the academy of Dijon, owing to the famous discourses of Rousseau, had given a stimulus to all the other provincial academies; and the Royal Society of Arts and Sciences, at Metz, now proposed the following subject:—"What is the origin of that opinion which extends to all individuals of a family a part of the shame attached to a criminal? That opinion, is it more dangerous than useful? and (should it be decided in the affirmative) what would be the means of preventing the danger?"

This was just the sort of subject Robespierre gloried in; and although his discourse did not obtain the prize (that was awarded to Lacretelle), it was nevertheless thought worthy of honorable mention, and obtained a medal of 400 francs.

The following year we see him again a competitor. The academy of Amiens had proposed as its subject, the "Eloge" of Gresset (the charming author of "Ver-Vert"), one of those graceful writers peculiar to French literature; a man of fashion tinctured with religion; a man of wit, with just enough seriousness to give momentum to his wit; of whom Voltaire said,

> Gresset, doué du double privilége
> D'être au collége un bel esprit mondain,
> Et dans le monde un homme de collége;
> Gresset dévot, long-temps petit badin,
> Sanctifie par ses palinodies;
> Il prétendait avec componction
> Qu'il avait fait jadis des comédies,
> Dont à la Vierge il demandait pardon.

The verses, and the letter previously given, will have prepared the reader for Robespierre's admiration of such a writer as Gresset. The ease, the gaiety, frivolity, and wit which distinguish Gresset, are graces to have captivated one less ambitious of literary success; and Robespierre in his "Eloge" shows that he was captivated by them. There is, moreover, another aspect of Gresset's mind, as Voltaire indicates—I mean the religious aspect. That also Robespierre appreciated, and with an earnestness which was not common in those days.*

If it is difficult to imagine Robespierre a poet, still more difficult is it to picture him in love. Nor, indeed, have my researches enabled me to discover any chapters of youth's romance during this dull, dark, Arras period. I suppose that all boys have loved; especially boys who write verses, however bad. And I assume, therefore, that some affection did shed its sunny influence over a brief portion of this Arras period. His heart, doubtless, beat for some blue-eyed girl; and I am sorry that I have only a fleeting rumor to record of his having won the affections of one who

---

* The curious reader is referred to the "Eloge" itself; extracts to support the assertion in the text would occupy too much space, and would not justify it by their merit.

appears to have had the virtue of constancy in the smallest possible degree; on returning after a short absence, Maximilien found her as beautiful as before, but she had given her beauty to another. It is to her the motto points which is inscribed under the earliest portrait of Robespierre, that, namely, in M. Saint Albin's collection, where he is represented with one hand holding a rose, the other placed upon his heart. Underneath the portrait are these words—"Tout pour mon amie." Maximilien was not of a nature to be greatly affected by this inconstancy. He consoled himself with his law books, and continued to earn the applause and esteem of his fellow citizens.

CHAPTER V.

Robespierre named member of the Criminal Court—Resigns, from opposition to capital punishment—"L'Affaire du Collier"—Convocation of the notables—States General—The press loud for liberty—Robespierre's memoir on reform—Opposes his benefactor, the bishop—His pleading Dupond's cause—Writes against "lettres de cachet"—Address to the king—Letter about Canary birds—Chosen as deputy.

THE clergy were proud of their protégé; and the Bishop of Arras named him a member of the Criminal Court. Not long did he enjoy the honor and emolument of this elevation, for having been obliged, in the course of his duties, to condemn an assassin to death, he was so painfully affected by it as to send in his resignation. The man who was so soon to drown France in blood, the man at whose right hand stood the guillotine, whose watchword was terror, who brought to the block a king, a lovely queen, a royal princess, princes, noblemen, and prostitutes, was at this time an advocate for the abolition of capital punishment; and so disinterested an advocate, that he gave up emolument, rather than countenance the system. Those whose invincible dislike to Robespierre will not permit them to be impartial, regard this resignation as a pitiable affectation. They cannot understand the apparent contradiction of his horror at blood, and his share in the "Terror." Whoso looks deeper than the surface, will find no contradiction here. Robespierre was by nature not a sanguinary man; but he was a fanatic who would sacrifice everything to the triumph of an idea, and who pushed onwards to his goal, though his passage might be through a sea of blood. Remorseless in the name of liberty, a drop of blood shed for any other cause was sickening to him.

It was now that the infamous-famous *Affaire du Collier* startled France. Her queen, a prince of ancient name, together with the Countess Lamotte, the degraded descendant of the House of Valois, were implicated in a contemptible piece of fraud and felony. Whether Marie Antoinette were guilty, as Louis Blanc and the Republicans believe, or whether, as I confess it seems to me more probable, that she was in nowise concerned in it—the effect upon France was, in either case, fatal to the interests of royalty. Are these our rulers? Are these our aristocrats? Are these the highest people in our realm? A queen and a grand cardinal, to be dragged into a court of justice, as no better than pick-pockets! Is there really then no divinity hedging them? Are they to be tried in our courts of justice like simple mortals?

Not only on that did France ponder, but on many other things. Its whole social existence was decaying. The great fabric of the middle ages, reared with so much toil, cemented with so much blood, was now crumbling to pieces, and a new-birth of society was at hand. Robespierre, in his little province, was not untroubled. Looking, with the eyes of Rousseau, at the coming future, he felt his heart expand within him, beating with wild hopes. He deplored the state of society, and determined to join his efforts with those who would sweep away the abuses which existed.

France convoked her Notables, but neither the Notables, nor the administration of a dexterous Calonne, an unprincipled Brienne, and a virtuous Necker, could bring a remedy. At last, it was resolved to convoke the States-General.

The Convocation of the States-General, 1789, is, as Michelet truly observes, the era of the birth of a people; it called the whole nation to the exercise of their rights; it allowed them, at least, to utter their complaints, their wishes, and to choose for themselves their own electors. Small republican states had already admitted all their members to a participation of political rights, but never had a great kingdom, an empire, like that of France, done such a thing. It was new, not only in French annals, but in those of the world. It is affirmed, that 5,000,000 of men took part in the election. It was a grand, surprising spectacle, to see a whole people emerging at once from nonentity to existence; who, silent until then, suddenly found a voice. Curious also it is to think, that the ministers and Parliament, who convoked the people, only meant, by this solemn convocation of the great lifeless mass, to frighten the privileged classes. This lifeless mass, however, had a voice, many voices; and they spoke out. Every citizen had been authorized to publish the result of his studies, of his reflections and researches, on the mode of convocation, and the form of the States-General. The press became the voice of the people.

Kersaint in *Le bon Sens*, Brissot, Clavière, Condorcet, Target, Cérutti, Volney in the *Moniteur*, Thouret, Servan, and Mounier, ardently invoked the rights of the Third Estate, and spoke with eloquence in the name of justice, right, and reason. In the *Orateur pour les Etats Généraux*, a pamphlet, the vehemence of which obtained for it an immense popularity, Carra protested indignantly against the name of subjects given to the members of the assembled states. He said that the nation was the real sovereign, and the king was but its delegate. Energetic and eloquent pamphlets passed from shop to shop, from village to village, and, in spite of every effort to repress them, penetrated even to the hearths of the poor. Cérutti wrote this memorable sentence:—
"The People is the only body which does not live by abuses, and which sometimes dies from them."

Robespierre seized the occasion, and published a memoir on the necessity of reforming the Artesian States. The Artesian Third Estate was a mere mockery. It was composed of all the municipals of provinces which were chosen by the deputies of the states: and what were these deputies? nine individuals, selected by others, in each of the three orders. Thus: three deputies of the nobility, three deputies of the clergy, concurred with the three deputies of the third estate, to choose the municipals: that is to say, the electoral body of the third estate.

This injustice Robespierre boldly attacked. He demonstrated the corruption and venality of the system, with an audacity and a logic which astonished and silenced opponents. It made him a notable man: indeed he was gradually becoming more and more of a public character. He had incurred the lasting hatred of the prelates, and the contempt of the lords of Artois. What! he, the miserable advocate, brought up by charity, patronized by us the clergy, dare to raise his voice against us! Dare to think our acts unjust! It is preposterous! Ingratitude was charged to him; for though he owed so much to the Bishop of Arras, yet did he not flinch from espousing the cause of the bishop's opponents. Some peasantry came to Robespierre, as to the friend of the people, as to an honest advocate upon whom they could rely, to entreat him to plead for them against the bishop. He examined their case, found it just, and at that period, when no other advocate would have had the boldness to plead against the sovereign of the town, he, the *protégé* of that sovereign, considering an advocate as a magistrate, and placing justice before personal feeling, cast sentiment and gratitude aside, and, in the august name of justice and eternal truth, pleaded against his protector.

I know of no episode in his life which better characterizes him than this. The world did not, and will not, forget the ingratitude, but the world will recognize in it that great love of truth and justice, which, trampling under foot all ordinary notions of personal predilections, made him stand forth as the defender of the oppressed against the all-powerful oppressor. Here we see the germ of a fanatic; here we see the man who was ready to sacrifice the whole world to an idea; the man who recognized no claim of sentiment; no piety, but piety towards truth and those eternal principles of justice which human affections may pervert, but cannot wholly subdue. Brutus condemning his son to death was never lovable; and yet no one pretends to deny what was admirable in his act. Such stern adherence to abstract right is a suspicious virtue, and may sometimes turn out to be a kind of vice; for in this world of ours, living, as we do, amidst imperfect human beings, and having to work out our ends by human means, abstract principles of justice, irrespective of all human affections, never have, and never will, command unmixed admiration. We can never love such virtue. Our admiration of it springs from the intellect and not from the heart. The point is worth noticing in Robespierre, as it furnishes us the key to his whole subsequent career.

A few months before the opening of the States-General, Robespierre was appointed President of the Academy of Arras; a sufficient indication of the esteem in which he was held in his native town. Shortly afterwards, he had to plead a cause, which once more fixed public attention upon him. A certain Dupond had been the victim of a most infamous spoliation. His brother, brother-in-law, friends, the small authorities of the village, and in fact, the whole province seemed to be united against this unhappy man, to deprive him of fortune and liberty. After an absence of twenty-six years from his country, he endeavored to regain possession of his property. His claims were first received in silence, then by evasions. His enemies, alarmed at the risk of a law-suit, found it more convenient to lodge against him a *lettre de cachet*. It was his cause that Robespierre undertook to plead, and in a memoir, singularly bold, he attacks the whole system of *lettres de cachet*.

It was high time, for that system had reached the apex of its enormity. So crying was this abuse, that some of those historical philosophers who look upon the great events of the world's history as produced by accident or individual measures, have not hesitated to pronounce the *lettres de cachet* to have been the principal cause of the French Revolution;—an absurdity, since the *let-*

tres de cachet were but the produce of a far wider, far deeper system. Nevertheless, consider that fathers could then quietly imprison refractory sons; that noblemen could evade their debts, by sending their troublesome creditors to the Bastille; that wives who had husbands ridiculous enough to entertain scruples respecting the seventh commandment, had only to solicit a *lettre de cachet* to enjoy their amours in peace! St. Florentin alone gave away as many as 50,000! It was no difficult matter for Robespierre to expose this invention of despotism. Not content with demonstrating the illegality of these letters, he demonstrated, that real authority was not benefited by them, that they were only useful to satisfy the petty vengeance of the subordinate agents, or the cupidity and base passions of a reckless nobility. There is matter for reflection in the fact, that in this very memoir, in which he raises his voice against an infamous system of despotism, he has inserted a pompous eulogium upon that king whom he was afterwards to guillotine; and that in his peroration he presented a brilliant picture of the future prosperity of France, when governed by wise and popular laws, such as the convocation of the States-General could not fail to produce. He called upon the king to complete the work of Charlemagne and Henry IV., and thus realize the happiness of France.

"'To lead men to happiness through virtue, and to virtue, by a legislation founded on the eternal principles of justice, and so framed as to restore human nature to all its rights, and all its dignity; to renew the immortal compact which is to bind man to his Creator and to his fellow-citizens, by removing all the causes of oppression which now create throughout the world fear, distrust, meanness, selfishness, hatred and cupidity; behold, sire, the glorious mission to which you are called! It was to you, sire, that the achievement of a revolution was reserved, which neither Charlemagne nor Henry could accomplish. It was necessary for the harvest to have been prepared, and matured by ages which have preceded ours; it was necessary that reason, awakened from its long slumber by the crimes and excesses of ignorance, should gradually revive and diffuse amongst us a knowledge of the principles of public morality, too long misunderstood, and of the claims of humanity too long neglected."

This has been looked upon as hypocrisy. Very unjustly, I believe. It would be wrong to suppose that Robespierre did not really think the king would reform France; for although faith in royalty was then in its last stage, there was still a vital spark in it; many believed in it, or at least thought they believed in it. The enthusiasm of the people for the king was a genuine enthusiasm; and we shall find, much later than this, Robespierre still a royalist.

It is in allusion, I suppose, to this memoir that he speaks in the following letter, selected from among those in the possession of M. Louis Blanc, the original of which he has printed in his "Histoire de la Revolution Française;" the letter itself is only worth preserving from the piquant contrast of its tone with the idea usually formed of Robespierre's mind.

"1788.

"MADEMOISELLE,

"I have the honor to send you a mémoire, the object of which is interesting. Such homage is permissible even to the Graces, when to all their charms they add the gifts of thought and feeling, and are equally capable of sympathizing with misfortune as of conferring happiness.

"Apropos of so serious an object, mademoiselle, may I be allowed to speak to you of the Canary birds? They are very pretty, and we anticipated that, being educated by you, they would be the sweetest and most sociable of Canary birds. What was our surprise when, approaching their cage, we saw them dash themselves against the wires with an impetuosity which made us tremble for their lives! That is what they do whenever they see the hand which feeds them. . . . . What plan of education have you adopted with them? and whence their wild character? Do the Doves which the Graces rear for the chariot of Venus display this fierce disposition? A face like yours, has it not reconciled the Canaries to the human countenance? Or is it that they can support the sight of no other, having once seen it? Pray, explain this strange phenomenon. Meanwhile, we shall always think them charming, with all their faults.

"My sister particularly desires me to testify her gratitude for your kindness in making this present.

"I am, with respect, mademoiselle, &c.,
"DE ROBESPIERRE."

Dupond's was the last cause Robespierre pleaded in Arras; and almost the last intimation we have of him there. I regret that my researches have not furnished more details regarding this period of his life, on which I would gladly have lingered ere accompanying him into the turmoil of the Revolution; but over it there hangs provoking obscurity, and I fear the obscurity will for ever remain. This has led some to believe that he himself was an altogether insignificant person there; a conclusion which is contradicted by the few facts which have been brought to light regarding him. He was no insignificant man, whom the *Tiers-Etat* of Artois chose as their deputy to the States-General, appending this note to his name:—"*Ce dernier se charge de parler tout le reste.*" He was no insignificant man who was elected President of the Arras Academy, and whom M. de Fosseux, the Mayor of Arras, could call—

"Appui des malheureux—vengeur de l'innocence,
Tu vis pour la *vertu*—pour la douce amitié."

And, even in the exaggerated language of verse advise him—

"Ne vas pas, cependant vouloir priver ta tête
Des lauriers immortels que ta gloire t'apprête."

Ignorance of his whereabouts has given rise to many absurd stories, which have been collected into Memoirs. There is one, in the "History of Robespierre, Political and Personal" (London, 1794), which, amongst other absurdities and scandals, says that Robespierre was a shop-porter in Dublin; there, forging a will, he was sent to prison, where he became acquainted with Marat!

As I before intimated, a man may be of importance in a small town, like Arras, and yet utterly unknown to France at large. The point is of no great consequence. Suffice it for our purpose, that he was elected as one of the deputies to the States-General.

Now that he was to leave his native town for the great capital, one may ask: "Why did the poor advocate, with a family greatly depending on his exertions, leave his practice to throw himself into the turbid stream of politics, where he had so little prospect of distinguishing himself?" The *why* is found in that passion for truth and justice, which Cicero says is implanted in our souls:—
"Tantam esse necessitatem virtutis generi hominum à naturâ, tantumque amorem ad communem salutem defendendam datum, ut ea vis omnia blandimenta voluptatis otique vicerit."

CHAPTER VI.

Causes of the Revolution—The Tiers-Etat—Opening of the States-General—Description of Robespierre's appearance—Loyalty of the deputies—Struggle between the court and the Tiers-Etat—Robespierre makes his first motion—Received in silent disdain.

THE most eventful period of Robespierre's life, and one of the most eventful periods in the history of France, is now about to open. The States-General are convened; the States-General, which many men regard as the beginning, and some as the cause, of the French Revolution; as if history had any beginning, except that of the world's creation: as if any one event could be taken as the sole cause of a great revolution!

The States-General are here; and what brought them here? Some will say, inconsiderate feebleness of the king, rash demands of innovators, and anarchical schemes of reckless demagogues. It requires, however, no great sagacity to see that the States-General are the inevitable product of all that has gone before them. Historical philosophers and essayists may discourse glibly about the causes of the French Revolution, but in truth, no man can name them. They are countless: old as the world; beginning at the remotest eras of history, and have not yet ceased operating on society. To hear men talking of *this measure* arresting the revolution, and *that man* altering its course:—to hear them say, if *this* had been done, the course of all things would have been altered:—to hear them attribute to one man the direction of the whole nation in its mad career, is to those who regard history as the growth and development of a world, a matter of some astonishment. Master the Revolution? To master it you must control all history, you must undo all that ages before you have done; wash from the tablets whereon are recorded the annals of mankind, all the folly, all the madness, all the cruelty, all the wisdom, all the myriad concurring circumstances which went to build up that one event we name—The French Revolution.

The causes of the Revolution are not to be named. The proximate causes are indeed easily discernible. We do not, we cannot, know how the gunpowder was made; but we can perceive the sparks which produced the explosion, and it is because we can thus determine what were the accidental trifles which stimulated the outbreak, that so many shallow explanations of this great event have been proposed by various writers who have overlooked the fact so admirably stated by Aristotle in his "Politics," that revolutions are produced *by* trifles but not *out of* trifles: γίγνονται δε αἱ στάσεις οὐ περὶ μικρῶν, ἀλλ' ἐκ μικρῶν. The French Revolution was the great struggle of the oppressed against the privileged. It was a cause to be tried before the great tribunal of history; a cause such as no man can look on without painful interest. The many, instructed in their rights by the philosophers, and stimulated by hunger and misery, now prepared to assert their rights. There can be little question that the philosophers, although they did not produce the Revolution, certainly did awaken the many to the true sense of their own position; nay more, to the true sense of their strength. "The state?" said Louis XIV., "I am the state, *L'état c'est moi!*" It would have been heresy to doubt it. But now the people said, "*L'état c'est nous*—We are the state;" and when once that is said, it will not be long before it is acted on.

Chamfort, that subtle thinker and celebrated wit, once said in the salons, "What is the Third Estate? Everything, yet nothing." This epigram originated the famous pamphlet of the Abbé Sièyes on the *Tiers Etat*. This pamphlet was the "manifesto" of the middle classes; it put the three great questions, and gave the answers.

What is the Third Estate? Everything.

What has it been hitherto in the political constitution? Nothing.

What does it demand? To become something.

A pamphlet more cogent, more obvious, or more modest, at the same time more terrible, was never published. It was a flash of thought which illumined the whole kingdom. In it, these three fatal expressions perpetually recurred, as texts to the great sermon which the priest of humanity was preaching. He undertook to prove that which now-a-days no one will deny, but which was then a daring novelty, that the Tiers Etat formed the complete nation; that the millions really *did* count as an element in society, and that a few privileged units did not form the whole nation. Nay more, that the millions really could do without the privileged orders, and yet society not fall to pieces; but that the privileged orders could not exist without the nation. One of the daring phrases of this work was: "If aristocracy is created by conquest, the Third Estate will become noble by conquering in its turn." Sièyes also said,—and this, perhaps, was the deepest insight in all his work,—that there was no constitution in France, and that it was necessary to create one; that the nation alone had the power and the right to create it; and that so far from imitating the English constitution, which thinkers of that day, following Montesquieu, were so prone to imitate, the nation must create one entirely adapted to its own nature. "In the English constitution," he said, "instead of the fabric of order, I perceive nothing but a scaffolding of protection against disorder."

With our free press, our free elections, our open trials, and civic liberty, we cannot, without an effort, throw ourselves back into that age of tyranny, of privilege, and of political ignorance. To paint that age by one stroke, it is enough to say, torture then was legal! That fact alone is sufficient to indicate the immensity of the progress that has since been made.

The greatness of the evils which the Revolution came to remedy, is to be measured by the madness of the Revolution itself; by its crimes, by its horrors, by its extravagances. Had not the sense of injury been so keen, the vengeance would not have been so terrible. The Revolution would only have been a change of government. But the vengeance of the people was fierce, partly because their wrongs had been so great, and partly because the resistance which opposed them was so powerful. So little did the privileged classes understand political justice, that they fought for their injustice as for a pure truth. We have only to compare the Revolution of 1830 with this first and bloody Revolution of 1789, to perceive that the horrors which stained the last-named arose not from doctrine, but from social evils. *Then* the Republic had to contend against three great elements of resistance: Royalty, which, though feeble, had still an existence in men's minds; Aristocracy, which was a devout faith among all the well-born; and Religion, which, although the clergy were shamelessly corrupt, and even some archbishops did not believe in God's existence, still chose to identify itself and its welfare with the preservation of established governments. Since that day faith in royalty has become wholly extinct; faith in the aristocracy has scarcely an existence; and religion has seen that its interests and well-being are not necessarily bound up with any form of government. Hence in 1830, there really was no opposition: nothing to fight against, consequently there was no vengeance. Whatever we may think of the methods adopted by the republicans, however we may shudder at their crimes and sneer at their folly, the Revolution had its holy work to do, and did it. It waded through blood to its attainment, but the blood was forced on it by those who opposed it.

It is the 4th of May, 1789; the sun pours floods of rays upon this earth; the whole sky is cloudless. All France, as they say, is at Paris, and the *élite* of France is at Versailles. The States-General are to open on the morrow; and it has been decided to open it by a National and Religious Fête. The broad streets of Versailles are lined with French and Swiss guards. The crown tapestry hangs from the windows; the very roofs of houses are loaded with people; the balconies are adorned with costly stuffs, and filled by brilliant women in the coquettish costume of that period, variegated with feathers and flowers. But that which makes the grandeur of the spectacle is not the streets glittering with thousands of bayonets, nor the heads of lovely women gazing from the windows, nor the rich draperies floating from the balconies, nor the grave sad voice of the priest, mingled with the sound of church bells solemnly mounting towards heaven, amidst the roll of drums, the clanging of trumpets, and the sharp loud commands of officers. No; the real grandeur, the thrilling novelty, is in the language spoken amongst the crowds, in the enthusiasm of their looks, in the unaccustomed haughtiness of their demeanor.

All that mass of men is strangely affected, and full of anxiety; an unknown something is before them, and their hearts tremble at its awful approach. What will be its progress? what its result? No one can tell; few can pretend to guess.

The beauty of the scene is varied and majestic. The music, mingling with the sounds of arms and infinite hubbub of voices, produces an effect which no spectator ever forgets. One deputy of the nobility confesses that he wept for joy.

Behold the doors of St. Louis' Church are flung open, and the procession advances, amid shouts which rend the air. First appears a mass of 500 men, clothed in black, with white cravats. It is the deep battalion of the Third Estate, or rather of the *Communes*.* In that battalion more than 300 are jurists, advocates, or magistrates; a proportion which will raise the scornful ire of a Burke, when, in the forlorn splendor of diction befitting

---

* In one of Robespierre's unpublished letters, dated 11th of May, 1789, the words Third Estate are proscribed as a token of ancient servitude.

an ancient priest wailing over the destruction of his gods, that great writer will stigmatize the Revolution. To him, and to others, it will seem as if the predominance of lawyers was the truest indication of the coming anarchy. What! shall pettifogging lawyers presume to take into their hands the reins of government, when Nature has so kindly furnished hereditary legislators: men *born* to the office! It is even so. This "new birth of time" is the advent of Law: and lawyers are its mouth-pieces. These States-General are to proclaim, that Law and Justice in place of privileges and classes shall rule the world.

In that battalion of the Third Estate strange figures may be seen, figures of men already famous, or to become so hereafter. There Beauty gazes with its wondering eyes upon the modern Gracchus, Mirabeau:—scanning his fearful but meaning countenance—his scarred, distorted face—his flashing eyes, and lion mane. He is a man in whom it has been truly said everything is great, even his vices; who gives heroic proportions even to his degradation; who unites a cool head to an ardent temperament; and preserves, amidst all the infamous traffic of his powers, the incorruptibility of his genius! "At the foot of the tribune," says Lamartine, "he was a man destitute of shame or of virtue; in the tribune he was an honest man. His eloquence, popular in its style, was the eloquence of a patrician."

There, also, Beauty might have seen (if it had cared to look) a sickly man, whom none observed. He perhaps is the only one in that battalion, who, illuminated by the light of his own convictions, foresees the real consequences of the States-General. It is the advocate of Arras. If Mirabeau was the most illustrious among these men, Robespierre was certainly one of the most obscure; so obscure that he had, to so vain a man, the great annoyance of seeing his name perpetually mis-spelled by journalists and writers. Mirabeau always called him Robertspierre. Prudhomme writes it "Robert Pierre." He is not unfrequently designated in the *Moniteur* by M.* * *. It is so in the report of his speech on the 6th of June.

Here is Lamartine's portrait of that advocate.

"Robespierre had not the advantages of birth, of genius, nor of exterior, to arrest men's notice. There was nothing striking about him; his small talents had only shone at the bar or in provincial academies; a few wordy speeches, filled with a tame and almost pastoral philosophy, some stanzas of cold and affected poetry, had carried his name into the insignificant periodicals of the day: he was more than unknown, he was mediocre and despised. His features presented nothing which could attract attention in a large assembly: there was no visible characters of the power which was within; he was *le dernier mot* of the Revolution, and no one could read it.

"Robespierre's figure was small, his limbs feeble and angular, his step irresolute, his attitudes affected, his gestures ungraceful; his somewhat shrill voice sought oratorical inflexions, but was only fatiguing and monotonous; his forehead was good, but small and projecting over the temples, as if enlarged by the mass and embarrassed movement of his thoughts; his eyes, much veiled by their lids and very sharp at the extremities, were deeply buried in the cavities of their orbits; they were of a soft blue color; his nose straight and small, was very wide at the nostrils, which were high and too expanded; his mouth was large, his lips thin and disagreeably contracted at each corner; his chin small and pointed, his complexion yellow and livid, like that of an invalid or a man worn out by vigils and meditations. The habitual expression of his face was the superficial serenity of a grave mind, and a smile wavering betwixt sarcasm and sweetness. There was *softness*, but of a sinister character. The dominant characteristic of his countenance was the prodigious and continual tension of brow, eyes, mouth, and all the facial muscles. One saw that the whole of his features, like the whole of his mind, converged incessantly on a single point, with such power that there was no dissipation of will, and he appeared to foresee all he desired to accomplish, as though he had already the reality before his eyes. Such was the man destined to absorb in himself all those men, and make them his victims after having used them as his instruments. He was of no party, but of all parties which by turns served his ideal of the Revolution. In this his power consisted, for parties paused, but he never paused. He was the entire embodiment of the Revolution,—principles, thoughts, passions, impulses. Thus embodying himself wholly in it, he compelled it one day to incorporate itself in him. That day was yet distant."

This strange Battalion of the Third Estate is accompanied in its march by enthusiastic applause. The applause suddenly ceases as the brilliant little troop of Deputies of the nobility now approach, and dazzle the eye with their dancing plumes, their glittering ornaments, and rich laces. This body of the aristocracy, the depository and guardian of France's military glory, boasts of no single celebrated general. "Obscure men of illustrious origin are those grand lords of France." Among them, however, is a figure of no little interest, that namely of the young Lafayette, the hero of the American war.

The clergy advance in the same silence. In this order two orders are distinctly perceptible: namely, the nobility, the prelates of the Church; and the Third Estate, the plebeians of the Church. Thirty prelates in lawn sleeves and violet robes keep themselves distinctly separated, by a choir of singers, from the modest 200 curés in their priestly black.

Lastly come the King and Queen, accompanied by the Holy Sacrament, which glitters in the hands of the Archbishop of Paris, beneath a magnificent dais, of which the Counts of Provence and Artois, the Dukes of Angoûleme and Berry, hold the *cordons*.

The King is applauded; but the Queen, an object of the people's hatred,—whom they sarcastically call the "Austrian woman," and "*Madame Déficit*,"—is received with murmurs; a few women shouting, "Long live the Duke of Orleans!" thinking to hurt her more by praising her enemy. The insult nearly overcomes her, but she quickly recovers her wonted courage; and from that moment forth attempts to meet the people's hatred with a steadfast and disdainful stare. Ah! how different these murmurs and this insult, from the shouts of acclamation and delight which so little while ago welcomed her lovely face, when France rejoiced in its young Queen!

Arrived at Saint Louis, the three orders take their places in the nave. The King and Queen are seated under a dais of violet-colored velvet, ornamented with the fleur-de-lys of gold. A chorus of melodious voices chants "*O salutaris hostia*." Then the Bishop of Nancy rises; but the people, instead of animating words such as they expected, have to listen to a long harangue, which is little more than an amplification of this idea: religion is the force of States. An idea singularly inappropriate to the occasion;

especially when addressed to an assembly, the majority of whom were infidels.

One thing is peculiarly noticeable at this period; namely, the blindness and frivolity of the Court, which on the eve of such great events could not forget its most puerile distinctions. Even now, with this Convocation of the States-General, it busied itself among old books, to find out the miserable details of a Gothic ceremonial, and the distinctions of a past age, which should rather have been buried in oblivion, hurriedly trodden under ground, not raised into the face of day. The truth is, however, as Michelet has seen, that it was not so much the mania for old customs which guided the Court, as the secret pleasure of mortifying and lowering the petty people, who, at the elections, had been acting the part of kings. It was thought well to remind them of their low origin. Weakness was playing at the dangerous game of humiliating the strong.

Who would believe that this mad Court insisted upon the absurd custom of making the Third Estate harangue kneeling? They would not dispense with this ceremony, and preferred deciding that the President should make no speech whatever; that is to say, at the end of 200 years of separation and silence, the King convokes his people and then forbids them to speak!*

On the 5th of May, the doors of the Salle des Menus are opened. It is a vast rectangular building, with two rows of marble columns, capable of containing upwards of 2000 spectators. The ceiling lets in the light through a curtain of white silk. At the bottom of the Salle is placed a magnificent throne, the fauteuil of the Queen, and the stalls of the princesses. Below is the seat for the secretaries of state, and before them a table covered with violet velvet. To the right are the seats destined for the clergy; to the left, those of the nobility; in front of the throne those of the Commons. The King has superintended these arrangements himself, choosing the carpets and the hangings. On the eve of so solemn an event, his thoughts were occupied with decorations, and with studying the intonations of his voice for his opening discourse. Yes, that was the occupation of France's ruler at such a time!

A foolish incident marked the opening of this first Assembly. Instead of receiving the three orders together, the King made them enter separately. First the clergy, then the nobility, and lastly, after a pause, the Third Estate. These distinctions were only exasperating, not humiliating; and that the Court might have known by the murmurs of applause which saluted Mirabeau, who, with a haughty and domineering manner, his head thrown back, marched across the Salle like one who knows his power. He was, indeed, the true King of that Revolution, and on him were all eyes fixed. Poor, feeble, good-natured Louis, in spite of his diadem, his royal robes and feathers, was abashed at the sight of the severe and firm countenances of the Assembly. Mirabeau was heard to say to those around him, pointing to the King, "Voilà la victime."

The King's speech was weak and unsatisfactory. He grumbled about the spirit of innovation, and expressed his sensibility for the two superior orders "who showed themselves disposed to renounce their pecuniary privileges."

Strange must it have appeared to the bilious advocate of Arras, now that he was face to face with his sovereign on so momentous an occasion, to hear in the speeches of his King and the King's minister, so great a predominance of the question of money, so little on the question of right! The King and his minister talked as if the Assembly there had nothing to do but to settle the question of taxation. They absolutely believed that if the privileged few would grant, as alms, to the Third Estate, an equality of taxation, everything would be amicably settled. Not only did they believe this, but they were eloquent in eulogium upon the sacrifice made by the privileged few, in declaring themselves willing to forego their exemption from taxation; in declaring themselves generous enough to pay their share of the state expenses; a sacrifice of which Necker says, "No heroism in history is comparable to it." How profoundly did they misunderstand their age, its wants and tendencies! The States-General were not there to receive alms, but to extort rights:—nothing more, but nothing less!

Paris was in constant communication with Versailles. The Assembly of the Electors of Paris, and the irregular tumultuous crowd, daily collected in the Palais Royal, were asking every moment for news of the deputies. They questioned eagerly all comers from Versailles. The Third Estate saw that the Court was surrounding itself with soldiers; but they also saw that the crowd was listening to them, and that their true army, the press, was fighting their cause all over the kingdom.

From his unpublished letters, I find Robespierre making a motion, which is not mentioned in the *Moniteur* nor the *Histoire Parlementaire*. While some members were for supplicating the nobles, he rose and entreated them to abstain from such an act which could only make the nobles triumph more. He urged them to address themselves to that order, where, beside the prelates, stood the modest and popular preachers of the Gospel. Robespierre had drawn out a scheme, and demanded that they should deliberate on it. But who would listen to this obscure Robespierre, with his cracked voice, and uncongenial aspect? He was so insignificant that they disdained to consider the proposal. The proposal is, however, not without interest to us, as indicative of the religious tendency of Robespierre's mind, a tendency which has too often been mistaken for hypocrisy, but which, in truth, was one of the distinguishing points in his character.

CHAPTER VII.

Distress of the country—Robespierre bids the clergy sacrifice their superfluities—The "Jeu de Paume"—Attitude of the court—Mirabeau and Robespierre—Troubles of Paris—The Palais Royal: scene in, reported by Desmoulins—The cockade—Apathy of the court—Fall of the Bastille.

THE Assembly was sitting idle, or discussing the vain frivolities of etiquette, instead of accomplishing the work it had to do: namely, to redress the wrongs of the people, and propose measures for the salvation of the country. But famine was not idle. Work ceased. He who had but his hands and daily labor to supply his daily bread, sought work; found it not; begged; got nothing; robbed. The rich spent as little as they could. Starving gangs overran the country. When they found resistance, what wonder if they became furious? if they killed, and burned? Terror spread far and near. A prelate came into the Assembly, to weep over the poor, and to declaim upon the misery of the rural districts. There, in the presence of 4000 persons, he drew from his pocket a hideous lump of black bread. "Such," said he, "is the bread of the peasant." The clergy proposed to form a commission on the subject of food. The proposition was but a snare; for either the Assembly must yield, and thus consecrate the separation of the Orders—a separation they were determined not to admit; or else it would seem to declare itself insensible to public misery. The usual orators were silent. It was time for Robespierre to speak:—

"Go and tell your colleagues," said he, "that if they are so impatient to assuage the sufferings of the poor, let them come to this Hall to unite themselves with their friends. Tell them no longer to retard our operations by affected delays. Tell them it is vain to employ stratagems like these, to induce us to change our firm resolution. We must recall the clergy to the principles of the primitive Church. The ancient canons authorized, for the relief of the poor, to sell even the sacred vases; but happily it is not necessary to recur to so sad a sacrifice. It is only necessary that the bishops should renounce that luxury which is an offence to the modesty of Christianity, dismiss their carriages, their horses, and the insolent lacqueys who attend them; to sell, in fact, if need be, a quarter of the ecclesiastical property."

A very radical proposition, truly! "subversive of all sound morality," and drawing from the prelates looks of withering contempt. As he concluded, a confused murmur of applause ran through the Assembly. Every one asked his neighbor, "Who is that speaker?" The question went round, and at last the speaker's name was discovered. Reybaz, turning to Dumont, said:—

"That young man wants practice. He is too verbose, and knows not when to stop; but he has a fund of eloquence and bitterness which will soon distinguish him."

From his unpublished letters it appears that Robespierre watched in silence and in sadness the troubles which existed within the bosom of the Communes. In those letters he signalized the dangerous designs of Malouet, the partisan of the *bourgeoisie*, and rejoiced over the perceptible decline of those reputations which were not at the service of the people; such, for instance, as those of Target and Mounier. Mirabeau he little feared, reading well his character, and foreseeing that even his genius would not keep him pure. On the whole, however, he did not despair of the Communes; for although he foresaw divisions, perhaps even treachery, yet he consoled himself with the knowledge that there were around him "upwards of a hundred citizens disposed to die for their country."

On the 10th of June, Sièyes, entering the Assembly, said, "Let us cut the cable: it is time." It was time. Sooner, the nation had not been sufficiently convinced of the obstinacy of the privileged classes; and on this Wednesday, the 10th of June, Sièyes proposed to summon the clergy and the nobility for the last time, and to say that the call would be made in an hour. This summons was an unexpected blow. The deputies, with wise audacity, assumed towards those who contested their equality, the superior position of judges. The nobility of course treated the call with haughty contempt. Of the clergy ten only went over. Great was the merriment at Court about this fine conquest made by the Third Estate: a conquest of ten priests! The merriment was but short-lived. The Assembly took another and a bolder step, and called itself by its true name, the National Assembly.

The Assembly proceeded immediately to take the oath in the presence of some 4000 deeply interested spectators. These 600 deputies, on whom rested the destinies of France, standing in profound silence with upraised hands, contemplating the calm, honest countenance of their President, listened to him whilst reading the formula, and then exclaimed, "We swear!"

The Assembly was constituted. The cardinal and the archbishop returned to Marly, and, falling at the feet of the King, exclaimed, "Sire, religion is ruined!"

Next came the Parliament, believing its religion, too, was ruined, exclaiming, "The monarchy is lost unless the States be dissolved!"

This was on the 19th of June. The King, to prevent the clergy from uniting with the Third Estate, commanded that the Hall should be shut on the morrow. A pretext was easily found in the preparations for a royal meeting, to be held on the Monday. It was settled during the night, and placarded at Versailles at six in the morning.

A memorable morning! The rain fell, and the sky was overcast. Groups were seen wandering about the town, seeking an asylum: "Their name? *The National Assembly.* Their aim? *To make a free people.*"*

The deputies stand grouped on the Paris road, on the umbrageous avenue of Versailles, complaining aloud of the indignity. "Courtiers, it is supposed, look from their windows and giggle."†

But neither giggling, nor closed doors, sufficed to thwart these men. They resolve to organize at once their interrupted work, at the risk of a terrible struggle, at the price even of life itself. If a place of meeting is not to be found, they will assemble in the open air. Some shout, "Let us go to the Place d'Armes." Others shout, "To Marly;" others, "To Paris." Conspicuous amidst this indignant crowd is one Dr. Guillotin,* whose name is hereafter to become famous, as the inventor of that machine which plays so terrible a part in the history of the Revolution. Dr. Guillotin proposes that they shall repair to old Versailles, and assemble in the Tennis Court.

This was the celebrated *Jeu de Paume.* It formed a strange contrast to the Hall in which they had met before. No ornaments, no draperies, no insignia of royalty, there met their eyes; nothing but four naked walls, a few tables, and wooden benches.

The people hurry "like cranes on the wing," fill the galleries, and crowd at the windows. From the wall-top, from the adjoining roof and chimneys, their faces are visible. There the Tiers Etats has met, and the President Bailly, rising, says, "The members of the National Assembly must swear never to separate till the constitution of the kingdom, and the regeneration of public order, are established upon a solid basis." In his character of President, he demands the honor of swearing first. In an instant every arm is raised, and a cry escapes from every mouth, spontaneous, irresistible, thrilling all hearts.

That scene lives still on the canvass of David. Standing on the table, calm and imposing as the law, is Bailly. You see one man with garments in disorder, looking towards the President, holding a pen, and prepared to write:—it is Bertrand Barère, editor of the *Point du Jour.* There, also, you see Pétion, Garat, Chapelier, Thouret, Guillotin, and Barnave. Mirabeau, with his head on high, striking the earth with his foot; and Robespierre,

---

* The story current about Dr. Guillotin is, that he was one of the first to suffer by his own machine—like Phalaris, by his own brazen bull; but the worthy doctor was alive in 1812, and died in his bed.

pressing both hands upon his breast, "as if he had two hearts for liberty."*

This was the celebrated oath of the *Jeu de Paume*. In contemplating this imposing scene, let us not forget, that, as Michelet remarks, the whole assembly was, without exception, royalist. Even Robespierre was a royalist, as I learn from his unpublished letters, wherein he still expresses belief in the good faith of Louis. Nay more, even Marat was a royalist, till 1791; so little did those who were most republican then know whither they were tending!

This meeting at the Tennis Court should have been a lesson to the aristocracy; but it was not. For some time there had been a party forming round the Queen, which affected to place in her all their hopes of France. They never spoke of Marie Antoinette but as the intrepid daughter of Maria Theresa. They despised the King for his indecision and bourgeois habits. He was not *un roi gentilhomme*. "What nonsense," they said, "it was, talking to the people. Had not the court soldiers? And if French regiments should be disaffected, had they not foreign regiments who would drive before them this insolent ragged crowd?" Mirabeau was pestered with challenges, which he contented himself with inscribing on his tablets, deferring these small combats till the morrow after the grand battle. He was too haughty to conceive himself bound to offer any proofs of courage. These challengers were the young cavaliers of whom Burke thought that 10,000 of their swords must have leaped from their scabbards, to avenge even a look which threatened their Queen with insult. Yet these were the very men who first fled from danger, deserted their Queen and their country, and passed over to Coblentz; there to fight duels, seduce women, cabal, and bring upon France the disasters of the coalition.

To show how little the Court understood their position, it is enough to record the plan imagined by the Count of Artois, which was to crush the Assembly, and prevent the consequences of the

* The saying of David, in explanation of his picture.—Louis Blanc. Vol. ii. page 254.

oath taken in the Tennis Court. This plan was nothing less than retaining the Tennis Court for himself; so that the Communes, during the whole day, should be thrown upon the streets, and thus present the spectacle of an illegal gathering. How puerile a plan! as Madame de Staël well said, "it was opposing playthings to fire-arms." Not thus were the people to be put down. Meet they would. They first went to the *Récollets;* but the monks were afraid to compromise themselves. Fortunately the 134 curés, with a few prelates at their head, had already taken up their quarters in the morning in the church of St. Louis. There the Assembly was introduced into the nave, and the ecclesiastics took their seats among its members. "The Temple of Religion," says an orator, "became a Temple of the Representatives."

I have no space to narrate this long, teasing history of the struggle between the Assembly and the Court; suffice it to say, that the Assembly was firm; and that a Mirabeau could tell the King's embassy, "I declare to you, that if you are ordered to drive us hence, you must demand orders to employ force, for we will quit our posts only at the point of the bayonet."*

The King could not dissolve the Assembly; and Sièyes, with fine oratorical concision, said, "Gentlemen, you are to-day what you were yesterday. Let us deliberate: *délibérons!*"

So triumphs the Third Estate. The States-General are become the National Assembly, and all France may sing "*Te Deum.*" "It is the last night of June. All night you meet nothing in the streets of Versailles, but men running with torches, with shouts and jubilation."

In spite of the jubilation, in spite of the firmness of the Assembly, the King had not revoked anything. He kept the Assembly like a prisoner among his troops; and excluded the public from its sittings. What thought Paris of all this? On the 24th the

---

* This is the real reply of Mirabeau, which historians have all disfigured and made more revolutionary. The phrases they insert of "Go, tell your master"—and, "We are here by the will of the people," belong to the spirit of a later day, and could not have been pronounced at that epoch.—See Louis Blanc, vol. ii. p. 261.

ferment was terrible. Paris sent a deputation to the Assembly, with the expression of its approbation, and with encouragements to continue firm. From the Palais Royal there came an address, covered with signatures, breathing war, and intimating that the French Guards were preparing for revolt. Versailles was also greatly agitated, and founded its *Club Breton* with Mirabeau, Sièyes, Pétion, Barnave, Buzot, Lanjuinais, the Abbé Gregoire, and Robespierre, among its members: a club which afterwards, in Paris, will become the *Club des Jacobins*.

Robespierre, who as yet could make no figure in the Assembly, where his opinions met with little response, and his person with no consideration, passed the greater part of his time in the cafés and the restaurants, amongst the crowd of idlers and adventurers every day flocking from Paris. There he was always to be found, proclaiming in his trenchant, dogmatic style, the maxims of liberty and equality which he had learned from Rousseau.

Not only Paris and Versailles, but all France was in a ferment. Paris became the seat of the Revolution. On the 25th it broke out in three different ways, by the Electors, by the Crowd, and by the Soldiers. The electors had agreed to meet together after the elections, to complete their instructions to their deputies. The ministers refused them permission to meet; but at their own peril they met on the 25th, in the Rue Dauphine. Their assembly-room was at that moment occupied by a wedding-party, which, however, gladly gave way to them: and this was *their* jeu de paume! It is not to be overlooked that these electors were, for the most part, rich citizens; nay, even members of the aristocracy were among them. Two men we may single out as interesting: the Abbé Fauchet, and his friend Bonneville, the translator of Shakspeare. It was Bonneville who, on the 6th of June, proposed that Paris should fly to arms. A wag then present suggested that the young man should postpone his motion for a fortnight. The fortnight is scarcely over, and now this motion has become serious. The electors propose three things. First, the constitution of a citizen guard; secondly, the early organization of a true elective and annual commune; thirdly, an address to the

King for the removal of the troops and the liberty of the Assembly.

While these electors clamored for civic liberty, there was another party—that of the million—clamoring for food. Famine was advancing in its gaunt march over France. The little bread which the people were enabled to buy was so bad that it caused inflammation of the throat and stomach. Every morning bands of unknown ragged wretchedness stalked into Paris; holding in their hands long *batons;* seeking for food and for work, where no food and no work were to be found. Yet they too, the starving millions, demanded liberty. At the very bakers' doors they discussed the Constitution; and vowed to defend the National Assembly. In their misery they hoped that government would relieve them. They hoped that the National Assembly *could* assuage all their wants; and that it *would* do so. Let the Assembly be free, and their stomachs would be full! It has ever been so. The wretched throw their wretchedness upon government; as if political measures could arrest a famine, as if parliamentary eloquence could assuage hunger. The government is supposed to do everything. It is curious to see men thus fiercely demanding liberty of thought and act as the solace of all their woes. Whatever confusion might have been in their minds, whatever chimerical hopes and indifferent political economy, yet were these men formidable, for they were pressed on by want. They sternly demanded that their wants should be relieved. It was no easy task to devise how this should be done.

There was, moreover, a third party, the soldiers: and they looked to the National Assembly. French guards formed secret societies, and swore they would obey no orders contrary to those of the Assembly. The Court was so astonished that it could only explain this, by saying that the guards had been debauched by money and women. But surely, when the King had exclaimed in the strongest manner that he would never change the constitution of the army, the French guards, in that state of political excitement, needed no other stimulus than that very speech. What was the principle of this constitution? That the nobility should for ever monopolize every rank, and the plebeian live and die a common soldier. A Jourdan, a Joubert, a Kléber were obliged to quit the profession, hopeless of advancement. It is worth bearing in mind, that in the budget of that time, officers were reckoned at 46,000,000 of francs, while the soldiers were only reckoned at 44,000,000. The fact speaks volumes. What was more natural, therefore, than that the troops should stand by the electors and the people? On the 20th of June long files of them, headed by their sergeant, appeared at the Palais Royal, and were welcomed with *Vivats*, presents, and pledges of patriotic liquor; embracing, and embraced, they declared that the cause of France was their cause.

Eleven of the ringleaders are confined in the Abbaye prison; but they send intimation thereof to the Café de Foy, "where patriotism harangues loudest on its table;" and there a young man, jumping on the table, shrieks "To the Abbaye! Let us deliver those who would not fire upon the people!" Soldiers offer their aid; but citizens thank them and declare they will do it alone. On the road the crowd increases; workmen join them with crowbars. They are 4000 strong by the time they reach the Abbaye. There they break open the doors and liberate the victims. A body of dragoons gallops up. The people lay their hands on the bridles and explain the whole matter. The soldiers will not massacre the preservers of soldiers; but sheathe their swords, take off their helmets, and drink to the King and the nation with great cordiality. Among the liberated it is found that there is one real criminal. Him they lead back again to prison; but the others march in procession to the Palais Royal, amidst shouts of *Vive la nation!**

On the 26th, the court, trembling with anger and indignation, still more with fear, resolves to grant the reunion of the orders. "M. de Luxembourg," said Louis, "I pray that the order of the nobility may unite itself with the two others. If it is not enough for me to pray, *I insist.*" Great rejoicings welcome this news at Versailles. The people make bonfires and even shout "*Vive la*

---

* Carlyle, Michelet, Louis Blanc.

reine!" The Queen is obliged to appear on the balcony and show them the Dauphin. All will go on well, now the Orders are united; the reign of peace and of plenty is at hand! So think enthusiastic deputies. Robespierre is not quite so enthusiastic. Silent and unmarked amongst the crowd of deputies, he expresses himself boldly in the cafés. He begins to see the weakness of the Court; he begins to see the strength of the people!

Although the nobles were now assembled in the self-same hall with the Communes, could that be called union? It was contact, not union. The nobles had been vanquished, not convinced. Those who came did not condescend to sit, but wandered about, or stood gazing like simple spectators. And yet it was fast becoming clear to all men, as to Robespierre, that the power was not in the palace, but in the states. Even the soldiers themselves thought so, and while the *Gardes du Roi* refused to make their usual rounds in the courts of the Châteaux of Versailles, two of them came disguised into the Assembly, to place in the hands of the President, as to a real monarch, a complaint against their colonel.

While the Assembly was losing precious time in idle discussions, and preparing the declaration of the rights of man, the Club Breton became bolder and bolder, and more and more agitated. "It was," says an observer of those days, "a stormy, heavy, gloomy time, like a feverish painful dream, full of illusions and anxieties. There were false alarms, false news, and all sorts of fables and inventions."

The great news-market and centre of disaffection was the Palais Royal. Under its pleasant colonnades, under the shade of its trees, men crowded, gesticulated, and gossiped. That place which most of my readers have so often seen filled with idle loungers—with bearded smokers, and tripping grisettes—with *bonnes*, and their infant charges playing about—and small French boys (diminutive Frenchmen) with hands in their pockets, and casquettes shading their intelligent eyes;—that Palais Royal, with its restaurants—its cafés—its politicians sitting in the open air reading the last debate—and its miscellaneous crowd of strangers thronging in the Café de la Rotonde, devouring the last *feuilleton* of Alexandre Dumas, or watching children toddling about;—that Palais Royal was, in the time I now write of, the centre of political agitation.

In the correspondence of Camille Desmoulins, I met with this anecdote, which is worth telling for its own sake, as well as for the glimpse it gives us of that crowd in the Palais Royal. "In the midst of the vehement discussion, one of the orators ended by demanding that the mob should burn the house of D'Eprémenil, his wife, his children, and himself. Voted unanimously. Then up rose a man saying, 'Messieurs, the upholsterer of M. D'Eprémenil demands to be heard.' Cries of '*La parole au tapissier!*' 'I demand,' said the speaker, 'an exception in favor of M. D'Eprémenil's furniture. That all belongs to me, seeing that I have not been paid for it. Is not my demand just?' 'Perfectly just,' they exclaim, 'perfectly just.' 'Since,' he continues, 'you grant my request, dare I represent to you that the architect has not been paid for the house, so that the house ought also to be spared.' 'The house is spared.' Then the orator continues, 'As to M. D'Eprémenil's wife, wherefore should you burn that which belongs to you? It is notorious that his wife is public property. And, messieurs, have you no fears of imitating the crime of Œdipus, and becoming unconscious parricides if you burn the children of D'Eprémenil? 'Yes, yes,' shouted the mob, 'pardon for wife and children.' The pleasant part of the anecdote," adds Camille, "is, that it is said D'Eprémenil himself was the orator."

And now on this Sunday morning, the 12th of July, the news comes to the Palais Royal that Necker is dismissed. What! Necker, the citizen minister, the idol of the nation, the detestation of the court. He dismissed? It is false! The bearer of the news is called an aristocrat, and escapes being ducked in the basins only because his news is confirmed; "and then," says the *Ami du Roi*, "a gloomy feeling of terror pervaded every soul." The report is too true. We have a new ministry. Marshal Broglie, and Breteuil, and old Foulon, "who said the people might eat grass." Shall we submit to this? No! From out of the Café du Roi a young man rushes; his hair streaming; in each hand a pistol. He springs on a table, the police satellites eyeing him. People ask who it is. The name is Camille Desmoulins, a name which will become notable. Indignation and audacity fire his speech, "To arms! to arms!" he cries. Then snatching a leaf from a tree, he makes a cockade of it—a cockade the color of hope. In another instant all the leaves are stripped from the trees, every patriot has his cockade. Green ribbons are snatched from the neighboring shops and imperfectly paid for. Everything green is turned into cockades; the crowd rush to the shop of Curtius, the plaster-cast maker, and demand from him the busts of the Duke of Orleans and of Necker, the two popular favorites. With these busts they make a procession through Paris. Arrived at the Place Vendôme, a detachment of dragoons charges them, puts them to flight, and destroys their bust of Necker.* Only one man is killed, yet Paris is filled with indignation at what it calls "this brutal attack of the hated Germans, driving their horses against our women and children." Everything is exaggerated by loud and credulous rumor. It is said that the dragoons fired upon the passers-by; that the Prince de Lambesc had slain an old man, begging for quarter on his knees. Some said that the capital was to be burned. False as these words were, they exasperated the people as much as if they had been true.

On Monday, the 13th, Dr. Guillotin, with two electors, went to Versailles and entreated the Assembly to concur in establishing a citizen guard. They gave a terrible description of the crisis in Paris. The Assembly voted two deputations, one to the King, the other to the city. That to the King obtained from him only a cold, unsatisfactory answer: that he could make no alterations in the measures he had taken; that he was the only judge of their interests; and that the presence of the deputies of Paris could do no good. The indignant Assembly decreed, first, that M. Necker bore with him the regrets of the nation; secondly, that it insisted on the removal of the troops; thirdly, that not only the King's ministers but the King's counselors, of whatever rank they might be, were personally responsible for the present manifestation; fourthly, that no power had the right to pronounce the infamous word bankruptcy.

The third article sufficiently designated the Queen and the princes; and the last article branded them with reproach. The Assembly thus resumed its noble attitude. Unarmed, in the middle of the troops, without any other support than that of the law; threatened that very evening to be dispersed; it yet bravely branded its enemies on the brow with their name of bankrupts.

The apathy of the Court during all these riots is very remarkable. Now was the time to act, if ever; but the Court did nothing. It only continued its system of exasperation. That the King meant well, no one can honestly deny; it was his misfortune to have been born in a time when his very virtues told against him. These nobles, too, who rallied round the Queen, and strove with insolence to quell a revolution, were they not honest? Did not they mean well? It cannot be said that they meant ill. They had been bred up to look upon themselves as the rightful lords of creation; to look upon France as their domain; to look upon the well-being of France as indissolubly connected with their privileges. It may be difficult for the republican to understand the honesty of these men; yet he may be assured that it was no less difficult for these men to understand the honesty of republicans. Thus it is. Each man sees his own truth, and looks with horror upon those who will not see it with him. What can be more clear? Have you eyes that you see it not? It is so clear to me that it must be only your prejudice, or bad passions, that can prevent your seeing it also. A great lesson of tolerance may be learned from witnessing the fierceness with which antagonistic opinions can be maintained: each man so fiercely confident in the truth of his own!

But let the King and his counselors mean well or mean ill,

the crisis is now rapidly approaching. The cry of "To arms!" raised by that wild Camille thrills all Paris. His Majesty's repository is ransacked, arms are taken from the Hôtel de Ville, snatched up wherever they can be found; and in that tumultuous crowd you may see antique tourney lances amidst indifferent firelocks, and princely helmets amidst modern hats; ragged coats amidst glittering hauberks; typifying the breaking up of the whole middle ages. With these weapons in hands, moved by such convictions as were then universal, a turbulent crowd will take an impregnable Bastille. Certainly the attack on the Bastille looked like madness, it was so utterly impracticable—yet it succeeded. The storm and fury of an enraged people tore down that monument of despotism; and, after a bloody fight, the cry was raised, "The Bastille is taken!"

CHAPTER VIII.

Agitation of Paris—Kings learn no lessons from experience—"Not a revolt, a revolution"—The King comes over to the Assembly—New hopes!—Creation of a national guard: Lafayette General—Bailly, Mayor of Paris.

THE night which followed this success was one of extraordinary excitement. Although the troops had all been withdrawn from the capital, and were quartered around Versailles and the adjoining villages, yet the agitation was still extreme. The houses were all illuminated; less from triumph than from a dread of being left in the dark. In spite of the wearisome labors of the day few eyes were closed that night. Men congregated in the streets, and on the quays, and in the squares, discussing the probability of an attack. It was not natural that a military monarchy should so soon abandon the contest, or should tamely submit to such an insult as the destruction of its great fortress and prison. All night the mournful clang of the tocsin was heard, interrupted by the cries " Don't go to bed !" " Keep your lamps burning !" A second St. Bartholomew seemed at hand; to meet which the people barricaded the streets, tore up the pavement, carried stones to the tops of houses, and established guards at all the principal quarters. At the Hôtel de Ville, Moreau de Saint Méry, before rising from his chair, had dispatched no less than 3000 orders—a striking instance of the prevailing agitation, and of the energy which animated the people. Amidst this agitation and this fear, the alarming clang of the tocsin continued its doleful *boom! boom!* through the night. It is difficult for those who have not heard the tocsin sounded to conceive the terror it inspires. A ceaseless sound boding ceaseless danger, and that danger vague, unknown! A terrible enemy is at your gates, but what enemy you know not. You only know that he is terrible. Imagine all the churches of London suddenly to begin booming a cry of danger, and this cry to be kept up throughout the night, and you will then have an idea of the tocsin.

If Paris was agitated, not less so was Versailles. The Court was indignant, the Assembly timorous. Before the news came, the Assembly was distracted by the chances of an insurrection in Paris, and by the violent measures adopted by the Court. They thought that Paris was to be attacked that night on seven points simultaneously. The Queen and Madame de Polignac went into the Orangery to encourage the troops, and to order wine to be given to the soldiers, who were then dancing about and singing roundelays. The officers were conducted to the Queen's apartment, where they were excited by liquors, by sweet words, and murderous glances. Who would not fight for so lovely a Queen ? A thousand swords *are* ready to leap from their scabbards! The effervescent loyalty would have gladdened a Burke.

But there is a cloud of dust in the Avenue de Paris. A body of cavalry comes tearing along with the Prince de Lambesc and his officers flying before the people of Paris. De Noailles arrives with the news " the Bastille is taken;" afterwards arrive two Envoys of the Electors, who acquaint the Assembly with the alarming state of Paris. The Assembly is furious, and invokes the vengeance of God and man against Court and ministers. "Heads!" exclaims Mirabeau, "we must have Marshal de Broglie's head."

A deputation waits upon the King, but gets only equivocal answers. The Assembly is clamorous, and sends a second. The King is heart-broken, but he can do no more. They talk of sending a third deputation, but Clermont-Tonnerre says, "No, leave them the night for counsel. Kings, as well as other men, must *buy* experience."

Unhappily, kings cannot buy experience at any price. The terrible strokes of destiny fall upon them not as lessons, but as outrages. They never hear the truth, they cannot hear it. From childhood upwards, surrounded by flatterers (which means liars), they are to be pitied, deeply pitied, rather than blamed. They so seldom hear a true word spoken that they know not how to distinguish it from falsehood.* They are treated so like gods upon earth that we must not wonder if they believe in their own divinity. Experience teaches not kings; it only exasperates them! What king ever had so ample an experience as Louis Philippe? He lived through the first Revolution. He saw the Consulate and the Empire, the Hundred Days, the Restoration, and the Revolution of July, which placed him on the throne. He had known adversity, and struggled for his existence. He had lived in free states: in Geneva, in England, in America; yet he, too, when on the throne, went the old way, fell into the old foolish rut; lied, equivocated, and fell. All his large experience had not made him wiser. With regard to the relation between kings and their people, he was no clearer-sighted than the stupidest man in his whole dominions. And yet Louis Philippe is a man of considerable talents and great energy. If *he* could not be taught, how should that poor, somnolent, indolent, amiable, vacillating Louis, at a time when kings were worshiped?

The night brought no counsel. The King retired early to rest;

---

* Lange gab es einer wirklich betitelten Narren des Königs; niemals hat Jemand den Titel Eines Weisen des Königs getragen.—GÖTHE.

but the Duke de Liancourt, whose duties gave him the privilege of entering at any hour into his room, who loved the King, and could not see him perish thus in his apathy, awoke him and told him the extent of the danger. Louis, half-asleep, yawned out, "What, then! is it a revolt?" "Sire," said the Duke, "it is a revolution!" and then depicting the questionable fidelity of the troops and the formidable state of public opinion, the Duke advised him to take one step towards the nation. What bitter satire on kingship is written in the fact, that that very night Bailly was sent for and was requested to compose the speech for the King to deliver to the people on the morrow!

I have said before that the Assembly was decidedly royalist. It heard, therefore, of the taking of the Bastille with profound sorrow, and spoke of it as " *Les malheurs de la capitale.*" The maddened people who, without troops, without discipline, could take an impregnable fortress, had become really alarming! Where was this spirit of insurrection to stop? Accordingly, when the deputies met on the morrow at eight o'clock, they were animated with but one desire, that, namely, of coming to an understanding with the King. He did not appear; and it was decided that a third deputation should go and demand of him the removal of the troops and the dismissal of his ministers.

But before the deputation departs, the Duke de Liancourt announces that the King is coming. How shall he be received before we know what are his sentiments? Let us maintain the dignity of silence. "The silence of the people," Mirabeau exclaims in his grand way, "is a lesson to kings."

The King arrives, accompanied by his brothers, and without his guards. He announces that the troops shall be removed, and assures the Assembly of its safety. "People have dared to spread a report," he said, "that your persons are not in safety. Can it be necessary to re-assure you against such vile rumors, so contrary to my well known character? *I who am but one with my nation, I come to entrust myself to you.*"

The hall rung with acclamations. The deputies crowded upon him, and followed on foot as he passed out. Locking their hands together as if to keep off the multitude, they passed out into the sultry day. The people without made the welkin ring with shouts. The Swiss band played the air, "Où peut on être mieux qu'au sein de sa famille." The King, who was very corpulent, was almost exhausted in crossing the Place d'Armes under that July sun; but his heart was gratified at these testimonies of the people's love. One woman approaching him had the naïve audacity to say, "O my King, are you really sincere? Won't they make you change?" "No," replied the King, "I will never change." Marie Antoinette appeared in the balcony with the Dauphin in her arms, hardly knowing what to think of such enthusiasm.*

The hundred deputies are now on their road to Paris to communicate the joyful intelligence. The Revolution is finished! The King has trusted himself to his people! It was time to recall to the people that they had a King, for they were beginning to forget him. In the Hôtel de Ville, the Marquis de la Fayette, after a rapid narrative of events, exclaimed, "The King has been deceived. He is so no longer. He knows our miseries, and will prevent their recurrence." And when Lally-Tollendal exerted his eloquence in behalf of the King's generosity, of the goodness of that prince who had said, "*Je me fie à vous*," all hearts were touched, and the orator was crowned with flowers.

This enthusiasm gave birth to the idea of a National Guard. A bust of Lafayette, which had been in the salle of the Hôtel de Ville ever since the American war, was pointed out by Moreau de Saint Méry, whereupon Lafayette was named general, and Bailly named Mayor of Paris, amid shouts of applause, *Vive Lafayette! Vive Bailly!*

The Mayor and the Commandant of Paris appointed by the

---

* A passage from one of the numerous pamphlets of the day will best illustrate with what delight the news was heard in the provinces:

"La première et la plus importante de ces vérités Louis l'a fait entendre de sa bouche, lorsque n'écoutant que l'impulsion de son cœur il s'est présenté à l'Assemblée Nationale, avec toute la simplicité de ses mœurs, avec toute la beauté de son caractère, pour annoncer qu'il n'était que le Chef de la nation Française."—*Addresse aux gens de Bien du Languedoc.*

electors without asking the King's consent—those places accepted by such men as Bailly and Lafayette,—their nominations confirmed by the Assembly,—this, indeed, was no longer a revolt, but a well and duly organized revolution!

It is necessary for the King to take some decided step. He must go to Paris. Paris wishes for him. The King will go; and on the same evening writes to recall Necker; two popular acts in one evening.

On the 17th of July, after hearing mass and taking the communion, the King departed for Paris, pale and serious. He had named MONSIEUR, Lieutenant-General of the Kingdom, in case he should be killed or detained prisoner. Without guards, but surrounded by 300 or 400 deputies, he arrived at the barrier about three o'clock. Bailly, as mayor, presented him the keys of the city, saying, "These are the same keys that were presented to Henry IV. He had conquered his people. Now the people have re-conquered their King." This epigrammatic speech—the full force of which no one saw at the time—was received with immense applause. In front of the King's carriage rode Lafayette, sword in hand, cockade and plume in his hat, everything obedient to his slightest gesture. There was no disorder, there was no noise. Unhappily, not even one cry of "*Vive le Roi!*"—only now and then a cry of "*Vive la Nation!*" Bailly and Lafayette were the only men applauded. The deputies marched, surrounding the King's carriage, sorrowfully, uneasily.

Nevertheless, when the King told the people they might rely on his affection, when they thought they had re-conquered their King, when they learned that Necker was re-called, they shouted "*Vive le Roi!*" A market-woman flung her arms round his neck. Men stopped the horses, poured wine for the coachman and valets, and drank with them the health of the King. The King smiled, but still said nothing. Michelet thinks that the least kind word uttered at that moment would have been re-uttered and circulated with immense effect. Perhaps so; but like many other words, which in those days created a momentary ferment, it would have been forgotten on the morrow, and the King would have had a lie on his conscience.

All this while the Breton Club was becoming more violent. Sièyes called it a den of political banditti. Robespierre was a constant attendant there; though not as yet making a distinguished figure. He was insignificant beside his two schoolfellows Camille Desmoulins and Danton.

CHAPTER IX.

Robespierre's energetic protest against the reaction—Horrors commencing: massacres and burnings—Labors of the Assembly—The counter-revolution—Declaration of Rights of Man, compared with that of 1848—Robespierre on the veto—His republicanism becomes avowed—Two of Robespierre's letters—Agitation in Paris respecting the veto—The famine—The insurrection of women.

THE moderate portion of the Assembly was frightened into a stronger adherence to royalty, while the democratic portion of it was daily becoming more bold. On the 20th of July, Lally Tollendal conjured his colleagues to guard themselves against the emotions raised by the new spirit of innovation. Within a few paces of that Tennis Court where they had made so noble a stand, within a few miles of that Bastille which a people had torn down, Lally rose to say that the great danger of the moment was the spirit of revolt; that the King was the father of his people and the real founder of liberty; and that the representatives of the people should only look to the King! He proposed that every man wanting confidence in the Assembly, or fidelity to the King, should henceforth be looked upon as a bad citizen; and that every suspected person accused and arrested, should be consigned to the hands of his natural judge; and finally, that the municipalities should exclude from the citizen militia all those who were capable of doing harm to their country. His speech was loudly applauded, and its resolutions would have been adopted, if some energetic members of the Breton Club had not vehemently protested. Among these protestors, was one man known to journalists as *Robert Pierre*, who, irritated and astonished, rose and demanded, "What has then occurred that can authorize M. Lally Tollendal to sound the tocsin? He speaks of a right. That right, messieurs, is liberty! Do not deceive yourselves: the combat is not yet finished. To-morrow, perhaps, will be renewed those dangerous projects of the Court; and who shall then repel them, if we begin by declaring rebels all those who arm themselves for our safety?" His commanding gestures, the fire which flashed from his eyes, the convulsive movement of his thin lips, the earnestness of his pale and bilious face, the brief, but menacing appeal which he made to the force of the insulted people, so impressed the Assembly, that the project, before so applauded, now got no one to defend it. It was becoming evident to those who cared to observe, that this Robert Pierre was not so insignificant a person after all.

Meanwhile the aspect of Paris was sad in the extreme. In the Faubourg St. Antoine, thousands of starving men demanded some occasion on which to employ their energy. "If we must die," said they, "we would rather die from a cannon-ball than from want."* The distress was terrible. Subscription-lists were opened. Beaumarchais gave 12,000 francs; the Archbishop of Paris 20,000 francs. But individual efforts were powerless to assuage the general hunger. Bread was dear. The Assembly had fixed it at a lower price; but even at that lower price, the poor had no money to buy it. Still worse, there was little corn to make bread. To these real evils were added imaginary evils. Reports of plots to poison the French Guards circulated everywhere. The people became exasperated. A convoy of grain coming from Passy, on the 16th, was seized by the multitude,

---

* Almost the identical words were uttered in the fearful *émeute* of June, 1848. "Better to die by a bullet than by want!" was the cry of their despair.

and with it Sauvage, a farmer, accused of being a monopolizer. Quickly the drum went through the town with this announcement: "Citizens! by order of the King and the Third Estate, Notice is hereby given, that Sauvage will be hanged at three o'clock." At three o'clock he was hanged. His head was then cut off, fixed on the top of a pike, and paraded through the streets, preceded by a butcher, who, having cut off an arm, brandished his bloody knife, while he occasionally opened the lips, to make them receive the stream of blood which flowed down the ghastly cheeks. Old Foulon, too, of whom it was said, truly or falsely, that he had declared the people might eat grass, was clutched by the enraged multitude and slung up. Twice the cord broke, and twice the poor old man fell to the ground, amidst peals of laughter and shouts of joy. He was despatched at last. Berthier, his son-in-law, soon after met with the same fate. Their heads were paraded on the ends of pikes. The heart and pieces of the body of Berthier were thrust into a goblet of wine, in which they were boiled, and, standing round the caldron, the savages drank the fuming liquor, their naked arms uplifting the glasses, while they shouted a song, the burden of which was "Death to those who opposed the will of the people."

The fearful days of the Revolution were commencing Insurgent peasants, in the first transports produced by the taking of the Bastille, sacked and burned the châteaux. In the space of a few days, sixty-seven were destroyed in the districts of Maconnais and Beaujolais. In the Dauphiné, thirty-six shared the same fate. Most of the inhabitants were burned or massacred.

The National Assembly was painfully moved by the intelligence of the death of Foulon and Berthier. Alarmed at this rise of the people, they saw themselves powerless to arrest it. Indeed one may say that no man, no body of men, could stay the Revolution. Its flames were spreading far and wide. The Assembly wanted a recognition of the rights of man. They only demanded civic liberty; but they had called to their aid the People; and the starving People wanted above all things work and food, which no Assembly could give them. Revolution or no revolution, France would at all events have suffered deeply from her financial difficulties. Nay, so deeply seated were the social evils, so complicated the difficulties, that we should be surprised at any man, or masses of men, having looked to the National Assembly for a solution, did we not know how, in all ages of history, man has been led by abstractions; how the great periods in human development have been uniformly opened by a consideration of questions the most abstract, and apparently the most remote from immediate interests. New ideas have ever been the heralds and creators of new eras. The mystery of all this is that man has a soul, and that in all moments of enthusiasm, his convictions really are dearer to him than his interests.

One may look upon the peculiarity of the Assembly, as being a singular faith in the power of ideas.* That was its greatness. It firmly believed that truth shaped into laws would be invincible. Two months—such was the calculation—would suffice to construct the constitution. That constitution by its omnipotent virtue would convince all men and bend them to its authority, and the revolution would be completed. Such was the faith of the National Assembly.

The attitude of the people was so menacing that many of the courtiers fled. Thus commenced the first emigration. The Count of Artois made himself the centre of a counter-revolutionary party. Some letters to him having been seized on the person of the Baron de Castelnau, were brought to the Assembly. What was to be done with them? Could the seals be broken? It was a delicate question. The Assembly had every reason to suspect the correspondence to be a dangerous one; still there was something sacred in a sealed letter, which deterred them from opening it. Many, Mirabeau amongst the number, decided in the negative. The contrary opinion was maintained by Rewbell and others, to whom the Bishop of Langres opposed several examples drawn from antiquity. Then Robespierre uprose, and according to the expression of Gorsas, *foudroya l'argument de L'Evêque de Langres*, "It was not antiquity," he said, "they should there invoke; it was the supreme law of public safety."

Public safety: what words! They had not, however, yet become words of terror.

And as if the minds of men were not sufficiently agitated, there now were heard cries of a great conspiracy of the aristocrats. The papers announced that a plot had been discovered which was to have delivered Brest to the English. Brest, the naval arsenal, wherein France for whole centuries had expended her millions and her labors: this given up to England! England would once more overrun France! Conceive the rage and horror of a Frenchman at the mere mention of the English in France! But England, to her honor be it said, disdained the temptation, and revealed the plot to the ministers of Louis XVI., without, however, mentioning the names of the parties. Of course French writers see in this only another instance of Albion's "perfidy." It was not generosity in England, it was not honor, it was nothing but profound calculation. England "wanted to set France by the ears!" This is the liberal interpretation Frenchmen put upon her conduct!

It was amidst these cries of alarm—with on one hand the emigration of the nobility, on the other the hunger of a maddened people; with here an irresolute aristocracy, startled at the audacity of the *canaille*, and there a resolute Assembly, prepared, at the hazard of their lives, to work out the liberty of France; amidst reports of famine, of insurrections, and wild disorders of all sorts, that we find the National Assembly debating upon the rights of man, discussing every article with metaphysical quibbling and wearisome fluency, and having finally settled each article, making their famous Declaration.

This Declaration, which was solemnly adopted by the Assembly, on the 18th of August, was the product of a whole century of philosophical speculation, fixed and reduced to formulas, and bearing unmistakeable traces of Rousseau. It declared the original equality of mankind, and that the ends of social union are liberty, property, security, and resistance to oppression. It declared that sovereignty resides in the nation, from whence all power emanates; that freedom consists in doing everything which does not injure another; that law is the expression of the general will; that public burdens should be borne by all the members of the state in proportion to their fortunes; that the elective franchise should be extended to all; that the exercise of natural rights has no other limit than their interference with the rights of others; that no man should be persecuted for his religious opinions, provided he conform to the laws and do not disturb the religion of the state; that all men have the right of quitting the state in which they were born, and of choosing another country, by renouncing their rights of citizenship; that the liberty of the press is the foremost support of public liberty, and the law should maintain it, at the same time punishing those who abuse it by distributing seditious discourses, or calumnies against individuals.

During the discussions on the Rights of Man, Robespierre was not idle. Hitherto we have seen him a royalist; but now the republican begins to appear. In these discussions of abstract questions, the philosophy of Rousseau carried him beyond the limits of royalism. He said nothing important until they came to discuss the question of the veto. This brought the whole existence of monarchy into question. Is the King the absolute ruler of the nation, or is he only its accepted delegate? The lovers of England and the English constitution all voted in favor of the veto. Even Mirabeau was for it. In a famous speech on that occasion, he said, "I would rather live in Constantinople than in France, if laws could be made without the royal sanction." He could conceive of no other state than one in which the King had supreme voice and power!

It was then that Robespierre, as the disciple of Rousseau, stood boldly forth, and spoke:—

"He who says that one man has the right to oppose himself to the law, says that the will of one man is above the will of all. He says that the nation is nothing, and that one man is everything. If he adds that this right belongs to him who is endowed with the executive power, he says that the man chosen by the nation to execute the will of the nation, has the right to contradict and enchain the will of that nation. He has created a monster, inconceivable in morals and in politics: and that monster," added Robespierre, earnestly, "is nothing else than the royal veto. It is idle to tell us continually that France is a monarchical state; and from this axiom to derive the rights of the King as the first and most precious part of the constitution; as if the rights of the nation were but a secondary matter. Let us first know what the real signification of monarchy is. It merely expresses the state in which the executive power is confided to a single man. We must remember that governments, such as they are, are established *by* the people, and *for* the people. That those who govern, and consequently the kings themselves, are only proxies and delegates of the people."

Strange language this to hear in an assembly, and from an obscure member! But this obscure member, instead of occupying himself with the verbiage of political or parliamentary eloquence, had gone back to first principles.

"We must remember," he continued, "that the functions of all political powers, and consequently of royalty, are public duties, and not personal rights; and therefore we must not be startled to hear, in an assembly of the representatives of the French nation, citizens who think that the liberty and the rights of a nation are the first objects which ought to occupy them; the real aim of their labors, and that royal authority merely established for their preservation, ought to be regulated in the manner most fitting to fulfil that destination.

"The representatives of the nation may abuse their authority, it is said, consequently we must give the King a power of opposing himself to the law.

"This is just as if one said: 'The legislator may err, therefore we must abolish him.'

"It presupposes a great want of confidence in the legislative body, and an extreme confidence in the executive power. Let us examine how far that opinion is well-founded."

There was no man, except Sièyes, who could have spoken in this manner; who, calm amidst these stormy discussions, could have pursued this logical sequence of ideas; and summed them up in so clear, distinct, and comprehensive a formula.

"Without doubt," he continued, "the laws of a wise policy prescribe that we should prevent the abuses of all powers by just precautions. The severity of these precautions should be proportioned to the probability and facility of those abuses; and by a necessary consequence of this principle, it would be unreasonable to augment the force of a most redoubtable power, at the expense of that power which is weaker and more salutary. Now let us compare the force of the legislative body with that of the executive power.

"The first is composed of citizens, chosen by the people, clothed with a peaceful magistracy, and for a limited time. After which they return into the crowd, and are subjected to the stern or favorable judgment of their fellow-citizens. Every thing guarantees their fidelity—their personal interest; that of their family; of their posterity; of the people whose confidence had elected them."

Having thus drawn a picture of the calm majesty of Law, and the might of a representative assembly, Robespierre proceeded to place beside it the picture of a despotic monarchy. To place the two in opposition was inevitably to condemn the latter. Hear him:—

"What, on the contrary, is the Executive power? A monarch clothed with an enormous strength which disposes of armies, of tribunals, of all the public affairs of a great nation, and is armed with all the means of oppression and of seduction. How many facilities to satisfy the ambition so natural to princes: above all, when the hereditariness of the crown permits them to constantly follow their project of extending a power, which they regard as the patrimony of their family! Then calculate all the dangers which beset them, and if that is not enough, run your eyes over history. What a spectacle there presents itself! Nations everywhere robbed of the legislative power, become the plaything and the prey of absolute monarchs, who oppress and degrade them: so difficult is it for liberty long to defend itself against the power of kings. And we who are scarcely yet escaped from the same condition—we whose present reunion is perhaps the most striking evidence of ministerial power, before which our ancient National Assemblies have disappeared; hardly have we recovered them, than we wish once more to place them in tutelage and dependence.

"The representatives of the nation appear then to you more suspicious than the ministers and courtiers? If I examine the dangers which you appear to dread from the former, I believe they may be reduced to three:—Error, Precipitation, Ambition. As to Error, besides its being a strange expedient to render the legislative power infallible, that we should render it null; I see no reason whereby monarchs in general, or their counselors, should be presumed more enlightened on the wants of the people, or on the means of alleviating them, than the representatives of the people themselves.

"Precipitation! Neither do I conceive how the remedy of this evil consists in condemning the legislative body to inaction: and before recurring to such a method, I would at least desire that we should examine if there is another which might lead us to the same end.

"Ambition! But is that of princes and courtiers less redoubtable? And it is precisely to that, that you confide the care of enchaining the authority of your representatives: that is to say, the only one that can defend you against the attempts of princes and courtiers."

The majority of the Assembly shared Robespierre's views; and the King's counselors were at length forced to propose a compromise in the shape of a suspensive veto; namely, that the King should not have the absolute right of preventing any law, but only the right of suspending it for two, four, or six years. And it is very characteristic of the fluctuating vague ideas of the Assembly that they should have accepted such a compromise; that, after having voted against the absolute veto, they should have really thought this suspensive veto rational and acceptable. It was carried by a large majority! Robespierre skillfully exposed its absurdity.

"The palpable absurdity of the veto in general," he said, "has produced in this Assembly the invention of the suspensive veto:

a new expression imagined for a new system. I must avow that I have not yet been able perfectly to understand it: all that I know is, that it gives the King the right of suspending, according to his pleasure, the action of the legislative power, for a period on the duration of which opinions are not unanimous. That which induces me to combat this doctrine, although maintained by very excellent citizens, is, that a great number of them have not denied that they regard all royal veto as contrary to true principles, but persuaded that it was adopted in all its rigor by the majority of the Assembly, they fancied that the only mode of escaping such an infliction was to find refuge in the system of a suspensive veto. I have only differed from them on one point, and that is, that I have not despaired of the power of truth, and of public safety. It seemed to me that it was not right to compound with liberty, with justice, with reason; and that an indomitable courage, an inviolable fidelity to great principles, was the only resource which was becoming the present situation of the people's defenders. I say, therefore, with frankness, that both the absolute veto and the suspensive veto appear to me to differ far more in words than in effects : and that they are both equally capable of annihilating our liberty."

From this time forward we may date Robespierre's republicanism. The germs sown by Rousseau were now beginning to flower. Yet so little was republicanism the distinct creed of the Assembly, that at this very time they enthusiastically voted the hereditary succession of the crown, and the inviolability of the royal person. And when, on the 8th of October, as they were discussing the formula to be observed in the royal edicts, Robespierre proposed to do away with the terms of ancient despotism, he was only met with inextinguishable laughter. "Liberty," he said, "should exist in the words by which you express things, and in the form of the law, no less than in the law itself." He demanded that all the decrees of the Assembly should be expressed by the uniform terms of *law*. He demanded the suppression of ancient formulas, such as "Pleine puissance et autorité voyant—car tel est notre plaisir," &c., and that these formulas should be replaced by this:—

"Louis, by the Grace of God, and by the will of the nation, King of the French, to all citizens of the French Empire; people, this is the law that your representatives have made, and to which I affix the royal seal."

But so burlesque did this commencement appear, that they would not hear the end of it. The *Moniteur*, in reporting it, described it as a "*formule très plaisante.*"

When the King sent his reply to the declaration of rights, Robespierre demanded that it should be more explicit; and he made this bold speech: "The reply of the king is destructive, not only of all constitution, but also of the national right to have a constitution. Constitutional articles are only adopted positively; not conditionally. He who has the right to impose a condition on a constitution, has the right to annul that constitution; and he places his will above the right of the nation. You are told that your articles do not all present the idea of perfection: *ne présentent pas tous l'idée de la perfection.*

"On the declaration of rights, *on ne s'explique pas!* Is it for the Executive power to criticise the constituent power, from which it emanates? It belongs to no power on earth to subvert principles: to raise itself above the nation, and to censure its wishes. I consider, therefore, the reply of the king as contrary to principles; contrary to the rights of the nation; and as opposed to the constitution."

In the course of this speech, he let fall an aphorism which may be taken as the motto of his whole life: "*Vous n'avez d'autre moyen d'éviter les obstacles qu'en brisant les obstacles.*"*

I may here insert two of Robespierre's letters written at this period, and addressed to M. Buissart, Assessor of the Marshalsea at Arras. They are sealed with red wax, bearing the impression of a head of Socrates on an antique cameo.

---

* "There is but one way of avoiding obstacles: to crush them."

"Thursday, 5th September, 1789.
"Paris, Rue de l'Etang, No. 10.

"SIR,.

"I arrived in safety, though not without alarm. Twelve leagues from Paris I heard a rumor well calculated to inspire terror. It was said that 15,000 men had marched to Versailles to force the National Assembly to issue decrees such as should assure French liberty. My courage was shaken at this terrible news; I thought, however, of the antique courage of the *communes*, and I flew to Paris, resolved to carry a musket in defence of the nation. The reports turned out to be false, and there was no need for me to take up arms. There was, however, some foundation for the rumor. On arriving in the capital, I saw a vast concourse of people, not in the least tumultuous, and astonishing only from its immense number. Dearth of bread was the cause of this assemblage. You must know that there are at Paris a set of monopolizers of bread. These avaricious wretches rush to the bakers', buy up all the bread they can, and then resell it at an exorbitant price. I get this fact from an elector, and member of the present *comité* (M. Desessarts, a physician).

"The States-General, which were acquiring greater strength, are dissolved. It was decreed here that 15,000 men should be sent to Versailles to recal the Assembly to reason, and to intimidate the priestly and noble aristocrats, who are beginning to have a manifest superiority in all the deliberations. Three letters written from the Palais Royal were read to the Assembly, which have somewhat lowered the pride of the Calotins and the . . . . . But they will soon resume their former tone, because the Palais Royal is cleared by the militia of Paris. Good patriots will really find no support but in the ardent breasts of the Palais Royal.

"The majority of the National Assembly is the declared enemy of liberty; at this moment the most interesting questions are discussed there. The permanence or periodical recurrence of the States-General, their organization, and the veto, or royal sanction. There appears to be no difficulty about the first question, and all the orators are agreed as to permanence. The legislative power should not slumber a moment, since the executive power is always wakeful. The second question, whether there shall be one or two chambers, encounters more obstacles. There are several systems of organization; some want a senate which should revise what the National Assembly decreed. Others want two chambers; others again wish for one chamber alone. God grant that the latter plan be adopted. The third question,—the royal sanction, is discussed with much ardor. It appears by the questions examined that they recognize the necessity of a royal sanction, for the only division is on the question whether the King's veto shall be absolute or suspensive. The most mediocre minds feel perfectly that this veto would paralyze the legislative power, but what they cannot perceive is, that the suspensive veto has the same effect, and would be even more dangerous. Reflection will certainly suggest peremptory reasons which will make you reject any species of veto.

"There is but a very small minority which opposes itself to every sort of royal veto. The greatest majority is in favor of the suspensive veto. The Bretons have received orders, forbidding them to subscribe to any veto. Our Artesians will follow their courageous example.

"I mourn over the docility of that National Assembly; its dignity is compromised by the revolting pasquinades of the Vicomte de Mirabeau. A number of those narrow minds do not feel their true position, and dare not tell the National Assembly that it is not the nation; that the King is a part of the nation; that by giving him the veto, it is opposing one part of the nation to the other; and a thousand other things of the same kind.

"Present my thousand-and-one respects to Madame Buissart. I hope you will not forget to continue her in her office of secretary."

The second runs thus:—

"Versailles, Sept. 10, 1789.*

"SIR,

"I wrote to you so hastily, that I hardly remember the subjects which I mentioned to you. I will inform you of the decrees of the National Assembly. Yesterday (I do not know the day of the month), the Assembly decided that the legislative body should be permanent. The second question agitated was whether the National Assembly should be composed of one or two chambers. This important question, which seemed to have been solved by most of the orators who had spoken on that interesting subject of the constitution, made all the aristocrats uneasy. Their leader, who was also president of the Assembly, tried to put off the deliberations, in hopes of seeing opinions change on this subject. The Assembly decided that the question had been sufficiently discussed; this did not prevent his granting to two frenetic aristocrats, M. de V—— and M. de Lally, leave to speak again. The former, in a discourse which tended to the establishment of two chambers, used expressions and gestures which revolted a portion of the *commune;*—the most sensible portion. He said that two were needed to restrain *popular violence,* and he pointed, as he pronounced those words, to that portion of the *commune* to which the aristocrats have given the name of *Palais Royal.* One man alone persisted, during three-quarters of an hour, in calling M. de V—— to order; and in spite of the decree of the Assembly, which had given him leave to speak, he obtained that he should speak no more, because he had offended the Assembly. The president acknowledged that M. de V—— had used extraordinary expressions, and yet he allowed him to continue speaking. The first aristocrat thus got rid of, the Comte de Lally still remained. He was not allowed to speak, notwithstanding the cries of the nobility and clergy. It was known that the president had written a work in favor of the two chambers. A member of the commons asked him if he was not tired of wearying the Assembly. He was accused of having given M. de Lally leave to speak, only to favor his opinion upon the two chambers. The poor Bishop of Langres could not stand these reproaches. He rang his bell, and tried to end the sitting. This was opposed. He at last grew abashed, and withdrew, telling the Assembly to name another president. His departure was applauded. M. de Clermont Tonnerre, who was called upon to succeed him, made a few exclamations of factitious sensibility before ascending the president's seat. The Assembly is, for the moment, presided over by that Clermont Tonnerre, whose aristocratic shrewdness renders him as dangerous as lightning. Let us congratulate ourselves, however, on the fact that he will not be able to do all the harm that he might have done. Although he followed the same track as his predecessor, he could not manage to set aside the question of the unity or plurality of the chambers; and this morning, Thursday, the Assembly decided there should be but one chamber, by a majority of 802 against 89. The Curé of St. Pol was for the two chambers. Several did not vote. Many bishops retired. The Abbé Maury continues to play his infamous part. He would not vote, because, he said, the question was not sufficiently clear. Malhouet excited the indignation of the Assembly by voting for the two chambers.

"The *veto* is no longer so much to be dreaded as it would if there had been two chambers. The suspensive *veto* will be but the error of a moment —the nation, better represented, will soon swamp the *veto*. It may, however, still give rise to great evils. It will always be a matter of astonishment that the legislative power should have fettered itself for an instant, and should have given the power of opposing its decrees to the executive; which is in constant activity, and has a natural tendency to oppress the legislative body. It is surely absurd that the executive should be the judge of what is given him to execute. The very power of judging destroys his existence. These principles, although evident, have not been perceived, owing to the distrust which reigns in the Assembly, and flagrant injustice has endeavored to smother them.

"The suppression of tithes and feudal rights is most necessary to the general welfare. Nothing is rarer than a generous priest or a disinterested noble. The former has only become a priest in order to levy tithes on people and property; the latter only came into the world a noble, in order to shine.

"I forgot in my last letter to inform you of the offering of a box-full of jewels; eleven wives of artists dressed in white, came to present their little holocaust. This offering has been looked upon with various feelings. Some looked on it as a farce, others as the effect of well-intentioned patriotism.

"The criminal instruction is taking a good turn; it is to be ended to-day or to-morrow.

"I trust the commutation is infallible. I would have obtained (begging your assessorial and provostal majesty's pardon) the nullity of the proceeding and of the judgment, had it been necessary. The penalty is too arbitrary to be allowed to stand. We should soon be condemned to go and kiss the moon, if the judges were allowed to follow their own imaginations! This is between ourselves; I would not jest in this way with any one else, but I know you too well not to permit myself this ebullition of mirth. I beg you to remind your amiable secretary that she has not fulfilled her functions. I denounce her to you. I do not forget that she has undertaken that office, and can no longer neglect it without your consent. I have not written to the Robespierre part of my family. I leave it to your prudence whether to communicate my letter, or not.

"My brother has made amends for his errors towards me. Excuse this scrawl; it is already dark.

"Rue de l'Etang, No. 16."

The reader will not fail to notice the altered tone of these letters, and to contrast it with that of the letter from Carvins. What a change has come o'er his spirit since a journey of six leagues afforded matter for a long and pleasant epistle! and how different this grave pre-occupation of politics—the great question of the veto, of the unity of the Assembly, and the suppression of feudal rights—from the pleasantries about the hunchback T——, who held the balance of Themis and the lancet of Esculapius, or the rhapsody in honor of the inventor of tarts!

Let us return to Paris.

Vast and incalculable was the misery: crowds of peruke-makers, tailors, and shoemakers, were wont to assemble at the Louvre and in the Champs Elysées, demanding things impossible to be granted: demanding that the old regulations should be maintained, and that new ones should be made; demanding that the rate of daily wages should be fixed; demanding, in anticipation of 1848, that all the Savoyards in the country should be sent away, and only Frenchmen employed. The bakers' shops were besieged, as early as five o'clock in the morning, by hungry crowds who had to stand *en queue;* happy when they had money to purchase miserable bread, even in this uncomfortable manner! Famine went on increasing. "Parliamentary eloquence; discussion of the rights of man; discussion on the veto; these grew no corn; they only kept the nation agitated, and prevented men from growing corn." Yet the nation was as deeply interested in all these discussions, as if their vital interests were inseparably bound up with them. Paris was living at the mercy of chance: its subsistence dependent on some arrival or other: dependent on a convoy from Beauce, or a boat from Corbeuil. The city, at immense sacrifices, was obliged to lower the price of bread: the consequence was that the population for more than ten leagues round, came to procure provisions at Paris. The uncertainty of the morrow augmented the difficulties. Everybody stored up, and concealed provisions. The administration sent in every direction, and bought up flour, by fair means, or by foul. It often happened that at midnight there was but half the flour necessary for the morning market. Provisioning Paris was a kind of war. The National Guard was sent to protect each arrival; or to secure certain purchases, by force of arms. Speculators were afraid; farmers would not thrash any longer; neither would the miller grind. "I used to see," says Bailly, "good tradesmen, mercers and goldsmiths, praying to be admitted among the beggars employed at Montmartre, in digging the ground."

Then came fearful whispers of the King's intention to fly to Metz. What will become of us if the King should fly? He must not fly; we will have him here; here amongst us in Paris!

This produced the famous insurrection of women, of which Carlyle has given us so stirring a narrative. It was on the 5th October: there were 8000 or 10,000 women crowding to Versailles. The National Guard forced Lafayette to lead them there the same evening. They stormed the palace; they entered the presence of the King, exclaiming "Bread! bread!" They forced him to return to Paris. "Courage!" they cried, "we shall not want bread now. We are bringing back the baker, his wife, and the baker's boy, *le boulanger, la boulangère, et le mitron.*" It seems to them that with their King in Paris they can no longer want: all must go well!

In the midst of this insurrection of women, Robespierre is dimly seen, for a moment or two, supporting their orator against the Assembly, and quieting their turbulent fears. He was rising daily into importance; made several motions in the House, which, although rejected, still served to fix attention on him. The eagle eye of Mirabeau had discerned the one element of greatness in that man. "He will go far," said he, "for he believes all he says." Nothing was wanting for him to become eminent, than that France should also believe what he said; and that time was fast approaching.

CHAPTER X.

The Assembly transferred to Paris—The Jacobine Club—Murder of François—Robespierre opposes martial law—Speaks on the distribution of church property—His style of eloquence—Speech on the right of voting—Defends the rights of Jews and comedians—Dr. Guillotin on the penal code—His machine—The King declares himself the friend of the Constitution.

On the 19th October, the Assembly was transferred from Versailles to Paris, and held its first sittings in the halls of the Archbishop's palace. All distinctions in costume and places were suppressed. The nobles and ecclesiastics lost those futile marks of supremacy, now no longer in harmony with those principles of equality which the Assembly had proclaimed. *Le Club Breton* also followed, and took up its abode in the ancient convent of the Jacobins, in the Rue St. Honoré, and was henceforth named the Jacobin Club. People were admitted by tickets only; but they were freely given to all persons of known republican principles. Something like 1300 chosen patriots, with many of the Assembly, were there. Barnave, Mirabeau, the two Lameths, were to be seen there. Robespierre was a constant attendant. This Jacobin Club soon divided itself into three other clubs: first, that party which looked upon the Jacobins as lukewarm patriots left it, and constituted themselves into the Club of the Cordeliers, where Danton's voice of thunder made the halls ring; and Camille Desmoulins' light, glancing wit, played with momentous subjects. The other party, which looked upon the Jacobins as too fierce, constituted itself into the "Club of 1789; friends of the monarchic constitution;" and afterwards named *Feuillant's* Club, because it met in the *Feuillant* Convent. Lafayette was their chief; supported by the "respectable" patriots. These clubs generated many others, and the provinces imitated them.

But let us return to the King. It is the 7th of October, and the Tuileries this morning are crowded with an excited multitude, impatient to see their monarch. "Look, there he is!" exclaims some happy mortal, having caught a glimpse of the father of his people, who was obliged to show himself from the balcony, to be received with unanimous acclamations; and then to descend into the gardens, and mingle, as it were, still closer with his people. When the King and Queen appeared by torchlight at the Hôtel de Ville, a hurrah like that of thunder rent the air; shouts of joy, love, and gratitude, arose from that fierce crowd towards the King who had come to live among them. The men, with true French sensibility and enthusiasm, wept like children, shook each other by the hands—even strangers embraced. "The Revolution is ended," they cried. "Here is the King delivered from the palace of Versailles, delivered from his courtiers and advisers: he is with us." Alas! this enthusiasm, like so much that we have seen before, was to evaporate in a shout of joy, in the wringing of hands and fraternal embrace. It all passed away like the spurious friendship of after-dinner toasts: noisy and meaningless. For, although Paris had their *baker*, they had not food : hunger goaded them as severely as before. Street riots demonstrated that even the presence of the baker brought no food.

A real baker on the 21st fell a victim. François was just commencing his seventh batch on that day, when a woman, who had been unable to procure bread at nine in the morning, and who was told to wait until the seventh batch was completed, entered his house to assure herself that all the bread had really been sold. She found three stale loaves which had been reserved for the men. She rushed into the street, holding one in her hand, loudly accusing the baker of only distributing a part of his stock. Riot began : he was accused of wishing to keep bread from the people. They burst into his shop, seized the unhappy man, and, disregarding his cries, hanged him.

Mr. Alison declares that the mob, enraged at finding the return of the King had not immediately lowered the prices of provisions, murdered this baker in revenge.

The murder was quite shocking enough, without attributing to it any such motive. They paraded his head on a pike through the streets, compelling every baker they met to kiss the remains. The unhappy wife of François, far advanced in pregnancy, running about in a state of distraction, met the crowd. At the sight of the bloody head she fainted. The mob had the barbarity to lower it into her arms, and press the lifeless lips against her face.

Surely such scenes require no aggravation from prejudice. Even Toryism, one would think, could find no satisfaction in making them worse. The people were mad—starving. Reports that the aristocrats bribed the bakers not to furnish food were rife. Such had been the accusation against François. It was enough to condemn him. Mr. Alison, not content with maligning the mob, maligns the National Assembly; and says, that the Assembly, " elected by universal suffrage," were " paralyzed at every step by the dread of losing their popularity, and did nothing to prevent, or punish this barbarity." So false is this, that Mr. Alison himself, at the opening of the succeeding paragraph, declares, " The Assembly, acting under the impulse of the indignation which this murder had excited, entertained a motion for a decree against seditious assemblages." He does not attempt to reconcile this flat contradiction; of "an Assembly, indignant, and passing decrees to prevent the recurrence of such scenes," and, "an Assembly, elected by universal suffrage, paralyzed by fear, and taking no step to prevent them."

The Assembly, indeed, proposed a decree of martial law. On every occasion of serious public disturbance, the municipality were to hoist the red flag; and immediately every group of citizens should disperse, on pain of military execution. It was tantamount, in fact, to our reading the Riot Act. "Mirabeau, Buzot, and Robespierre," says Mr. Alison, "vehemently opposed the measure." He then adds this ungenerous insinuation: "They felt the importance of such popular movements to aid their sanguinary designs." Now, what proof has he that these men had, as yet, any sanguinary designs? None; absolutely none. In fact, his sentence " denotes a foregone conclusion." Because Robespierre was subsequently sanguinary, it is asserted that he was so then! The reverse is the truth. Robespierre, indeed, opposed the motion, but upon high grounds. He said it was necessary to create a high national court. "Are we," he said, "in this discussion, to consider only an isolated fact; a single law? If we do not embrace at once every measure, our liberty is at an end. The deputies of the municipality have drawn an afflicting picture: they have demanded bread and soldiers. Those who have followed the Revolution, have foreseen the point at which you have now arrived. They have foreseen that food would be wanting, and that you would be shown to the people as its only resource. They have seen that terrible situations would cause you to demand violent measures, in order to immolate at once both you and liberty. Bread and soldiers are demanded: that is to say, the congregated people want bread. Give us soldiers to immolate the people. You are told that the soldiers refuse to march. Well: can you expect them to attack an unhappy people, whose misery they share? It is not, therefore, violent measures that we must take; but wise measures, to discover the source of our evils; to disconcert that conspiracy which, perhaps, in the very moment that I now speak, leaves us no other resource than a splendid devotion. We must name a tribunal, which shall be really national. We have fallen into a great error, in believing that the representatives of the nation cannot judge crimes committed against the nation. These crimes, on the contrary, can only be judged by the nation; or by its representatives; or by members taken from your body; and we should organize a tribunal, in this Assembly, to take a final and definite cognizance of all state offences. We should trust nothing to the Procureur du Roi. If we do not this, the constitution will be stifled in its cradle, amidst all our deliberations."

This national court, which Robespierre thus proclaims, may be looked upon as the germ of the famous Revolutionary Tribunal: but, although Mirabeau supported him, the martial law was proclaimed by a large majority.

In the discussion on the better distribution of ecclesiastical property, Robespierre was not silent. He had before boldly spoken out his opinion on the necessity for the rich clergy doing something to assuage the general want. He had told them even to sell their sacred vases; and now that the Assembly began to consider the propriety of a more equal distribution of ecclesiastical property, Robespierre rose, and said:—

"This property belongs to the people: to demand from the ecclesiastics succors for the people, is to return those goods to their first destination." A sophism very intelligible in the mouth of a disciple of Rousseau; and as applicable to the estates of the aristocracy, as to the goods of the Church. Looked at calmly, any one may see that ecclesiastical property really did not belong to the people, and therefore the people could have no claim upon it; but as property had been defined by Rousseau to be in itself a spoliation; and, as his disciples all concurred with him in believing that everything in the nation belonged to the nation at large, Robespierre was only consequent in his demand. Michelet puts it much better, when he looks upon ecclesiastical property as a patrimony in reserve for the people. "It was on their account, and to feed them, that our charitable ancestors exhausted their fortunes in pious foundations; and endowed the ecclesiastics, the dispensers of charity, with the best part of their possessions. The clergy had so well kept, and augmented, the property of the poor, that at length it comprised one-fifth of the lands of the kingdom, and was estimated at 4,000,000,000 francs (160,000,000*l.*)"

In all times, the attempt to touch the property of the Church has been more fiercely resisted by the Church than any attempt to attack its doctrines. The clergy have been so accustomed to confound their interests with their convictions, that we find their thorough-going defender, Mr. Alison, gravely declaring, that religion speedily falls into discredit, unless its teachers are amply maintained at the public expense. "The marked and almost unaccountable irreligion," he says, "of a large proportion of the French, ever since the Revolution, is a sufficient proof that the support of property, and a certain portion of worldly splendor, is requisite to maintain even the cause of truth." Unhappy truth that needs such support! The clergy, however, thought with Mr. Alison, and when the project of the Assembly was made known, which would give to country curates and vicars about 60,000,000 francs, and to the bishops only 3,000,000 francs, the cry was raised, "Religion is destroyed! The Virgin is weeping in the churches of the south." And in *La Vendée*, in desperation, the clergy circulated pamphlets among the people, declaring that the project of the Revolutionists was to attack the Catholic religion. And from that moment the formidable power of Religion was arrayed against the power of the Revolution; exasperating the already exasperated minds of men; setting province against province; father against son.

Robespierre's speeches during these discussions are by no means striking. Indeed, as yet, we see little of that power which he subsequently displayed. His delivery was monotonous and disagreeable; his language pedantic, heavy, verbose: unrelieved by any play of fancy, unembellished by any pictorial power. He was a logician, not an orator. In looking into what he then said, all the merit we can trace is the merit of consistency of earnestness.

He struggles confusedly to express what he thinks; but makes no attempt at display. He is there to utter a thought, and he utters it in the best manner he can. He is not there as an orator, to charm an audience with his attitudes, to thrill them with the inflexions of a musical voice, or to delight them with the play of fancy. He stands fast by the Declaration of the rights of man. It seems to him that the Assembly, having once accepted that Declaration, having once put it forth as the formula of their convictions, have nothing more to do than to carry out those convictions, and to apply them to every case. He is always seen going back to that irrefragable text; recalling to the members the fact that those principles have been promulgated by them, and should be maintained by them. *E. g.*:—when, on the 22d of October, the Assembly decreed that no man could be an elector unless he paid in *direct* taxes, as proprietor, or as tenant, the value of three days' labor—thus with one line sweeping away 1,000,000 of rural electors; Robespierre rose to remind them that, according to the dictates of natural law, all men were equal and ought therefore all to vote.

"The constitution establishes," he says, "that sovereignty resides in the people, and in all the individual members of the people. Every individual has therefore the right to consent to the law which he is to obey, and to the administration of public affairs which is to be his. Otherwise, it is not true that all men are equal in rights: that every man is a citizen: if he who only pays a tax equivalent to one day's labor, has less right than he who pays the value of three days' labor, that man who pays ten days' labor has more right than he whose direct taxes only equal the value of three. Hence, he who has 100,000 francs rental, has 100 times as much right as he who has only 1000 francs of revenue." In this confused style, but with this pertinacious adherence to the rights of man, did Robespierre correct the Assembly. On the 23d of December, the Count de Clermont-Tonnerre brought forward a motion on the admissibility of all citizens whatever to civil employment, without respect to their condition, or to their religion. The Jews and comedians were those principally alluded to. M. Clermont-Tonnerre observed, that if these two classes were excluded, it would be in flat contradiction to the Declaration of rights, which said that all citizens are equal. The Jews, indeed, who had hitherto been smitten on the cheek, or hung between two dogs, now came forward, modestly to ask whether they were men; and the comedians, who had been enveloped in the same aristocratic prejudice, also wished to know if they were citizens. Robespierre, in a very feeble, heavy speech, defended the motion; but he seems to have done so rather as a matter of principle than of sympathy. He stands upon the abstract ground of humanity; and admits the Jews and comedians, as men.

The winter of 1790 was fortunately milder than the preceding: still the general misery increased, for there was no labor—little food. At that period the nobles were emigrating, or at least quitting their castles, then hardly safe, and settling in the towns. Several of them prepared for flight. If they visited their estates at all, it was to demand money—not to give relief. In haste they collected whatever was owing to them. Hence a scarcity of money; a cessation of labor; and a frightful increase of beggars in every town. In Paris they counted something like 200,000!

It was during these winter months, that Dr. Guillotin read his long discourse upon the reformation of the penal code; of which the *Moniteur* has not preserved a single word. This discourse attracts our attention on two accounts:—First, it proposed a decree that there should be but one kind of punishment for capital crimes; secondly, that the arm of the executioner should be replaced by the action of a machine, which Dr. Guillotin had invented.

"With the aid of my machine," said the glib doctor, "I will make your head spring off in the twinkling of an eye, and you will suffer nothing." Bursts of laughter met this declaration; nevertheless, the Assembly listened with attention, and adopted the proposal.

Among the articles of the decree, this was the third:—

"A crime, being personal, the punishment of the culprit will impose no stain upon the family. The honor of those who belong to him, will in no sense be damaged; and they will all continue to be equally admissible to every sort of profession, of dignity, or employment." Remembering Robespierre's early essay on this very point: how he endeavored to do away with the prejudice which inculpated all members of a family in the crime of one, we can well imagine the feeling of triumph with which he witnessed this recognition by the Assembly of his cherished principles.

Dr. Guillotin's proposal had greater àpropos than may at first be imagined. Torture was not yet abolished. On the 11th of August of that very year, we read a sentence of the parliament, condemning Louis Tonnelier to be broken alive on the wheel: "The court condemns the said Louis Tonnelier to have his arms, his legs, his thighs, and loins broken by the public executioner, on a scaffold erected for that purpose, in the public place of the market, in the town of Château Landon. This done, he is to be placed on a wheel; his face turned towards heaven, and there to remain so long as it pleases God to preserve his life."

On the whole, Paris is quiet during these winter months: agitated, indeed, but undisturbed by riots, and looking forward to a bright future. On the 4th February, 1790, the King unexpectedly presents himself before the Assembly; and there makes an affecting speech, which fills everybody with emotion and surprise. "Can we believe our ears? The King was secretly in love all the time with our very constitution, which has stripped him of his power! He approves of our acts; only advising us to postpone a part of our reforms. He deplores the disorders; defends and consoles the clergy, and the nobility; is the friend of everybody; but is, he declares, before everything else, the friend of the constitution!"

The effect was prodigious. Barrère was drowned in tears. The Assembly seemed completely delirious. It rose in a mass, and swore fidelity to the constitution, which, by the way, as yet did not exist. The galleries joined in these transports with inconceivable enthusiasm. Everybody began to take the oath. A *Te Deum* was sung; and Paris was illuminated in the evening. The Revolution is effected, and, this time, thoroughly effected! So high ran men's hopes! The Revolution, it was said, was finished on the 14th of July: then again finished on the 16th October; and now finished on this 4th February. From the 5th to the 15th there was nothing but a succession of fêtes, both at Paris and in the provinces. On all sides, and in every public thoroughfare, the people crowded together to take the oath. "Surely," exclaims Carlyle, "except to a very hoping people, there was not much here to build upon. Yet what did they not build! The fact that the King has spoken; that he has voluntarily come to speak—how inexpressibly encouraging! Did not the glance of his royal countenance, like concentrated sunbeams, kindle all hearts in an august assembly; nay, thereby in an inflammable enthusiastic France? And still do not our hearts burn with insatiable gratitude; and to one other man, a still higher blessedness suggests itself, to move that we all renew the national oath?"

CHAPTER XI.

Robespierre a rising man—Chateaubriand's description of him—Ridiculed by the deputies—Letters and verses addressed to him—Defends the people —Tribune of the people—Was Robespierre honest?—The federation of mankind: fete of July—The Ca Ira!—The emigration—Robespierre in private—The Jacobin Club: his ascendency there—Speeches in favor of the clergy—The "incorruptible"—The Cordelier's Club.

DURING the year 1790, Robespierre's name is more frequently met with in the columns of the *Moniteur*. From them I will collect some indications of his views and of his rising importance: an importance created by the momentum of his convictions. Several are the motions he makes, but seldom does he get the Assembly to vote with him. It attempts to drown his voice with laughter, with murmurs; but he persists, and *will* be heard. "A la fin d'une discussion violente," says Chateaubriand in his Memoirs, "je vis monter à la tribune un député d'un air commun, d'une figure inanimée, regulièrement coiffé, proprement habillé comme le régisseur d'une bonne maison, ou comme un notaire de village soigneux de sa personne. Il fit un rapport long et ennuyeux : on ne l'écouta pas ; je demandai son nom : c'était Robespierre."

"Thus persecuted, he seized the more eagerly every opportunity of raising his voice; and this invariable resolution of speaking on every occasion, sometimes made him truly ridiculous. For instance : when the American, Paul Jones, came to congratulate the Assembly; after the président had replied, and everybody had considered his answer sufficient, Robespierre was obstinately resolved to give his reply likewise. Neither murmurs, interruptions, nor anything, was able to stop him. After a great deal of trouble he managed to say a few insignificant, useless words; but only by appealing to the galleries: claiming the freedom of opinion; and exclaiming that they were trying to drown his voice. Maury caused the whole Assembly to laugh by voting that M. de Robespierre's speech should be printed."* His attempts were not always well timed. For instance: after Mirabeau's splendid apostrophe to the massacre of St. Bartholomew, Robespierre had the astonishing vanity to mount the tribune; as if, after so thrilling a burst of eloquence from their greatest orator, the Assembly could listen to so poor a speaker as Robespierre! They would not hear him. Still, as I said, it is quite clear that he is a rising man; and when M. de Beaumetz attacks him, and circulates in the Province of Artois, libellous accusations against him, his reply not only completely clears his character, but, to testify their approbation of his conduct, his fellow-citizens raise his brother to the office of *Procureur de la Commune.*

Another indication of his popularity may be read in the letter of a priest, named Lefetz; in which, though a stranger, he appeals to Robespierre as a man who would argue in the Assembly the cause of the oppressed.

"Seeing you above the clamors," runs this letter, "of those

who find their advantage in abuses and in disorder, I entreat you, monsieur, to use your great talents towards the abolition of a law contrary to nature, to policy, and to religion—I mean the law against the marriage of priests. The enemy of all prejudices, you employ your eloquence to ruin them. What claims have you not acquired to the gratitude of France, and of all the earth! As incorruptible as you are courageous, you have always openly manifested your opinions: personal interest never has made you act, but always the general good."*

Allowing for the exaggeration of epistolary style, this letter still implies that Robespierre had become a man looked on as the protector of the oppressed, and as the stern advocate for justice. Nor was it in vain that he was looked on as the advocate of the oppressed. He spoke in favor of the marriage of priests; twice did he endeavor to make his proposal heard, but the Assembly would not hear him: his voice was drowned in the uproar. Nay, more, the journals agreed not to print his speech. But rumor caught up the echoes and spread them far and wide. Thousands of priests wrote to Robespierre, expressing their gratitude for the attempt; and many sang his praises in poems written in Latin, Greek, and Hebrew. He was excessively flattered at this enthusiasm. Dining with Villiers, he said, "People talk of there being no poets now; you see I can make some." Poor Maximilien!

On the 15th of February, in a discussion relative to the disturbances in the provinces, we see Robespierre standing out more distinctly as the tribune of the people than he has done hitherto. He rises to say that " M. Lanjuinais has proposed to exhaust all the means of conciliation before employing the military force against the people who have burned the châteaux." D'Espréménil interrupts him violently with, "It is not the people; they are brigands!" Robespierre calmly replies, "If you wish it, I will say, 'The citizens accused of having burned the châteaux.' " Again, he is interrupted by D'Espréménil and Foucould: "Call them *brigands!*"

* *Papiers trouvés chez Robespierre*, vol. i. p. 118.

Robespierre replies: "I will use the name of *men* only; and I will characterize them sufficiently in stating the crime of which they are accused. But military force, employed against men, is a crime, when it is not absolutely indispensable: and you must not forget that we are in a moment when all the powers are annulled; when the people find themselves suddenly relieved from long oppression. You must not forget that these local evils, of which an account has been rendered to you, have fallen upon men, whom, rightfully, or wrongly, the people accuse of oppression. Do not forget that these men, led away by the remembrance of their misery, are not hardened culprits; and you will then confess that exhortations will suffice to pacify them.

"Let us beware lest this love of tranquillity become a source of destruction to liberty. Let us beware lest these disorders only serve as a pretext for placing terrible arms in the hands of those who may one day turn them against liberty." In other words, Robespierre bids them exonerate the people; bids them look upon the people's crimes with a lenient eye; bids them beware above all things of distrusting that power which can alone carry the Revolution triumphantly through.

On the 22d of February, he again speaks on the same subject. "Forgive me," he says, "if I cannot conceive how the employment of despotism can in any way insure liberty. Forgive me, if I demand how a revolution, made by the people, can be protected by the ministerial employment of arms. You must demonstrate to me that the kingdom is on the eve of total subversion. This demonstration appeared necessary even to those who seconded the demand of the ministers. Let us see if it be true. We only know the situation of the kingdom from what has been told us by some members relating to the troubles of Quercy, and you have seen that these troubles consist only in a few burned châteaux.

"Let no one calumniate the people. I call all France to witness! Aye; let its enemies exaggerate all the violences that have been committed, and exclaim that the Revolution has been signalized by barbarities. But I call all good citizens, all friends of reason, to witness, that never did a revolution cost so little blood—

exhibit so little cruelty. You have seen an immense people master of its destiny, quiet and orderly amidst the destruction of those powers which have oppressed it for so many centuries. The gentleness, the moderation of the people, have been unalterable. They alone have disconcerted the manœuvres of our enemies; and they are accused here before their representatives. Whither tend these accusations? Do you not see the kingdom divided? Do you not see two parties, that of the people, and that of a despotic aristocracy? Let us hope that the constitution will be consolidated; but let us also recognize that there yet remain great things for us to do. Thanks to the zeal with which the people have been misled by libels, public opinion has not yet taken its proper ascendency. Do you not see that they seek everywhere to enervate the generous sentiments of the people; to make them prefer a peaceful slavery to liberty, purchased at the price of some agitations and some sacrifices?

" Let us not proclaim a martial law against the people who defend their rights. Ought we to dishonor patriotism by calling it the spirit of sedition and turbulence? Ought we to honor slavery by the name of the love of order and of peace? No: we must prevent troubles by means more analogous to liberty. If you really love peace, it is not by martial laws that you must present it to the people."

While other members were fluctuating, Robespierre alone was steady. Having adopted the principles of Rousseau, he was resolved to make those principles respected, and to endeavor to get them realized. Few were less eloquent: none were more decided. While the orators were indulging in imaginative flights, in adroit sophisms, in endeavoring to reconcile their interests with their convictions, Robespierre only thought of getting his convictions realized. Right, abstract, absolute right, was the thing he stood up for. Practicable or impracticable,—useful or dangerous, he never inquired; he always asked himself, What is the abstract truth of the matter? What is the proposition to be made on it? And, having settled that, he boldly professed it. The rights of man and the sovereignty of the people were principles to which he always brought back every discussion.

In the midst of one of the stormy discussions, when Robespierre in vain endeavored to obtain a hearing, M. Foucould sarcastically called him a "tribune of the people." Who shall say that that sarcasm did not designate to Robespierre his true mission,—the part he had to play in this perturbed society? Can we not follow him to his lonely home, in the dismal Rue de Saintonge, in the neighborhood of the Marais, where he had his cold and ill-furnished lodging, his heart proudly swelling at this designation, his mind stretching forwards into a dim futurity, and there picturing the great part he had to play as tribune to the people. Though insignificant amongst the nobles, soldiers, lawyers, orators, and *littérateurs* of the Assembly, could he not gain the highest eminence as a tribune?

The sovereignty of the people has been his creed; to be the orator of the people shall now be his part!

Mirabeau, the great Mirabeau, has been tampered with by the court,—has sold himself to it. When I say sold himself, I of course mean, he has been *paid;* for it was the distinction of Mirabeau, as Lamartine has said, that in the midst of the infamous traffic of his powers, he preserved the incorruptibility of his genius. All the contradictions in Mirabeau's political life seem to me thus explicable. He was willing to receive the salary,—he was willing to defend the court,—but he only defended it when he really felt with it, whenever he thought it necessary to neutralize the advancing anarchy. On all great occasions, the vicious politician disappeared; and, as Michelet says, the "God of Eloquence took possession of him." He cannot be said to have sacrificed his convictions to the court; all he did was, in return for its money, to lend it such influence as was in his power. I do not defend his corruption, I explain it. Corrupt he was, because he was paid; but he was not *bought*.

Opposed to this figure of the gigantic, but corrupt Mirabeau, it is not uncommon to see that of the "incorruptible" Robespierre. Was that epithet deserved? As far as mere money corruptibility is concerned, Robespierre was unquestionably pure. But is there no other means of corruption besides money? Is there not a greed of applause quite as despicable as a greed of money? May not a man sell his convictions for the good opinion of his small circle of friends, or for the loud hurrahs of a miscellaneous audience? Perhaps the nature of the bribe is not so distinct; the man is not so conscious of his corruption; but the taint is there.

Robespierre was bribed by that which tempted him. He was not a luxurious man, not a sensual man; to poverty he had been accustomed, and now when poverty was a virtue he could glory in being poor. But the voluptuous soul of Mirabeau was not more avid of pleasure than the vain ambitious soul of Robespierre was of applause. For popularity Robespierre sold himself. I do not say that he was a mere worthless demagogue. I believe him to have been actuated by deep sincere convictions. But I do accuse him of having flattered the mob which flattered him; of having shaped his convictions so as to gain the applause of men whom he should have ruled and enlightened. I accuse him of having disgraced his life with acts which no eloquence can adorn, which no sophistry can excuse. I accuse him of having uttered language which in his heart he knew was false, and that too at a time when such language was translated into bloody acts. I accuse him, in short, of that dishonesty which consists in not daring to speak the truth, preferring to speak what will flatter an audience. He was corrupt because he dared not be true.

Among the acts of the Assembly during this year, must not be forgotten the abolition of all titles contradictory to the idea of equality. It was proposed by a deputy from the South, in a moment of generous emotion; and adopted by the excited members, with an overwhelming majority. This notion, supported by Montmorency, de Noailles, and Lafayette, was principally opposed by Maury, the shoemaker's son! It decreed there should be no more transmission of merit. The acts of one man should not ennoble his successors.

On the day on which this abolition of nobility was decreed,

Anacharsis Clootz, a German from the Rhine, presented himself at the bar of the Assembly with a score of men from every nation, in their national costumes. This deputation styled itself that of the human race; and Clootz demanded in their name to be allowed to take part in the confederation at the field of Mars, "in the name of every people; that is to say, of the legitimate sovereigns everywhere oppressed by kings."

The day of this great confederation had arrived. It is the 14th of July, the anniversary of the fall of the Bastille. All the provinces send forth their deputies, and as these bands of patriots tramp through the towns and villages, they chant, with heroic cheerfulness, a song which the inhabitants re-echo from their thresholds. It is the *Ca Ira*—

> Le peuple en ce jour sans cesse répète:
>   Ah! ça ira! ça ira! ça ira!
> Suivant les maximes de l'Evangèle
>   Ah! ça ira! ça ira! ça ira!
> De legislateur tout s'accomplira;
> Celui qui s'élève, on l'abaissera;
> Et qui s'abaisse, on l'élévèra, &c.

This song, which afterwards became the murderous *Ca Ira* of 1793, was then of a very different character: it was the national song, and stirred every heart. Under the burning sun of July this song was indeed, as Michelet says, a viaticum, a support like the *proses* chanted by the pilgrims who, in a revolutionary spirit, built up the Cathedrals of Chartres and Strasbourg in the middle ages. The Parisians sang it in quick time, and with violent energy, when digging up the Champs de Mars to prepare it for the confederation.

From being a flat plain, the Champ de Mars was made to assume its present majestic form. The whole population worked at it; and day and night, men of every class and every age; soldiers, abbés, actors, sisters of charity, noble ladies, market women, even children, all handled the pickaxe, rolled barrows, or drove carts. Children bearing torches walked in front; perambulating musicians played to enliven the workmen; and the workmen themselves, while leveling the earth, continued still to chant their leveling song, *Ca Ira! Ca Ira! Ca Ira!*

This immense work, which converted a plain into a valley, was performed within a week; they began it on the 7th of July, and they ended it before the 14th.*

Paris is now filling on all sides with guests; every heart expands with an unknown sentiment of peace and concord. Even the journalists have ceased wrangling, and Camille Desmoulins proposes a confederation between writers, that there should be no more opposition,—no more jealousy,—no emulation but that for the public welfare. 160,000 persons are now seated upon the hillocks in that Champ de Mars, and 150,000 are standing in the field itself. About 50,000, of whom 14,000 are national guards from the provinces, those of Paris, the deputies from the army, the navy, and others, are ready to perform their evolutions. The eminences of Chaillot and Passy are crowded with spectators; the whole presents a magnificent amphitheatre, itself commanded by the more distant circus of Montmartre, St. Cloud, Meudon, and Serres.

At seven o'clock the procession advanced; the electors, the representatives of the municipality, the presidents of the districts, national guards, deputies of the army and others, moved on in order to the sound of military music, from the site of the Bastille, their banners floating patriotic inscriptions, themselves arrayed in various and gorgeous costumes. They crossed the Seine by a bridge of boats and entered the amphitheatre under a triumphal arch. There they were met by the King and the National Assembly, at the foot of a great altar, erected after the manner of the ancients in the middle of the plain. At its foot was a model of the Bastille, overturned. Talleyrand, Bishop of Autun, and 200 priests, dressed in tri-colored robes, celebrated high-mass in the presence of the assembled multitude. Lafayette, mounted on a superb white charger, advanced as commander-in-chief of the national guards, and took the oath in the following terms:—" We SWEAR to be faithful to the nation, to the laws, and to the King; to maintain with all our might the constitution decreed by the National Assembly, and accepted by the King; and to remain united to all the French by the indissoluble bonds of fraternity."

Immediately after, the president of the National Assembly and the King took the oath. The Queen, lifting the dauphin in her arms, also took it. Then the rolling of drums and discharges of artillery, the impassioned shouts of the multitude and the clashing of arms, rent the skies at that auspicious event. The monarch and his subjects seemed knit together by indestructible bonds of affection.

"Here, however, we are to remark, with the sorrowing historians of that day, that, suddenly, while Episcopus Talleyrand, long stoled with mitre and tri-color belt, was yet but hitching up the altar-steps, the material heaven grew black, and north wind, moaning cold moisture, began to sing, and there descended a very deluge of rain. Sad to see! The thirty-staired seats, all round our amphitheatres, get instantaneously slated with mere umbrellas, fallacious when so thick set; our antique cassoletts become waterpots, their incense-smoke gone hissing in a whiff of muddy vapour. Alas! instead of vivats, there is nothing now but the furious peppering and rattling. From three to four hundred thousand human individuals feel that they have a skin, happily *impervious*. The general's sash runs water; how all military banners droop, and will not wave, but lazily flap, as if metamorphosed into painted tin banners! Worse, far worse, these hundred thousand. Such is the historian's testimony of the fairest of France! Their snowy muslins, all splashed and draggled; the ostrich feather shrunk shamefully to the backbone of a feather; all caps are ruined; innermost pasteboard molten into its original pap; beauty no longer swims decorated in her garniture like Love-goddess, hidden-revealed in her Paphian clouds, but struggles in disastrous imprisonment in it, for the shape was noticeable; and now only sympathetic interjections, titterings, teeheeings, and resolute good humor will avail. A deluge, the insensate sheet or fluid-column of rain, such that our overseer's very mitre must be filled; not a mitre, but a filled and leaky fire-bucket, on his reverend head! Regardless of which, overseer Talleyrand performs his miracle; the blessing of Talleyrand, another than that of Jacob, is on all the eighty-three departmental flags of France, which wave or flap with such thankfulness as needs. Towards three o'clock the sun beams out again, the remaining evolutions can be transacted under bright heavens, though with decorations much damaged."*

In the evening Paris was illuminated, and festivities everywhere prevailed. On the site of the Bastille there was a ball given; over the gate was this inscription, *Ici on danse*. "They danced, indeed," says a cotemporary, "with joy and security, on that very spot where, formerly, so many tears had fallen: where courage, genius, and innocence had so often wept: where so often the cries of despair had been stifled." And this was the feast of Pikes! The festivities lasted out the week. Credulous men once more believed that all their troubles were to cease; that this universal swearing was a bond of brotherhood, which nothing could undo!

Unhappily, in opposition to this symbolical confederation of nations, was formed a confederation of kings. Europe had become alarmed. The progress of democratic ideas made every crowned head feel insecure. England and Prussia sided with Austria and Russia in hatred of this revolution; for the nations began to sympathize with France. The people everywhere began to ask whether they too ought not to put an end to the government of injustice and privilege?

The excitement created throughout Europe was intense. Burke sent forth his splendid and piteous wail over the destruction of order, and the advent, as he prophesied, of social disorganization; that grand and mournful protest, which Michelet, in his insane way, says, "was paid for by his adversary, Mr. Pitt!"

The nobles were emigrating; the Queen was carrying on correspondence with Austria; Prussia and England were threatening; Mirabeau was leaning visibly towards the court; and it became quite clear to every republican that the revolution was not yet finished; that terrible struggles were still to come.

Robespierre was not unmindful of all that was going on. Of his private life we gain but few glimpses. He lived parsimoniously on a part of his salary of eighteen francs a day as a deputy. One quarter of it he sent to his sister at Arras, for her support. Another quarter was given to his mistress, who loved him passionately, though she seldom saw him. His door was very often closed against her. He had little time for love; his heart was given to the republic; his ambition was to become a tribune of the people: that thought occupied him day and night. He could not, like Mirabeau, carry on his love affairs and political affairs at one and the same time. He did not treat the unhappy woman well, nor can he be said to have treated himself well. He was very frugal; and had scarcely money enough to purchase clothes. So poor was he, that when the Assembly decreed a general mourning for the death of Franklin, he was obliged to borrow a black stuff coat from a man much taller than himself. The coat draggled on the ground.

He was almost invariably at the Assembly, or at the Jacobin Club. The unwholesome, crowded rooms of the latter place causing him to suffer from frequent hemorrhage. He partook of no amusement; he saw no society; his greatest pleasure was to polish and improve his speeches; which, insipid as they were, he regarded with true paternal tenderness.

Hitherto Robespierre had followed, rather servilely, the Lameths, who, with Barnave, formed the leaders of the Jacobin Club, and were nicknamed by Mirabeau the Triumgueusat; and while they took the lead, Robespierre could maintain but a very secondary place. In time, however, they became rather alarmed at the progress of the revolution. Robespierre was perhaps not sorry for an opportunity of shaking off their equivocal friendship. He called one morning at the Lameths' house. They would not, or could not, receive him. It was enough for his susceptible pride; and he never returned there. He saw with some delight their leaning towards Mirabeau's party. That left room for him in the Jacobin's.

"The part he now had to play," says Michelet, "was prominent and simple. He became the principal obstacle to those whom he had forsaken. At every compromise these men attempted to make between principles and interests, a stumbling-block of abstract, absolute right was opposed to them by Robespierre: against their spurious Anglo-French and constitutional ideas he brought theories deduced from the Social Contract, the legislative ideal of Rousseau and Mably. They intrigued and agitated, but he remained immutable. They seemed like attorneys; he a philosopher, a priest of justice. He could not fail to weary them out in time. As a man of principles, and ever protesting in their favor, he seldom explained himself about their application, or ventured on the dangerous ground of ways and means. He said what ought to be done, but very seldom how it could be done."

As the revolution advanced the Jacobin Club rose gradually to higher importance. Michelet contradicts himself when he said that Club was one of mediocrities. He has himself named it, elsewhere, as a meeting of distinguished and educated men. French literature had a majority in it. La Harpe, Chenier, Chamfort, Andrieux, Sedaine, and others, were there. There also were several artists; David, Vernet, Larive, and the young Talma.

Through the yellow glare of the glimmering lamps, through the dull fog, in the Rue St. Honoré, may be seen a dark dense multitude, all wending to the door of the convent of the Jacobins.* It is there that the agents of insurrection every morning come to receive orders from the Lameths, or the money of the Duke of Orleans from Laclos.

Let us enter. The place is badly lighted, but the meeting is numerous and imposing. Voices which resound here, find echoes all over France, and France, from every one of her departments, pours in her news, true or false, and her accusations, just or unjust. This is the centre of all the clubs. The dark church is very so-

---

* I follow Michelet's description of the club.

lemn. There are a vast number of deputies present, and men who were hereafter to be famous and infamous. At the door, to examine the cards of admission, are two censors: Laïs the singer, and a handsome youth, the promising pupil of Madame de Genlis, the son of the Duke of Orleans, who will afterwards teach mathematics in Geneva, in England, in America; will be raised to the throne by barricades; and by barricades, after seventeen years of corrupt rule, once more to exile in England. It is the young Louis Philippe. At the bureau there is a dark-looking man, smiling. It is the agent of the Prince, Laclos, the too-notorious author of the *Liaisons dangereuses;* himself called *La Liaison la plus dangereuse.* In the tribune is another man, with sad and meagre visage, with threadbare olive-green coat (his only coat), with shrill weak voice, but earnest manner: there is no mistaking Maximilien Robespierre.

The anxious crowd are looking for an honest countenance. Some countenances express only intrigue, some fatuity, some insolence, others corruption; but Robespierre's seems to say *I am honest.* His face, which was always melancholy, wore not at this period the spectral and sinister expression which it assumed subsequently. The fine medal still extant expresses a certain benevolence and rectitude, with, however, a strong tension of the muscles.

His speeches are entirely on morality, and the interests of the people. He professes principles, nothing but principles. He is not entertaining: his person is austere and melancholy; his style academic and cold; no warm pulse of affection seems to beat in his heart. He is an incarnate syllogism, separating himself from all friends and colleagues: even his former college companions are kept at a distance. Entertaining the man certainly is not, nor is he what one would call attractive, yet he is popular. The partisan of absolute right, the man who constantly spoke of virtue, and whose sad and serious countenance seemed its very image, became the favorite of the people. The more he was disliked by the Assembly, where we have seen him laughed at, and coughed down, the more he was relished by the galleries. So he addressed himself more and more to this second assembly, which represented the people and claimed the right of interfering and hissing its delegates. Robespierre was an actor, who, failing in genius, and unable to move the pit and boxes, played to the gods; and their applause he won.

We can easily understand how naturally he would acquire an ascendency at the Jacobins. He was wonderfully assiduous, being ever at his post, and speaking on every subject. This not only kept him constantly before his public, but gave him that practice in debate which his want of genius rendered so necessary to him. Many members became tired, sick of the task, and deserted the club; but Robespierre, though he would sometimes tire his auditory, was never tired of hearing himself. Perhaps it was the instinct of his own mediocrity, rather than clear-sightedness, which early led him to see that real power resided in the people, and which made him constitute himself their tribune; and I attribute it to his sincere religious convictions, rather than to any political foresight, such as Michelet discerns, that he should have relied upon the lower clergy (a powerful body of eighty thousand priests), as well as the Jacobins, for his support. He believed that whoever had on his side the Jacobins and the priests, would be near possessing everything.

We have seen him raising his solitary voice in favor of the marriage of the clergy, and we hear him continually speaking on their side. On the 16th June he asked the Assembly to provide for the subsistence of aged ecclesiastics who had no benefices or pensions. On the 16th September he protested in favor of certain religious orders, which the Assembly had unjustly reckoned among the mendicants, and, to anticipate a little here, for the sake of completing these indications, I may add that, on the 19th March, 1791, when in open ecclesiastical warfare, the lower clergy, led away by the bishops, left but little hope of their being ever able to be reconciled with the spirit of the revolution, Robespierre protested against the measures of severity proposed, and said it would be absurd to make a special law against the factious speeches of priests. Priests, he said, were citizens, and no citizen ought to be prosecuted for his opinions; and that nothing was more vague than the words "*discours ou écrits excitants à la révolte.*" Loud murmurs continually interrupted him, and a member on his left exclaimed, "Go over to the right side."* He felt the danger, stopped short, reflected, and was prudent. He felt that he would have compromised himself; and he had not then sufficient audacity to persevere in his convictions when those convictions were unsupported by the majority. So little was he inclined to audacity, that he used to say of Camille Desmoulins and his comrades at the Cordeliers Club, "They are going too fast; they will break their necks. Paris was not made in a day, and it requires more than a day to unmake it." But if he had not yet shown himself the stern and inflexible republican, willing to go whole lengths, and sacrifice everything for the sake of realizing his opinions, he had become sufficiently prominent to be feared by the Lameths, and to be styled by the journals the Incorruptible. Incorruptible he was; but it was early yet to give him that title, seeing that he was not yet of sufficient importance for any party to buy him. *Casta est qui nemo rogavit;* and nobody, certainly, ever thought of bidding for Robespierre, whatever sums they might squander upon Mirabeau, or that Mirabeau of the Sans-culottes named Danton.

CHAPTER XII.

Robespierre's activity in the Assembly—Letter to Camille Desmoulins—Defends the Jews—Elected Secretary of the Assembly and "Juge de District"—Defends Camille—Struggles against Mirabeau—Speaks on the right of the people to choose the form of government—Robespierre challenged by royalists—Oath demanded from the clergy.

IN this chapter I shall bring together the scattered indications of Robespierre's political activity at this period. The reader must exercise his patience; for if these details are uninteresting in

---

* Robespierre sat on the *côté gauche* with the Revolutionists.

themselves, they are important in the genesis of Robespierre's career.

Although he looked upon the Jacobin Club as his true arena, he was also very active in the Assembly. In the discussion on the game-laws he took the liberal side; declaring that the right of killing game belonged to all citizens, and was not a right of property alone. He also took a decided part in the discussion on the question, whether the nation should place the right of declaring war in the hands of the King. Against the assertion that the King, as the representative of the nation, ought to have the right of declaring war, he said: "It is inexact to call the King the *representative* of the nation. The King is *le commis*,* and the delegate of the nation, to execute the national will." At this a storm of opposition arose; some members demanded that the speaker should be called to order, whereupon Robespierre replied: "There would have been no murmurs if my thought had been properly understood; I should not have been suspected of being wanting in respect to the majesty of royalty, since it is nothing else than the majesty of the nation. I wished to give a magnificent idea of . . . . If my expressions have hurt any one, I will retract them. By *commis*, I only meant the supreme office; the sublime charge of executing the general will. I have said that the nation is only represented when it specially charges some one to express its will; no other power, how august soever it may be, has the character of the representative of the people. I say, therefore, that the nation ought to confide in its representatives the right of peace and of war. To these reflections I add, that we must delegate such a power to him who has the least interest in abusing it. The legislative body can never abuse it, but the King may; armed as he is with the dictatorial power, which may render him formidable, and which may cripple liberty and the constitution. The King will always be inclined to declare war for the augmentation of his prerogative. The representatives of the nation will always have a direct interest, and even a personal one, in

---

* I know no English word which exactly represents this.

preventing war; for in another moment they will return into the class of citizens, and war affects all citizens." This was on the 18th May. In the *Moniteur* of the 29th, a subscriber addresses a letter to the editor, in which he says, "I have just read, Monsieur, that M. de Robespierre, having said that the King is the *commis de la nation*, MM. D'Estournel, De Murinais, &c., called him to order; but in your same number I read that on the evening before, M. de Montlosier made use of the same expression, and said to the Assembly, '*Le roi est le commis de la nation, et non le votre.*' These gentlemen then gave no signs of disapprobation. Explain to me, I pray you, why the members of the Assembly thought this expression so reprehensible in the mouth of M. de Robespierre, when they saw nothing to object to it the evening before in the mouth of M. de Montlosier. Is an expression good or bad, according as it is uttered from the right side or from the left?"

The editor gives no reply; but the reason is very simple. In the mouth of Robespierre the expression was decidedly anti-royalist, and tended to put the Assembly in mind of the real position of the King; and this was what the royalists would not accept.

We also find him at this time speaking against the *lettres de cachet*, which were still in use in the army, under the pretext of the necessity for passive obedience.

A few days afterwards, the Jews of Metz presented their petition against one of those odious abuses of the ancient order of things, which the revolution professed to abolish. Four hundred and fifty Jewish families had been suffered to fix their residence in Metz, upon condition of paying annually to the government the sum of twenty thousand francs. M. de Brancas, in espousing one of the court favorites, had obtained a concession of this tax, which was henceforward paid to him. The Jews now petitioned against this, and demanded the removal of a tax which was the sign of their personal servitude. Robespierre rose and defended them, arguing very justly, that the protection of government *se doit et ne se vend pas*. Even his old enemy, the Marquis de Toulongeon, says: "*Il s'éleva un moment au dessus de cette* POPULARITE *qui avait été son seul talent.*"—(Histoire de France, i. 193.)

On the 19th June, the Assembly elected Robespierre as one of its secretaries, giving him as colleagues MM. Delley and Populus, the latter a man now wholly forgotten, but whom we constantly find in the pages of the *Moniteur*, siding with Robespierre.

The ancient magistrature had closed its long career, by stupid resistance to the national authority, and everywhere elections replaced the judges with republicans; among them was Robespierre, who was named one of the *Juges de district* of Versailles. This shows us, especially when coupled with his election as secretary to the Assembly, that Robespierre was a rising man; that he was gradually making his way, emerging from that obscurity which had before enveloped him, and beginning to realize Mirabeau's prophecy. We even see him attacking Mirabeau in the Assembly, who, on bringing forward a motion, which called upon the Prince de Condé to declare whether or not he was the author of the manifesto published under his name, and remarking, that his silence would be regarded as an avowal, so that, after the lapse of the time fixed for his reply, his goods would be confiscated; to the astonishment of the Assembly, Robespierre rose: "I demand of M. Mirabeau," he said, "if it is certain that the manifesto exists, and what proofs he has that M. Louis Joseph de Bourbon is the author of it? I also demand of M. Mirabeau, why he sees no other author than M. Louis Joseph de Bourbon; why, when we march in the midst of plots, all his severity is directed against one man, to whom the prerogative of his birth, and so many hereditary privileges, have naturally given a distaste for our constitution; why he selects him, instead of taking those who, bound by their oaths and their functions to the constitution, every day endeavor to overturn it? Wherefore do you divert attention from these culprits who environ you, to seek one who is afar?"

Camille Desmoulins, with his reckless wit, had severely galled the Assembly, and Malouet had denounced both him and Marat before the Assembly. Robespierre manfully defended his colleague and friend. In the midst of the uproar, Malouet said, "I have denounced a number of Camille Desmoulins' paper, because he dared to justify himself;" and Camille, with his wonted audacity, said, from the gallery, "Yes; I dare;"* Robespierre demanded, in the name of humanity, that the Assembly should be calm; demanded that Camille should not be imprisoned, and he succeeded; "*maints beaux faits*," says Camille, in reporting the same, "*surtout ont signalé mon cher Robespierre.*"

A few days afterwards the Assembly had to judge not a journalist, but one of its own members. The affair was very serious. The Abbé de Barmont was accused of having assisted in the flight of the conspirator Bonne-Savaudin, who, in escaping from prison, had found refuge with the Abbé, who had not only given him a disguise, but had also accompanied him in his flight. The opinion of the *comité* was, that the Abbé should be placed under arrest. Robespierre applauded that project, and recalled to them that public safety was the supreme law, and that a revolution ought not to be subjected to the same laws which regulate the peaceful course of civil life. "We must distinguish," said he, "real humanity, which only looks at the general good, and which knows how to triumph over the most lively emotions of piety, from that weakness which is sensibility towards an individual, and barbarity towards society. Our first impulses can only be our excuse in certain cases. A man who threatened to denounce one who demanded from him an asylum would be nearer vice than virtue; but when the criminal has committed a crime against society at large, and one which compromises public safety; then to favor his flight, to give him an asylum, is not virtuous, but criminal; and our impulses of sensibility no longer excuse such an act."

On the news of the dreadful riot at Nancy reaching the Assembly, in the last days of August, Robespierre several times spoke to condemn Boillé and the officers, and to excuse the soldiers. This we might have expected. The soldiers were the *people* of the army; the officers the aristocracy. Right or wrong, therefore, Robespierre would have been sure to side with the people.

On the 1st of August the president read a letter from the con-

---

* The *Moniteur*, and the *Histoire Parlementaire*, barely mention that Robespierre shared in this scene.

querors of the Bastille, inviting the National Assembly to assist at a funeral service which was to be celebrated on the second, in honor of those slain in the taking that fortress.

The *Histoire Parlementaire* simply says that Robespierre demanded a deputation should be named to assist at the ceremony; but the *Moniteur* gives us his speech, which, though brief, is very remarkable. "You have decreed," said he, "that a deputation should be sent to the King to assure him of the attachment of the Assembly. I demand that at the same time a deputation should be named to assist at the funeral service which is now being prepared for those citizens who died in defending liberty."

The juxtaposition here of the King and the people, and the marked manner in which Robespierre stands up for the people, constituting himself their tribune, must not be overlooked. Such speeches would be commented on in all the clubs, repeated in all the cafés, and the people would feel assured that Robespierre let slip no opportunity of vindicating their cause.

So also in November, when a proposal was made of restricting the national guards to *active* citizens only, which was in fact constituting the national guard out of the bourgeoisie, and excluding the people, Robespierre, in a long speech, pointed out the injustice, adroitly asking, "Do you wish then that a citizen should become a rarity?" and proposed that all citizens without distinction should be admitted into the ranks.

On the night of the twenty-first he maintained the same thesis at the Jacobin Club, when Mirabeau was president. "Who," exclaims Camille, "would not share the holy indignation which burst forth in that admirable discourse of Robespierre at the Jacobins?" The applause which greeted it, and which was so loud a censure of the decree that had passed that morning, seemed to alarm Mirabeau, who dared to recall Robespierre to order, saying that no one was allowed to speak against a decree once passed.

This was a dangerous step for Mirabeau to take in presence of an impassioned auditory, entirely in favor of Robespierre; and shouts from all sides of the hall bade their orator continue. The tumult became excessive. It was impossible to hear anything.

Instead of putting on his hat, as president, Mirabeau mounted upon the arm-chair, and as though the decree attacked was identified with his own person, and the question was to defend and save it, he exclaimed, "Help, colleagues! Let all my friends surround me." Only thirty deputies obeyed his call. The whole assembly remained with Robespierre, who, as Camille says, "always so pure, so incorruptible, and, on this occasion, so eloquent, had around him all the real Jacobins, all republican souls, the *élite* of patriotism. Mirabeau surely did not know that if idolatry could be permitted among a free people, it was only the idolatry of virtue."

Charles Lameth now arrived. His arm was in a sling from his late duel with M. de Castries. Everybody was silent. The Jacobins were convinced that he would speak for Robespierre; yet he sided with Mirabeau! But the Viscount de Noailles rose and declared that the *comité* had understood the decree differently from Mirabeau and Lameth; had understood it in the same way as Robespierre; whereupon Robespierre resumed his speech amidst deafening applause.

On the discussion in the Assembly of the petition presented by the people of Avignon, to be separated from the papal government, Robespierre made an admirable speech, which was much applauded, a thing rare with him in that place. Not only was it applauded, but the Assembly paid it the compliment of ordering it to be printed. In it he defended the right which the people had to choose their own form of government; he told them that there was an absolute necessity for the representatives of the French people to respect those eternal principles of justice upon which they had based the edifice of their constitution; to defend as much as is in their own power that sacred cause of nations, which was their own cause, and which could hardly succumb without dragging with it in its fall the work of their own hands.

Here we have distinctly enunciated the principle which France has so frequently proclaimed of the mission which it has to revolutionize the world; that with it liberty is indissolubly bound up; that it is the guiding light of nations, and its sacred cause is to be carried by fire and sword all over the world.

Parties were becoming more and more exasperated, and the royalists, daily losing ground, formed a frivolous but characteristic plot of exterminating their principal antagonists in duel. Charles Lameth, after receiving several provocations, at last consented to fight M. de Castries, and was severely wounded in the arm.

Barnave, Roederer, Raband, and Bernard, all received challenges; and it is an indication of his rising importance, that Robespierre was also provoked, but wisely declined. "A gang of spadassins," says the "Révolution de Paris," "has been formed to exterminate the most ardent patriots of the National Assembly, and the most eloquent defenders of the people. Among these, Robespierre takes a high place." The royalists began to see that this man was not to be coughed down,—not to be turned aside by ridicule,—but having firm faith in the sovereignty of the people, was determined on all occasions to advocate their cause. He was not to be put down by a duel any more than by laughter; he continued undisturbed his patient course.

In that period of excitement men lived fast. Weeks were years. Important acts succeeded each other with frightful rapidity. Who could believe that only four months have passed since the federation of July? That jubilant France is once more despondent? The bright sun of July is dimmed, and the dark winter months are coming on, full of sad portents. Even the press is groping its way in obscurity; halting about, guessing wildly, denouncing wildly. The nobles have everywhere assumed the attitude of defiance and provocation, insulting the orators and the national guard. They rely upon the King's escape and upon the foreign powers.

On the 27th of November the National Assembly passes a dangerous decree, insisting on the bishops, curates, and vicars taking the oath to the constitution within a week. In case of refusal, it was enacted that they should be held to have renounced their benefices, which were immediately to be filled up in the mode prescribed by the civil constitution of the clergy. Those who, after taking the oath, should break it, were to be summoned to the tribunal of the district; and such as, having refused, should continue any part of their former functions, to be prosecuted as disturbers of the peace.

It is to be observed, that the Pope had expressly refused his sanction to the civil constitution of the clergy, as established by the Assembly, and had written to two bishops to that effect. Moreover, a consistory of the whole of the bishops in France had almost unanimously agreed that they would not take the oath to be faithful to the constitution, inasmuch as it vested the whole nomination of priests and bishops in a simple numerical majority of their several parishes or dioceses, to the entire exclusion of the appointment or control of the church. It became, therefore, a matter of conscience with the clergy to refuse the oath; but the Assembly was resolute.

"What is worthy of remark," says Michelet, " is, that neither Robespierre, Marat, nor Desmoulins, would have required the oath from the clergy. The intolerant Marat, who demanded that the printing-press of his enemy should be broken, desires that the priests should be gently treated. 'It is,' says he, 'the only occasion on which regard should be shown, for it is a matter of conscience.'"

All parties are now agreed that it was a sad blunder in the Assembly to pass this decree. It gave the refractory a grand, glorious, and solemn opportunity of bearing testimony before the people for the faith which they did not possess. The Archbishop of Narbonne afterwards declared, "We behaved like true noblemen, for it cannot be said of the greater number of us, that we did so from any motives of religion."

Robespierre, whose religious convictions we have always borne in mind, whom we have always seen taking the part of the clergy, as far as was consistent with his democratic opinions, was no doubt greatly hurt at this decree, but he makes no motion upon it; he is content to sit silent and see it pass. Was this cowardice?

CHAPTER XIII.

Marriage of Camille Desmoulins—The King meditating flight—Robespierre's royalism—The Club des Femmes—Robespierre's speech on the right of emigrating—Death of Mirabeau.

On the 29th of December, Camille Desmoulins presents himself before the curé of St. Sulpice to be married. The curé demands if he is a Catholic.

"Why do you ask me that question?" says Camille.

"Because, if you are not a Catholic, I cannot marry you."

"Verily, then, I am a Catholic."

"No, monsieur, you are not; since you have said in one of your articles that the religion of Mahomet was quite as evident as that of Jesus Christ."

"You won't marry me, then?"

"No, monsieur; not until you have made profession of the Catholic faith."

"I shall address myself to the ecclesiastical committee," replied Camille, "to see if what I have written suffices to prevent my marriage."

The notary who had accompanied Camille having written all these replies of the curé, they were taken to the ecclesiastical committee, and Mirabeau returned to his friend Camille a decision, by which it was established, that the outward profession of faith was the only test by which to judge a man's belief; and that Desmoulins' calling himself a Catholic must be accepted as such, and the curé was bound to marry him without delay.

Camille joyously takes this consultation of Mirabeau to the curé, who says,

"Since when, then, is M. de Mirabeau a father of the Church?"

"Ah! ah!" laughed Camille. "Mirabeau a father of the Church! I will tell him that! It will delight him."

The curé demanded that he should retract what he had said.

"Why, I don't exactly think of writing a number before my marriage," said Camille.

"It must be then afterwards."

"Well, I promise it."

"I also require of you that you will fulfil all the duties prescribed by marriage, and that you will confess yourself."

"Willingly, monsieur le curé, and it shall be to you yourself."

Having thus settled the affair, Camille was married. His witnesses were Pétion, Robespierre, and M. de Montesquiou. Mirabeau was to have been there, but was prevented.*

The curé delivered a short exhortation to the newly-married couple, during which Desmoulins began to cry. Robespierre was indignant, and said,

"Don't cry, hypocrite!"

Camille says, that three-fourths of the patriots deplored his marriage as if it had been his burial, thinking that love would turn him aside from politics. They little understood Camille, or that charming and beloved Lucille, who married him because he was poor, because he was in danger; who read every morning his fervent articles, so full of passion and of genius, so sparkling and so eloquent; who accepted his dangerous life, and was his guardian angel through the storm.

Camille himself, having nothing else to relate, enlivened the dulness of his paper with an account of his marriage, like the modern Camille, Jules Janin, a Camille without earnestness, who filled his *feuilleton* with an amusing account of his own marriage.

Robespierre, doubtless, was among those patriots who objected to Camille's marriage. He gave not up his time to love! That poor girl who had so strangely selected him as the idol of her heart saw but little of him. She had a terrible rival—Ambition.

* Michelet is in error when he says that Mirabeau and Danton were present. They merely signed the contract.—See the "Memoirs of Desmoulins," published by Berville and Barrière.

The year 1791 opened with a revolutionary fervor which colors all the writings of that time. Parties had become more separated by hatred, by menaces, by riots. They ceased to reason with each other, and began to threaten. There is a sound of arms in the words uttered, both in the clubs and in the Assembly. The resistance of the clergy, the insolence of the nobles, the menaces of foreign powers, all boded violence.

From November, the King had made a plan of escape from Paris. He had read much history, especially the history of England; and saw in the misfortunes of dethroned princes, analogies with his own unhappy position. A portrait of Charles I., by Vandyke, was constantly before his eyes; the history of Charles I. constantly lay upon his table. Two circumstances struck him. One, that James II. had lost his throne because he had left his kingdom; the other, that Charles I. had been beheaded for having made war against his parliament and his people. These reflections inspired him with an instinctive repugnance against the idea of leaving France, or of openly casting himself into the camp of the army.* But these reflections only served to foster his vacillating weakness. Neither the lessons of history, nor the warnings of his own fearful times, were sufficient to make him take a decided step. He had no will; he could not embrace the principles of the revolution; he dared not set himself against them. Irritated by the attitude of the Assembly, and the growing power of the bourgeoisie, he would neither side with it nor against it. It is idle to speculate what would have been the result, had he possessed more firmness. The historian has to deal with facts, with events, not with schemes and possibilities. This much, however, may be said, that at that period there was scarcely any republicanism in France. If I sometimes speak of the republicans, it is not that I mean to designate men who distinctly wished for, and foresaw the possibility of a republic being established in France, but rather as of men, who, having adopted the principles of Rousseau, were implicitly, if not explicitly, republicans in creed.

* Lamartine.

Robespierre himself was by no means averse from the idea of royalty. There were even rumors circulated of some endeavors on the part of the court to win him over; rumors which, although they never affected his reputation of incorruptibility, are sufficient to indicate the color of his opinions as not being distinctly republican. Indeed, in the "Défenseur de la Constitution," may be read articles in which Robespierre protests his repugnance against a republic, and declares that he will make no compact (*pactiser*) with parties who conspire against the monarchy.

In the Journal of the Jacobin Clubs there is a formal condemnation of republicanism. "A little state," it says, "may govern itself for a long while as a republic; a great empire once adopting this government, must inevitably become the prey of a usurper;" in which those fond of noting realized predictions, may see a reference to Buonaparte. Federalism was the doctrine of the first republicans, and they laboriously refuted the idea of separating France into a number of independent republics, and rejected as inapplicable the example of America.

Neither in Prudhomme nor in Marat can you find a trace of the word republic. The last spoke, indeed, of insurrections for the profit of the poorer class, and of a dictatorial government; and the former, or his editor, wrote an article on the rich and poor, in which it is clear that social reform was the idea which most occupied the patriot writers: "It is the poor who have made the revolution," he said; "but they have not made it for their profit; for since the 14th July, they remain much the same as they were before the 14th July, 1789." The writer then enters upon the subject of the distribution of property, much in the same spirit as men are now writing in France. The parallel, indeed, between the ideas which agitated France in 1791 and 1848 is very singular. The same hopes, the same formulas, the same extravagant errors, the same strong sense of necessity for more perfect social justice, may be read in the writings of both epochs.

Among these coincidences I pause to notice that of the establishment of female clubs. Theories respecting woman's "emancipation" were rife then; and on the 3d of January, at the *Cercle*

Social, a discourse was read from a certain Madame Palm, a Dutch woman; in which, with Wolstonecraft eloquence, and more than Wolstonecraft force of reasoning, she advocated the cause of her sex. She spoke against those prejudices which enveloped her sex, and which had created unjust laws, only giving to women but a very secondary position in society. Admitting that nature had given men greater strength, she maintains that women are equal, if not superior to men in morals, in force, in delicacy of sentiment, and generosity of soul. She cites the daughter of Cato, the mother of Coriolanus, the Greek women who fought in Salamis, the mother of the Gracchi, Elizabeth, Joan of Arc, Katherine II.; and then, coming down to her own times, she cites the corporation of the women of Paris.

Condorcet, before this, had published in the "Journal de la Société," 1789, a very remarkable article on the admission of women to the right of citizenship; he demands if the principle of equality has not been violated by men tranquilly depriving one half of the human race of the right of concurring in the formation of laws. His article is, perhaps, altogether, the most forcible and sensible word that has yet been spoken on this subject, in favor of the emancipation. He combats all the objections temperately, but cogently. Here is an example:—

"It is said that women, though better than men, more gentle, more sensitive, less subject to those vices which belong to egotism and hardness of heart, have nevertheless not properly speaking the sentiment of justice; that they obey rather their feelings than their conscience. This observation is true, but it proves nothing. It is not nature, it is education; it is their social condition which has caused this difference. Neither the one nor the other has accustomed women to the idea of that which is just, but rather to the idea of what is virtuous. Away from affairs, from all that is decided by rigorous justice according to positive laws, the things which occupy them, upon which they act, are precisely those which are regulated rather by natural propriety, and by feeling. It is unjust, therefore, to allege for the continuance of the refusal to women of the enjoyment of their natural rights, motives which have only reality, because they do not enjoy those rights."[*]

[*] See the whole article. "Hist. Parl.," ix. pp. 98–104.

That these were not isolated opinions, may be seen by the fact of the foundation of a club of women, *Les Amies de la Vérité*, opened under the auspices of the editors of the *Bouche de Fer* by Madame Palm. This club had several imitators both in the capital and in the departments.

I have endeavored to exhibit Robespierre's general rise in public estimation, and from time to time have noted the signs of his increasing popularity. He and Pétion (now for some time named the "incorruptible" and the "virtuous") have been growing more and more the marked men of the Assembly. In this month of February they are particularly celebrated by the patriotic journals; all of which are lavish in eulogies upon Robespierre's speech on the formation of the national guard; a speech which he had printed and distributed even before he spoke it at the tribune. It circulated in the provinces, and was enthusiastically received there. He was also particularly remarked for his vote on the formation of the juries.

I find St. Just, in a letter dated August, 1790, addressing him thus:—

"I know you not, but you are a great man; you are not only the deputy of a province: you are the deputy of humanity and the republic."

The young fanatic had thus early detected in Robespierre, a fanatic of a kindred spirit; thus early seen in him the latent republican, even before republicanism had become his explicit and accepted creed. The time, however, was fast approaching, when every vestige of royalty would be eradicated from Robespierre's mind.

The increasing emigration of the noblesse augmented the disgust and suspicions of the nation. Rumors of the King's projected flight had been rife. The departure of the Princesses Adelaide and Victoire, who had set out for Rome, gave rise to the report that the whole family was about to depart. The mob was furious, and forcibly prevented the King from visiting even St. Cloud. Lafayette endeavored in vain to prevail on his guards to allow the King to depart. His own troops disobeyed his orders, and the multitude laughed at him. "Hold your tongue," they exclaimed; "the King shall *not* go."

The Assembly, alarmed at the possibility of the King's escaping, passed a decree declaring that his person was inviolable; that the constitutional Regent should be the nearest male heir of the crown; and that the flight of the Monarch should be equivalent to his dethronement. This fermentation, far from stopping the princesses, only hastened their departure. Marat, Desmoulins, and the rest of the patriot editors, declared that they were carrying away millions of francs, and smuggling away the Dauphin. The princesses were first stopped at Moret, but their escort forced its way in spite of opposition. They were then arrested at Arnay-le-duc. They wrote to the Assembly: and the King also wrote to authorize them to continue their journey.

Mirabeau, ever on the side of generosity, and now very decidedly leaning towards the court, raised his powerful voice in their favor.

"An imperious law," exclaimed the Jacobins, "forbids their departure."

"What law?" said Mirabeau, fiercely.

"The safety of the people," replied Lameth.

"The safety of the people!" scornfully retorted Mirabeau—"as if two princesses, advanced in years, tormented by their consciences, could compromise the people by their absence or their opposition! The safety of the people! I expected to hear these words invoked in the presence of serious danger. When you act as tyrants in the name of freedom, who will hereafter trust your assurance?"

The democrats were silenced, and the two princesses were allowed to continue their journey.

A projected law was brought forward, entrusting to three persons to be appointed by the Assembly, the dictatorial right of authorizing or forbidding emigration upon pain of confiscation and of degradation from the title of citizen. The greater part of the Assembly arose in indignation on hearing it read, and rejected the odious inquisition of arrest which the proposed law conferred on it.

Chapelier, the reporter, having himself declared that his projected law was unconstitutional, demanded that the Assembly should previously decide whether it wished to have a law. Robespierre rose, and said:

"I am no more a partisan of the law on emigration than M. Chapelier himself, but it is by a solemn discussion that you ought to recognize the impossibility or the dangers of such a law." So saying, he remained a silent witness of this debate. Whichever way it turned, he thought it must turn to his advantage; for whether Mirabeau compromised himself, or Mirabeau's enemies, Dupont and Lameth (his own rivals at the Jacobins), there would at any rate be space cleared for him.

All, both friends and enemies, desired that Mirabeau should speak. In six notes which he received one after another in rapid succession, he was called upon to declare his principles, and was reminded of the violent state of Paris. He perfectly understood the appeal made to his courage, and read a powerful address which he had written eight years before to the King of Prussia on the liberty of emigrating. He demanded that the Assembly should declare that it would not listen to the project, but pass on to the order of the day:—

"The Assembly of Athens would not even hear the measure which Aristides had styled as useful but unjust. You, however, have heard it; but your indignation proves that in questions of morality you are equal to Aristides, and the barbarity of the proposition proves that a law on emigration is impracticable. (*Murmurs.*) I ask you to hear me! If there be circumstances when measures of police are indispensable, even against the written laws, there is an immense difference between a measure of police and a law. . . . . I deny that the project can be submitted for our deliberation, and I declare that I should believe myself freed from every oath of fidelity towards men who could be infamous enough to name a dictatorial commission. (*Applause.*) The popularity which I have desired to possess, and which I have had the honor

—(*Murmurs at the extreme left of the Assembly*)—which I have had the honor to enjoy, is not a fragile reed; it is into the earth that I would thrust its roots; it rests on the immutable basis of reason and liberty! (*Applause.*) If you make a law against emigrants, I swear I will never obey it."

The project was unanimously rejected. The Lameths murmured, and one of them asked permission to speak, but conceded it to a deputy of his own party, who moved an adjournment. Mirabeau persisted in passing to the order of the day, when a man exclaimed on his left, "What, is this dictatorship assumed by M. de Mirabeau?"

The orator, knowing well his assembly, and feeling sure that this appeal to envy would not fail of its intended effect, rushed to the tribune, and although the president refused him permission to speak, said:

"I beg those who interrupt me to remember that I always opposed despotism, and always will. It is not enough to complicate two or three propositions . . ." Here great disturbance was expressed, and Mirabeau, lion-like, turning upon the Jacobins, exclaimed in a voice of thunder, "*Silence aux trente voix!*" and Robespierre and his friends were dumb, crushed beneath the weight of this apostrophe. Yet when the meeting was over, Mirabeau went home, and said to his sister, "I have pronounced my death-warrant. It is now all over with me, for they will kill me." But although he was suffering from fever, and had been fatigued by the violent debate, he went that very evening to the Jacobin Club, there to confront his enemies, and see whether there was one who dared to attack him, either with words or with a dagger. Robespierre was there; angry, but silent.

Death was soon to snatch away the great orator, this greatest man the revolution produced. In a few days he was lying on his death-bed. It is Tuesday, the 29th of March, and the report flies abroad that Mirabeau is ill. The sensation that report creates throughout Paris, among all men, even among his adversaries, proves how much he is loved; how much he is admired. Anxious multitudes beset the street in which he lives: among them men of all parties and of all ranks. The King sends publicly twice a day to inquire; and the furious editors of the *Révolutions de Paris*, who were at that moment proposing the suppression of royalty, on reporting that the King had sent to inquire about Mirabeau, add, " Let us feel grateful that Louis XVI. did not go himself; it would have occasioned a fatal diversion, for the people would have adored him." A written bulletin is handed out every three hours; is copied and circulated among the crowd. The people spontaneously keep silence, suffering no carriage to enter the street, lest its noise disturb the sick man. There is crowding pressure; but the sister of Mirabeau is reverently recognized, and has free way made for her. The people stand mute and heart-stricken, feeling that a great calamity is nigh; feeling that their great man is about to be snatched away from them.

He lies on his death-bed; he whose fluctuations of opinion have not been greater than those of the people; who has from time to time incurred the people's fierce suspicion and loud disapprobation; but who has regained their love by some splendid burst of eloquence, such as he alone could utter. The great strong man whose strength they recognize even when it is against them; who, after exciting their execrations in the morning, has only to show himself at the theatre in the evening, and his very presence acts as a spell upon all hearts, changing curses into shouts.

He lies on his death-bed; and well may he say, in gloomy presentiments of the destiny of France, "I am carrying away with me the funeral of monarchy; its remnants will become the prey of the factious."

A report of a cannon is heard. He starts and exclaims, with a sort of grandiose truth, " Is this already the funeral of Achilles?"

And now on this morning, the 2d of April, he orders the windows to be opened, saying, " Friend, I shall die to-day. On such a day it only remains to perfume one's self, and then, crowned with flowers, and surrounded with music, to be lulled agreeably to that sleep from which there is no awaking." He orders his bed to be moved nearer to the open window, that he may contemplate the first symptoms of vernal vegetation on the trees in his little garden. The sun is shining on him; the world is bright without—dark, dark within! His sufferings become excessive, and he asks for laudanum to abridge the useless agony. When unable to articulate any longer, he writes the word "Sleep," and at half-past eight, having just turned round and raised his eyes to heaven, he expires; his face exhibiting only a sweet smile, a smile as of pleasant dreams in a calm sleep.

And now the mournful news spreads abroad, *Mirabeau is dead!* The grief inspired is universal, intense. His young secretary, who adored him, several times endeavors to commit suicide. Such was the love the people bore him, that during his illness a young man presented himself, asking whether they would try a transfusion of blood; and offering his own to reanimate and revive the great man!

For three days there is heard a low wild moan. In the mournful streets, orators, mounted upon stones, preach funeral sermons to silent audiences. There is weeping in the National Assembly itself. The Theatres are closed. No public amusements are allowed. A ball is broken in upon, and the company dispersed and hooted, as insulting the general grief. In a restaurant of the Palais Royal, a waiter remarks, "It is fine weather, monsieur." "Yes, my friend," answers the gentleman, "very fine; but Mirabeau is dead."

On the 4th of April there takes place the most extensive and impressive funeral procession that had ever been seen in France; nothing has since equaled it but that of Napoleon, on the 15th of December, 1840.

At the head of the procession walks Lafayette; next, surrounded by the twelve huissiers, comes Tronchet, the president of the National Assembly. After him the whole Assembly; immediately after the National Assembly, the Club of Jacobins marches in a dense mass, like a second Assembly. All the roofs are thronged with on-lookers; men climb up the trees and lamp-posts; a roll of muffled drums, and the long-drawn wail of music, the strange clangor of trombones, salute the ear. The immense procession cannot arrive at the church of St. Eustache before eight o'clock, where Cérutti pronounces the funeral oration. Twenty thousand national guards then discharge their arms, and the neighboring windows are shattered to atoms by the sound. For a moment the people think that the church will fall in upon the coffin. Then the funeral procession resumes its course by torchlight to the church of St. Geneviève, which has been consecrated into a pantheon for the great men of the father-land. "*Aux grands hommes: la patrie reconnaissante.*"

The character of the day had been calm and solemn; but in proportion as daylight disappeared, and the procession buried itself in the doubly obscure shade of night, and gloomy streets, lit by the glare of flickering torches, "the imaginations of men," says Michelet, "also plunged irresistibly into the dark region of futurity and ominous presentiment. The death of their only great man occasioned from that day a formidable equality amongst all others. The Revolution was from that time about to rush down a rapid declivity, by a dusky path, to triumph or to a tomb; and in that path it was evermore to be without a man; a glorious companion on the road; a man of noble heart, a heart devoid of bitterness, of hatred; magnanimous towards his most bitter enemies, he carried with him to the grave something that was not yet well known, and which was known but too late, a spirit of peace even in war; kindness, gentleness, and humanity even in violence."

A man among the people, on seeing the coffin pass, exclaimed, "Ah! if Mirabeau could see what we have done for him, he would be very grateful, and would make them give us good laws." Another man, on some one exclaiming "Down with Louis the Sixteenth!" replied, "*Oui, bon ami,* Louis may die when he will; he will never have such a burial as this." Truly no, for France has lost her king! a king not without human infirmities, indeed, some of them perhaps carried to a fearful pitch, but still "every inch a king."

I shall miss him henceforth in the columns of that weary *Moniteur*. No longer will his glowing eloquence cheer me in my research. Amidst the dull, quibbling, pedantic, tiresome discussions of the Assembly, Mirabeau's voice was always welcome. It was a ray of light in that murky element. Upon every subject his was the word best worth listening to; and there were accents in his voice which stirred one's very soul. As with our own Burke, whatever we may think of his opinions, we cannot resist the influence of that master-mind from which they emanate. His eloquence comes from the heart, comes from a large magnanimous soul; it is not mere clap-trap, there is a heart in its wisdom; it has the ineffaceable stamp of genius upon it, making even its errors splendid.

Now Mirabeau is dead, there is only one man whom we care to listen to; one man thoroughly *genial*, amidst all his extravagances; I mean Camille Desmoulins, and he more often speaks nonsense than sense.

CHAPTER XIV.

Robespierre's growing importance—Proposes the exclusion of the deputies from the coming Assembly—Speeches on the national guard, capital punishment, and on juries—His philanthropy—Appointed public accuser—Flight of the King—Robespierre's speech on that subject—The captive King—Riot in the Champ de Mars—Cowardice of Robespierre—Termination of the Assembly's labors—Robespierre defends the people and the right of universal suffrage—The King accepts the constitution—What had the Constituent Assembly effected?

MIRABEAU gone, there was a place suddenly made for Robespierre; not the place, indeed, which Mirabeau had filled, but there was a vacancy; and Robespierre, it is noticeable, two days after Mirabeau's burial, assumed a new, audacious, and almost imperious tone towards the Assembly. He violently reproached the constitutional committee with having unexpectedly presented a plan for the organization of the ministry; and spoke of the dread with which the spirit which prevailed at their deliberations inspired him, concluding with this dogmatical sentence, "Here is the essential *instruction* which I lay before the Assembly;" and the Assembly accepted his domination! He was no longer the hesitating, timid deputy: he had assumed authority.

On the 7th he proposed, and caused to be decreed, that no member of the Assembly could be raised to the ministry during the four years following the session. Five weeks later, on the 16th of May, he proposed, and caused to be decreed, that "the members of the present Assembly cannot be elected for the next legislature." He developed his thesis of political morality, that the legislator ought to make it his duty to retire into the ranks of private citizens, and even to shun public gratitude. "The constitution did not issue from the brain of this or that orator," said he, "but from the very opinions that preceded and have supported us. After two years of superhuman labors, it only remains for us to give our successors an example of indifference for our immense power, and for every other interest except that of the public good. Let us go and breathe in free departments the air of equality;" then adding these imperious words, "It seems to me that, for the honor of the members of the Assembly, this motion ought not to be decreed in too dilatory a manner."

Michelet supposes that Robespierre's motive was to curry favor with the Jacobin Club, the predominant members of which were not deputies, but wished to become such. He was not afraid of shutting himself out of the official Assembly, because he was sure of being able to direct that active and perhaps more efficacious assembly, the Club. The next legislature, having no longer such men as Mirabeau and Cazalès, would be feeble and torpid; while the life and strength would be with the Jacobins.

It may have been so; for when a man is as ambitious of power as Robespierre evidently was, it seems to me quite clear that, with all his sincerity, he would not lightly have proposed his own exclusion. But it mattered little to him, as tribune of the people, whether he spoke in the Assembly or at the Jacobins. He knew that he derived his power from the people; and perhaps he felt himself at a disadvantage in the Assembly, in the presence of cleverer men. Nevertheless, it is quite clear that, now the great orator is gone, the Assembly looks with more respect upon the consistent thinker. Orator, Robespierre certainly is not; but he has the undeniable merit of clear conceptions and of undeviating consistency. This is beginning to be felt, and he is looked upon as a man worth hearing.

Camille says, that when Mirabeau's question, "Is this already the funeral of Achilles?" was related to Robespierre, he drew a favorable augury from it, saying, "Achilles is dead, then Troy will not be taken!" meaning, perhaps, that now the court had lost their great warrior, the republic was out of danger.

On the 29th of April, Robespierre made a really remarkable speech, on the subject of the national guards.

"An institution at once both military and national," he said, "is the most difficult of all undertakings; for, if it is not the firmest support of liberty, it becomes the most dangerous instrument of despotism. We must first seek the real object of the organization of the national guard. Is it to resist enemies from without? No; for that you have a formidable army. It is quite certain that wherever the power of a military chief exists without balance, the people is not free. What is this balance? A national guard. From this fundamental principle we must organize the national guard, in such a manner that the executive power cannot abuse the immense force which is confided to it; nor that the national guard should be able to oppress public liberty, and the executive power. These two points of view must serve us as guides on the question which now occupies us. From the first point of view, we must organize the national guard, so that no one of its parties shall depend upon the executive power. The prince's agent ought not, therefore, to name the chiefs. The chiefs of the troops of the line must not, therefore, become chiefs of the national guard. The King must neither recompense nor punish the national guards. From the second point of view, we must recognize, as a general principle, the necessity of preventing the national guards from forming a body; from adopting a corporate spirit, which would soon menace either public liberty or the constitutional authority. To arrive at this, we must avoid every measure which would tend to confound the function of the soldier with that of the citizen; we must diminish as much as is possible the number of officers, and name them for a very limited period; not extend the command beyond one district; and establish that the exterior mark of grades should only be borne during the time of service. These decorations are carried only for public use, and not to satisfy an absurd pride. Those exterior distinctions, which formerly accompanied everywhere the public functionaries, excited the vanity of some, produced the humiliation of others, degraded the people, emboldened the tyrant, destroyed thus the energy of the people, and corrupted the national character. Defenders of liberty! you will not regret these baubles of despotism! Your courage, your devotion, your success, the sacred cause for which you are working, that is your glory, those are your ornaments! (*Applause.*) To confound the citizen with the soldier! We have still something to do. There is one real obligation. Equity, equality demands it!" (Here some noise is heard in certain parts of the Assembly; whereupon M. de Montlosier says, "What M. Robespierre has to say is worth listening to, therefore, messieurs who are now talking, I pray you silence." Applause followed this, and Robespierre continued:) "Every citizen should be admitted to fulfil the functions of the national guard. Those who do not pay certain contributions, are they then slaves? Are they strangers to the other citizens? Are they without any interest in the public affairs? They have all contributed to the election of the members of the National Assembly; they have given you rights to exercise for them. Have they given you rights to exercise against them? They could not wish it; they have not done it. Are they citizens? I blush to have to make such a question. They enjoy the right of citizenship. Will you alone enjoy the right of defending yourselves and defending them? Decree, then, that all domiciled citizens have the right to be inscribed on the registry of national guards. Do not calumniate the people by raising against them unjust fears! The people are good, courageous. You know the virtues of the people by what they have done for liberty. After having worked with so much courage for its conquest, they demand the right of fulfilling those duties which are imposed upon all citizens for the conservation. . . ." (Here M. Lucas interrupted him.) "I mean by *people* all the citizens." Robespierre continues: "I mean by *people* the generality of individuals who compose society; and if I have for a moment used this expression in a more limited sense, it is that I thought it necessary to speak the language of those whom I have to combat. Shall I reply to a very futile observation? It has been said that a party of the people are not *active;* that they cannot support the expenses, nor the loss of time, the service as national guards would demand. But the State ought to furnish the necessary means for every citizen to serve; the State must arm them, must pay them, as they do in Switzerland, when they quit their homes. The committee has misunderstood the unique and veritable object and the institution of national guards. It places the national guards in circumstances under which they must always make war according to the orders of the King. But are they not also instituted to defend liberty against the attacks of despotism? This word liberty has not been pronounced once in the whole project. To repress brigands, to bring the seditious to justice, these are the only ideas which, in the projected law, fix and indicate the functions of the national guards. It seems as if they were instituted merely to sustain the gendarmerie and the troops of the line. But to make a subsidiary army thus to combat citizens—is not that oblivion of all principles? The project of the committee interdicts the bearing of arms to all citizens who are not *active*. Is not that creating a vast armed body to repress the rest of the nation? Is it not putting the political power and the armed force in the hands of a single class, and that armed force at the disposal of the executive power? I demand, therefore, that the Assembly decrees that every domiciled citizen has the right to be inscribed on the registry of the national guards."

We have now notice of a strange discussion which took place in the National Assembly on the 30th of May. Strange, I mean, for the opinions put forth by Robespierre, on that momentous question, the punishment of death. Lepelletier St. Fargeau brought forward a motion, on a report of the committee, which said that punishment should be humane, justly accommodated in gradation to the crime, and in its infliction without regard to the rank of the criminal.

Duport made an admirable speech against the punishment of death.—"Does not society," he says, "which makes itself a legal murderer, teach murder?" Robespierre took up the same side:

"The news," said he, "having been brought to Athens that some citizens at Argos had been doomed to death, the people ran to the temple, and prayed to the gods to turn aside the Argives from such cruel and fatal thoughts. I am about to pray not the gods, but the legislators, who should be interpreters of those eternal laws which the Deity has implanted in the human heart, to efface from the code of the French, those laws of blood which command *judicial murders;* and which our feelings and the new constitution alike repel. I will prove that the punishment of death is essentially unjust; secondly, that it has no tendency to repress crimes; and thirdly, that it multiplies offences much more than it diminishes them. Before society is formed, and law established, if I am attacked by an assassin or a robber, I must kill him or be killed myself; but in civilized society, when the power of all is concentrated against one alone, what principle, either of justice or necessity, can authorize the punishment of death? The conqueror who kills his prisoner in cold blood is justly stigmatized as a barbarian. A grown man, who murders a child whom he can disarm and punish, appears a monster. An accused person whom the law has condemned, is neither more nor less than a vanquished and powerless enemy. He is more at your mercy than a child before a grown man. In the eyes of justice and mercy, therefore, these death scenes, which are got up with so much solemnity, *are nothing less than base assassinations;* solemn crimes, committed, not by individuals, but by entire nations, and of which every individual must bear the responsibility. The punishment of death is necessary, say the partisans of ancient barbarity. Without it there can be no adequate security against crime. Who tells you so?

Have you really estimated the springs which move the human heart? Learn to how many things does the catalogue of human woes tell you that death is a relief. The love of life yields to pride, the most injurious of all passions which destroy the heart. It is often sought after as a cessation from pain by the lover, the bankrupt, and the drunkard. The punishment, which is really overwhelming, is opprobrium; the general expression of public execration. No one seeks *it* as a refuge from the ills of life. When the legislator can strike the guilty, in so many ways, merciful yet terrible, bloodless yet efficacious, why should he ever recur to the hazard of a public execution? The legislator who prefers death to the milder chastisements within his power, outrages every feeling, and brutalizes the minds of the people. Such a legislator resembles the cruel preceptor, who, by the frequent use of punishment, degrades and hardens the mind of his pupil. Listen to the voice of justice and of reason. It tells us that human judgments are never certain enough for society to condemn a man to death; those who condemn him being men, and subject to error. If you had imagined the most perfect judicial procedure, if you had found judges the most honest and the most enlightened, there would still always remain some place for error. Wherefore will you then interdict all means of repairing your error? Of what use are sterile regrets, illusory reparations, which you accord to a vain shadow, to the insensible remains of your victim? They are the sad witnesses of the barbarous temerity of your penal laws. To take away from man the possibility of his expiating his misdeed by his repentance, or by acts of virtue, is pitilessly to close against him all return to virtue, to his self-esteem; and to hasten him to the tomb, covered with the stain of his recent crime, is, in my eyes, the most horrible refinement of cruelty."

Singular language this, from the mouth of one who is afterwards to deluge France with blood! It was, however, a serious conviction of his, dating from the Arras period; and when Duport, in his speech, had said, "Since a continual change in men has rendered a change in things almost necessary, let us at least contrive that our revolutionary scenes be the least tragical—let us render man respected by man"—Robespierre sincerely felt with him, and sincerely wished for that large tolerance which he afterwards so ill knew how to practice.

The question of juries had been brought before the Assembly; and Robespierre, true to his principles, proposed that every citizen should be admitted to exercise the functions of a juryman. The *Moniteur* gives but a meagre account of this séance; but in the *Journal de Paris*, Robespierre is praised for the part he took in it, as an independent thinker, who always brought questions back to the eternal laws of equality and natural right. "It is a great pity," says the journalist, "that there are not more minds of this stamp. There are already too many who know how to make their convictions bend to conventions, and who think more of artificial distinctions than of that ideal towards which we must always tend."

Robespierre spoke against giving the procureur-syndic the power of naming the jury. "It is," he says, "to violate all the principles of liberty, to abandon such a power to a single man; it is to violate all the principles of the constitution, to accumulate in the same hands both the administrative functions and the power of electing those who must exercise authority: that power belongs only to that party from which all authority emanates; it belongs to the Sovereign, to the people. The suffrage of the people is the only quality which must be required to call a man to the functions of a juror. It is a crime to hamper it in any manner. What sort of a guarantee can you ever find in riches? What relation is there between riches and virtue? between the advantages of fortune and the love of liberty and equality? Not only does the system of the committee outrage all reason, all justice, all humanity, but it annihilates the very essential characteristic of a jury, which is, that the accused should be judged by his peers. It divides the nation into two sections, of which one, the richer and less numerous, would be destined to judge the other; and the other to be judged; of which one will be raised above the other by all the distance which exists between the political and judicial power; and nullity, subjection, or, if you will, servitude. In a word, this system at once degrades and oppresses the French people, whom you represent. My opinion is, that all citizens ought to be chosen by the people to form a jury, without any other condition beyond the competence of the people."

In this journal we also find a very remarkable reply of Robespierre to Maury, relative to the dispensation of ecclesiastics from serving on juries. Maury demanded that they should be dispensed from it, because their office of charity makes blood so horrible to them. Robespierre replied, that to judge culprits was charity towards society at large.*

Here we see Robespierre's famous distinction between pity for an individual and pity for the masses; between individual sympathy and social devotion; a distinction which, later on, guided him in the Convention, and which not inaptly characterizes the whole man. Pity, indeed, was a thing he knew not: for all pity must spring from individual sympathy. He had faith in abstract ideas, and he had that sort of feeling for the masses which has moved certain philanthropists, who have combined perfect heartlessness towards every individual with a sentimental sensibility towards the mass; men who could weep over the miseries of distant negroes, but could find no tear for the misery at their door; whose charity was a phrase, and not a real feeling; whose benevolence was not an extension of kindness toward individuals, but rather the sophistical refuge of their consciences against the inculpation of their hearts. It is not that I deny philanthropy—that I disbelieve the sincerity of those who talk about the masses, who devote their lives to them and their cause,—but I have so often found it accompanied with such utter absence of sympathy and kindness towards the individual, that, unless accompanied by very undeniable evidences of kindness and sympathy, I always look upon it as a sort of excuse with which a man's conscience absolves itself.

In the discussion on the question of the colonies, and whether the black men were to participate in political rights, Robespierre not only took the side of the blacks, but almost rose to eloquence when he exclaimed, "Let the colonies perish rather than a principle!" And in his speech on the re-eligibility of the Assembly, he not only received continual applause, but the Assembly almost unanimously voted that his speech should be printed.

In the *Moniteur* of the 19th of June we find Robespierre appointed public accuser. Duport, who was named president of the *Tribunal Criminel*, refused to accept the office because Robespierre was named public accuser. Bigôt, who is named vice-president, and Dandré, substitute, also refused for the same reason. Duport was replaced by Pétion, Bigôt by Buzot, and Dandré by Favre. In Brissot's paper we read as follows: "We may examine M. Duport's motive, since he openly declares it. M. Robespierre is, according to him, a violent man (*un homme sans mesure*). This is a reason why the president, who believes himself to be very moderate, should accept office, as he will then be able to temper the warmth of the accuser. If M. Robespierre accuses without grounds, he will condemn him. He will accuse, you say, by flattering the people, and placing the judges in the dilemma of deciding either against the people or against the law; but whoever is afraid of such a dilemma is not fit to be a judge. Any one sitting in the president's chair must be resolved to condemn the people when wrong, to brave them even to death if necessary. A judge who, having justice on his side, fears the people, knows them but little, or knows too well his own weakness. M. Robespierre is a good patriot, firm in his principles, deaf to all considerations. That is what M. Duport ought to recognize and respect, and which ought to excuse the excesses of M. Robespierre's patriotism."

We see from this that Robespierre is now becoming feared; that his ascendency in the Assembly has grown dangerous. Respecting his conduct in that important office, we have the authority of his virulent libeler, Montjoie, to show that it was creditable to him. "To the great astonishment of all decent people, he performed the functions of president, and subsequently of public accuser, without scandal, and even without too marked a partiality" (which, in Montjoie's mouth, in spite of what follows, means with rigid honesty). "Nevertheless, it has come to my knowledge, that in both offices he committed some glaring acts of injustice—

des injustices criantes" (how can this be reconciled with the previous assertion of impartiality?) "and that he abused the authority which they gave him, to combat with the sword of justice those who did not share his political opinions."*

We now come to the King's flight. I shall not, after the incomparable narrative of Carlyle, attempt to describe the flight to Varennes; nor can I describe the state of ferment into which Paris was thrown by the news of the King's departure. The republicans were sincerely rejoiced at it. Prudhomme had a few weeks before written a furious article in his journal, proclaiming the necessity of the abolition of royalty, and the King's flight seemed to the republicans the easiest way of forever abolishing monarchy. But, as I have said before, the republicans formed a very small minority, and the consternation of Paris at the prospect of a civil war and foreign invasion opened by this flight of the King, is impossible to paint. The clubs of the Cordeliers and the Jacobins caused their motion for the King's dethronement to be placarded about. One of the placards of the Cordeliers declared that every citizen who belonged to it had sworn to poniard the tyrants. The Assembly seized on the dictatorship with a firm grasp, and declared themselves permanent; declared that, during the King's absence, all power should be vested in themselves, and that their decree should be immediately put into execution, without any further sanction or acceptance.

On the 22d of June, the members of the constitutional party felt it their duty to attend a meeting of the Jacobins, in order to moderate its fury. "Whilst the National Assembly was decreeing, decreeing, decreeing," says Camille Desmoulins, "the people were acting. I went to the Jacobins. Robespierre was in the tribune. Listen to his discourse, of which I did not lose a single word, and tremble."

"I am not the man," said he, "to term this event a disaster. This would be the most glorious day of the revolution did you but know how to profit by it. The King has chosen to desert his post at the moment of our peril.

---

* "Conjuration de Robespierre," vol. i. p. 38.

The Assembly is discredited; all men's minds are excited by the approaching elections; the emigrés are at Coblentz; the Emperor and the King of Sweden are at Brussels; our harvests are ripe for their troops; but three millions of men are under arms in France, and this league of Europe will easily be vanquished. I fear neither Leopold nor the King of Sweden; that which alone terrifies me seems to reassure all others: that since this morning all our enemies affect to use the same language as ourselves. All men are united, and in appearance wear the same aspect. But it is impossible that all can feel the same joy at the flight of a King who possessed a revenue of forty millions of francs, and who disposed of all the offices of state amongst his adherents and our enemies. There are traitors among us; there is a secret understanding between the fugitive King and these traitors who remain at Paris. Read the King's manifesto, and the whole plot will be there revealed. The King, the Emperor, the King of Sweden, d'Artois, Condé, all the fugitives, all the brigands, are about to march against us. A paternal manifesto will appear, in which the King will tell you of his love of peace, nay, even of liberty; whilst at the same time the traitors in the capital and the departments will represent you as instigators of civil war; a compromise will be made, and thus the revolution will be stifled in the embraces of hypocritical despotism, and intimidated moderatism.

"Look at the Assembly; in twenty decrees the King's flight is termed an *abduction*. To whom does it entrust the safety of the people? To a minister of foreign affairs, under the inspection of a diplomatic committee. Who is the minister? A traitor whom I have unceasingly denounced to you, the persecutor of the patriot soldiers, the upholder of the aristocrat officers. What is the committee? A committee of traitors composed of all our enemies disguised as patriots. And the minister for foreign affairs, who is he? A traitor, a Montmorin, who but a short month ago declared a perfidious *adoration* of the constitution. And Delessart, who is he? A traitor to whom Neckar has bequeathed his mantle to cover his plots and conspiracies.

"Do you not see the coalition of these men with the King, and of the King with the European league? That will crush us! In an instant you will see all the men of 1789—mayor, general, ministers, orators—enter this room. How can you escape, Antony?" continued he, alluding to Lafayette. "Antony commands the legions that are about to avenge Cæsar; and Octavius Cæsar's nephew commands the legions of the republic.

"How can the republic avoid destruction? We are continually told of the necessity of uniting; but when Antony encamped by the side of Lepidus, and all the foes to freedom were united with those who termed themselves its defenders, nothing remained for Brutus and Cassius but suicide.

"To this point this feigned unanimity, this perfidious reconciliation of patriots, tends. Yes, this is the fate prepared for you. I know that by daring to unveil these conspiracies *I sharpen a thousand daggers against myself. I know the fate reserved for me;* but if, when almost unnoticed in the National Assembly, *I, amongst the earliest apostles of liberty, sacrificed my life to the cause of truth, of humanity, of my country;* to-day, when I have been so amply repaid for this sacrifice by such marks of universal good will, consideration, and regard, *I shall look at death as a benefit if it prevents my witnessing such misfortunes.* I have tried the Assembly; let them in their turn try me."

This conclusion was all bravado: the talk about daggers which awaited him, the flourish about his martyrdom, and his sacrificing his life to the cause of truth, were but vulgar clap-traps. He was really in no more danger than every other patriot; but it was well to put himself into the attitude of a daring martyr; and his words told with such effect upon the assembly, who had listened to it in the most religious silence, that many eyes were suffused with tears.

"We will all die first," exclaimed Camille, extending his arms toward him; and eight hundred persons rose at once, and, by their attitudes, offered one of those imposing tableaux which prove how great is the effect of oratory and passion over an excited people.

After they had all individually sworn to defend Robespierre's life (a perfectly superfluous oath), they were informed of the arrival of the ministers and members of the Assembly, who had come to fraternize with the Jacobins.

Danton then rose, and shaking back his shaggy locks, exclaimed with his voice of thunder,

"Monsieur le President, if the traitors venture to present themselves, I undertake the solemn engagement—either that my head shall fall on the scaffold, or I will prove that their heads should roll at the feet of the nation they have betrayed!"

Lameth replied to Danton, and spoke in favor of unanimity. The violent resolutions proposed by Robespierre and Danton had little weight that day at the Jacobins. The peril which threatened them taught the people wisdom, and their instinct forbade their dividing their forces.

During the first transports of alarm, Lafayette was nearly murdered by the populace of Paris, who believed that he had connived at the escape of the royal family. An immense crowd assembled round the Tuileries; the streets were filled with agitated people; the popular anxiety for news was indescribable. The mob had inundated the palace; ransacked the private apartments of the King and Queen; and were much astonished to find no instruments of torture, no preparations for massacreing the people, in them!

At length the captives were brought back to Paris. The national guard were drawn up in lines; but nowhere presented arms. Fearful cries burst from the multitude; cries of rage and of menace. The day was burning hot. The scorching sun, reflected from the pavement and the bayonets, was almost suffocating to the unhappy occupants of the royal carriage, where ten persons were squeezed together. Clouds of dust, raised by the trampling of two or three hundred thousand spectators formed a sort of veil, which from time to time concealed the humiliated King and Queen from the people. The sweat of the horses, the feverish breath of this dense mass of men, made the atmosphere fetid. The royal travelers panted for breath; the perspiration rolled down the foreheads of the two children. The Queen let down one of the windows of the carriage, and addressing the crowd, said, "See, gentlemen, in what a state my poor children are—one is choking."

"We will choke you in another fashion," replied these ferocious men, and the poor Queen was silenced. Her appearance excited general surprise. During the anxieties of that awful journey, her hair had turned gray, in some places quite white. Merciless ruffians looked in upon the King and Queen in dread silence, rejoicing in the degradation of royalty. From time to time the mob attempted to break through the line, but the bodies of gendarmerie restored order, and the procession resumed its way, amidst the clashing of sabres, and the cries of men trampled under the horses' hoofs.

The King was a captive; and now the necessity of coming to

some decision as to his fate perplexed all parties. It led to the first open avowal of republican principles in the Assembly. The mob, with savage ferocity, demanded the King's head. The Cordeliers and Jacobins demanded a republic. Seditious cries were incessantly heard in the streets; and those frightful figures began to be seen there who had emerged from obscurity on the 5th of October, and who subsequently proved triumphant during the reign of terror. It was decreed that information should be drawn up by the tribunal of the arrondissement of the Tuileries concerning the King's flight; and that three commissioners appointed by the Assembly should receive the declarations of the King and Queen.

Robespierre, in the audacity of excitement, exclaimed, "What means this obsequious exception? Do you fear to degrade royalty by handing over the King and Queen to ordinary tribunals? No citizen, no man, no rank, however elevated, can ever be degraded by the law." But the Assembly outvoted him; respect prevailed over outrage, and the commissioners were named.

On the morning after his return, Louis was, by a decree of the Assembly, provisionally suspended from his functions, and a band composed of national guards was appointed to watch over him and his family. The service of the chateau went on as usual, but Lafayette gave the password.

The gates of the courts and gardens were closed. The royal family submitted to Lafayette the list of those whom they desired to receive. Sentinels were placed at every door, even in the corridors between the chambers of the King and Queen. They were prisoners, and watched by a jealous people. The King was completely bowed down beneath the weight of his humiliation. For ten days he scarcely exchanged a word with one of his family; but the Queen, whose stronger nature was better fitted to cope with misfortune, bore up heroically under all.

The report of the committees, to whom the examination of the King had been entrusted, afforded no foundation for an accusation against him. They showed that it was not his intention to have left the kingdom, but merely to have withdrawn to a place of safety within it. In the debate which ensued, the inviolability of the King's person, which had been solemnly agreed to by the Assembly, was the basis of the argument on the constitutional side; and the King was shielded at the expense of his accomplices. Robespierre said, "I will not stop to inquire whether the King fled voluntarily, or whether a voice from the frontiers irresistibly carried him away. Can the people believe that kings are abducted like women? I will not inquire whether this flight was a conspiracy against public liberty, or whether it was a voyage without an object. I will only speak of the King of France as if he had been the King of China. I will occupy myself only with the general hypothesis, and will discuss the doctrine of inviolability. To admit the inviolability of the King, for acts which are personal to himself, is to establish a God upon earth. We can allow no fiction to constitute immunity to crime, or to give any man a right to bathe our families in blood. But you have decreed, it is said, this inviolability. So much the worse. An authority more powerful than that of the constitution now condemns it—the authority of reason, the conscience of the people, the duty of providing for their safety. The constitution has not decreed the inviolability of the Sovereign; it has only declared him not responsible for the acts of his ministers. To this privilege, already immense, are you prepared to add an immunity from every personal offence—from perjury, murder, or robbery? Shall we, who have leveled so many other distinctions, leave this, the most dangerous of them all? Ask of England if she recognizes such an immunity in her sovereign. Would you behold a beloved son murdered before your eyes by a furious king, and hesitate to deliver him over to criminal justice? Enact laws that punish all crimes without exception; or suffer the people to avenge them for themselves.

"The King is inviolable, but so are you. Do you now contend for his privilege to murder with impunity millions of his subjects! Do you dare to pronounce the King innocent when the nation has declared him guilty? Consult its good sense, since your own has abandoned you. You may accuse me of republicanism if you will; I here declare that I abhor every species of government where factions reign. It is not enough to throw off the yoke of a despot if we are to fall under the yoke of another despotism. England only threw off the yoke of one of its kings, to put its neck under one more degrading; that, namely, of a small number of its citizens. I do not indeed see amongst us a mind powerful enough to play the part of a Cromwell, nor do I see people here disposed to submit to one."

As to the Assembly exonerating the King, and accusing his accomplices, Robespierre boldly said—

"The measures you propose will only dishonor you. If you adopt them, I insist upon declaring myself the advocate of all the accused. I will be the defender of the three *Gardes du corps*, the Dauphin's governess, even of M. Bouillé. According to your committee, there has been no crime; if there is no crime, there can be no *accomplices*. Gentlemen, if it be a weakness to spare a culprit, to punish a weaker culprit and let the greater culprit escape is cowardice, injustice. You must pass sentence on all the guilty without distinction, or pronounce a general pardon."

While thus seeming to advocate the cause of the oppressed, Robespierre was in truth only throwing on the Assembly the onus of braving the nation. The Assembly, however, voted the decree as proposed by the commission; that is to say, without explicitly declaring whether Louis XVI. was or was not inculpated.

Foiled in their endeavors to sway the Assembly the republicans next attempted to rouse the people. The clubs declared they would no longer recognize the King. "We will repair," said they, "to the field of the Federation, and a hundred thousand men shall dethrone the perjured King: that day will be the last of all the friends of treason."

On the 14th of July the crowd presented to the Assembly a petition, escorted by four thousand of the people, and attempted to intimidate them. The Assembly remained firm, and passed to the order of the day. On quitting the Assembly, the crowd hastened to the Champ de Mars, and there signed a second petition, couched in still more violent language. The people thronged round the Tuileries, the Assembly, and the Palais Royal. They closed all the theatres. That evening four thousand persons went to the Jacobin Club. When they arrived, the tribune was occupied by a member, who denounced a citizen for having spoken scurrilously of Robespierre. The accused endeavored to justify himself, but was driven tumultuously from the room. At this moment Robespierre himself appeared, and with cheap magnanimity begged them to pardon the citizen who had maligned him. This intercession met with the applause it sought, and Robespierre's generosity excited tremendous enthusiasm. "Sacred vaults of the Jacobins," said an address from one of the departments, "guarantee to us Robespierre and Danton, these two oracles of patriotism!" And the sacred vaults were now ringing with the praise of the magnanimity of their great oracle.

Laclos proposed a petition, to be sent into the departments. A member opposed this proposition, in the name of peace and order. Danton rose. "I too, love peace," he said, "but not the peace of slavery. If we have energy, let us prove it; let those who want the courage to confront tyranny, refrain from signing our petition."

Robespierre next rose, and said that Barnave and the Lameths were playing the same game as Mirabeau had played. "They plot with our enemies," said he, "and then they call us factious." He refrained, however, from giving any opinion as to the petition. Throughout this insurrection, we shall see him playing a timid, shifty part. Laclos pressed his motion, and it was carried.

On the following day, however, the clubs did little but discuss the terms of the petition. The republicans negotiated with Lafayette. The Assembly was on its guard; Lafayette and Bailly resolutely prepared to repress any outbreak.

On the morning of the 17th two different bands of people were in motion; one of decent appearance, grave in manner, and comparatively small in number, was headed by Brissot; the other, hideous in aspect, ferocious in language, and formidable in numbers, was under the guidance of Robespierre. At twelve o'clock the crowd assembled round the "altar of the country;" the commissioners of the Jacobin Club who had promised to bring the petition to be signed, had not yet arrived. The mob chose four commissioners to draw up the petition, which should call upon the Assembly to receive the abdication of the King, to convoke a fresh constituent power, to point out the criminal, and organize a new executive power. This petition was laid on the "altar of the country," and paper was placed at the four corners of the altar to receive the signatures. They amounted to six thousand. This document is still preserved in the archives of the municipality.

Two unhappy men, who had placed themselves under the steps of the altar, to observe the extraordinary scene, were discovered. A cry arose that they were assassins, placed there to blow up the leaders of the people, and instantly the unhappy wretches were beheaded, and their heads paraded on pikes.

The Assembly, in this emergency, took the most energetic measures to support its authority. Lafayette put himself at the head of the national guard, and proceeded to the Champ de Mars. Meanwhile, the red flag was boldly hoisted by the order of Bailly at the Hotel de Ville; and well-disposed citizens urged the proclamation of martial law. Arrived in sight of the insurgents, Lafayette unfurled the red flag, summoning the multitude in the name of law to disperse. Cries of "Down with the red flag!" "Shame to Bailly!" "Down with the bayonets!" "Death to Lafayette!" accompanied by volleys of stones and mud, were the only answers. Lafayette ordered the guards to fire in the air; but the people were only encouraged by this. He then resolutely ordered a volley point-blank, which killed and wounded six hundred persons (the republicans, with their usual exaggeration, say ten thousand). In an instant the crowd dispersed, and the Champ de Mars was deserted. Robespierre, Danton, Marat, Fréron, and the other leaders of the insurrection, disappeared. The national guard, headed by Lafayette, marched victorious but mournful again into Paris.

What figure does Robespierre make in this insurrection? The crowd bore him along, shouting "*Vive Robespierre!*" The shout was never less welcome to his ear, for the red flag was still flying, and he dreaded the prominence given to him by his popularity. As they passed along the Rue St. Honoré, a carpenter named Duplay, one of his ardent admirers, urged him to take refuge in his house. He tremblingly accepted, and remained there till concealment was unnecessary. Madame Roland gives a slightly different version of this affair; but she and all concur in expressing contempt for the cowardice he exhibited.

Even his inviolability as a deputy could not make him feel himself secure. Robespierre at no time exhibited courage: if he occasionally exhibited audacity, it was always the temerity of excitement, when conscious that he was backed by the people. Like most timid men he had occasional spasms of temerity, which have been sometimes mistaken for courage.

The leaders were not pursued; and a few days afterwards they took fresh courage and re-appeared.

The termination of the labors of the National Assembly was now approaching. Several of the committee to whom the different departments of the constitution had been referred, had made their reports. The members were wearied with their quarrels; the people again desirous of exercising the powers of an election. Nothing remained but to combine the decrees regarding the constitution into one act, and submit it for the sanction of the King. It was proposed to revise some of the democratic articles of the constitution. All the subordinate questions which remained were decided in favor of the royal authority; but courage was wanted to alter the cardinal points of the constitution.

The Jacobins, dreading the reaction in favor of order which began to show itself, agitated in every way. They demanded to speak to Robespierre. He appeared, but was discouraged, and exclaimed to them, "My friends, you have arrived too late. Everything is lost; the King is saved."*

Robespierre had several times endeavored to remove the unjust law respecting the condition of paying a *marc d'argent*, equivalent to three days' labor, as contrary to the declaration of the rights

---

* Mémoires du Marquis de Ferriéres, vol. ii. p. 453.

of man, and as making distinction amongst citizens. He now, in a long speech, asks them whether their declaration of rights was a formula, or whether it expressed the real principles of the constitution. "According to the declaration of rights," he said, "every man born and domiciled in France is a member of the political society of the French nation. He is so by the nature of things, and by the first principles of national right; that right not depending upon any fortune he may possess, nor upon the amount of taxes he may pay. If the present law subsists, the nation will be enslaved; for liberty consists in obeying laws which the people have given themselves, and servitude in being constrained to submit to the laws which others have made for us.

"I will crush your objections with one word. The people,—that mass of men whose cause I defend,—have rights whose origin is the same as your own. Who gave you the power of taking them away? 'General utility,' you say. But is there anything useful except that which is just and honest? And this eternal truth, does it not apply to the *whole* social organization? If the happiness of all is the aim of society, what must we think of those who wish to establish the power of some individuals upon the degradation and nullity of the rest of mankind?

"But you say, 'The people! Men who have nothing to lose, shall they exercise like us the rights of citizens?' Men who have nothing to lose! How unjust and false is this haughty language. Those of whom you speak are apparently men who subsist in the midst of society without any means of subsistence? For if they *are* provided with these means, they have, it seems to me, something to lose, and to preserve! Yes, the coarse clothes which cover me, the humble roof under which I retire to live in peace, the small salary with which I nourish my wife and my children, do not, I confess, rank as lands, chateaux, and equipages! Such miserable things, I know, are called *nothing* in the language of luxury and opulence; but they *are* something in the language of humanity. They are property, and as such, sacred as the splendid domains of the rich.

"What do I say! My liberty, my life, the right of safety or

of vengeance for myself, or for those who are dear to me; the right of repressing tyranny, the right of freely exercising all the faculties of my heart and brain; these things which nature has given to all men, are they not confided to me, as yours are, under the guardianship of laws? and you tell me, that I have no interest in these laws, and you will dispossess me of the power which I ought to have as well as you, of vindicating the administration of public affairs; and for the sole reason that you are richer than I am? Ah! if the balance cease to be equal, is it not in favor of the poorer citizens that it ought to incline? Are not the laws established for the protection of weakness against injustice and oppression? Is it not, therefore, violating all social principles to place this authority in the hands of the rich alone?

"But the rich have reasoned otherwise. By a strange abuse of words, they have restricted the term property to certain objects: they have called themselves alone proprietors. They have pretended that only proprietors were worthy of the name of citizens. They have made their particular interest the general interest, and to insure the success of this pretension, they have seized upon all social power. And we, oh weakness of men! we, who pretend to reduce all things to the principles of equality and of justice, it is upon such absurd and cruel prejudices that we endeavor to raise our constitution! But what, after all, is this rare merit of paying a mark of silver or any other tax to which you attach such prerogatives? If you pay into the public treasury a greater contribution than mine, is it not because society has procured for you greater advantages than for me? What is the source of this extreme inequality of fortunes which assembles the riches of a nation into a few hands? Is it not bad laws and bad governments, in a word, all the vices of corrupt society?

"Why then must those who are the victims of these abuses be still further punished by the loss of their dignity as citizens?

"But the people! But corruption! O! cease, cease to profane the touching and sacred name of people by connecting it with the idea of corruption! Who is he among equal men who dares declare his fellow-men unworthy of exercising their rights? And if you permit yourself such a restriction upon the mere presumption of corruptibility, what a terrible power you arrogate to yourselves over humanity! Where will be the end of your proscriptions?

"Do you really believe that a hard and laborious life generates more vices than idleness, luxury, and ambition? And have you less confidence in the probity of our artisans and our laborers (who, according to your tariff, will scarcely ever be *active* citizens), than in courtiers and those whom you call *grand seigneurs*, and who, according to the same tariff, would be six hundred times better citizens?

"Let me rescue those whom you name the people from such sacrilegious calumnies. Are you fit to appreciate and to know the people? You who, ever since you have thought at all about them, have only judged them in accordance with the absurd ideas of despotism and feudal pride? You, who, accustomed to a bizarre jargon, have found it convenient to degrade the greatest part of the human race by the words *canaille* and *populace*. You, who have revealed to the world that there existed men of *no birth*, actually as if all men who lived had not been born! Thus we have heard of *men of nothing* who were, nevertheless, men of merit; and men, *comme il faut*, who were the vilest and the corruptest of beings!

"Ah! doubtless you may be permitted to deny the people that justice which is due to them! For me, I call to witness all those in whom the instinct of a noble and sensitive soul has led to communion with the people, that in general there is nothing so just nor so good as the people, when not irritated by the excesses of despotism! The people are grateful for the smallest respect, the smallest benefit that you confer on them; they are even grateful for the harm that you abstain from doing them. It is among the people that you will find, beneath an exterior which we call coarse, upright and open souls, good sense, and an energy which you might seek in vain amongst the class which disdains them.

"The people only demand that which is necessary; they only wish for justice and tranquillity. The rich aim at everything;

they wish to have all, and to domineer over all. The abuses are the work and the wealth of the rich, the scourges of the people. The interest of the people is the general interest; that of the rich but a particular interest; and you wish to render the people nothing, and the rich all powerful!"

One may imagine the effect of such words upon a democratic and excited populace; how the man who uttered them would be looked upon, not only as the tribune of the people, the advocate of the oppressed, but as the only wise and incorruptible defender of the sacred rights of man. Accordingly, the Society of the Indigent Friends of the Constitution voted an address to him, expressive of their admiration of his speech, and their attachment to his person.

Before finally submitting the constitution to the King for his acceptance, Robespierre proposed a motion, declaring that none of the present members of the Assembly should be capable of being elected into the next legislature. This act of renunciation, which was praised by some as Solon-like magnanimity and disinterestedness, was condemned by all sensible people, as assuring the triumph of mediocrity.

Camille Desmoulins, in the very last article which he wrote, had said that "The whole National Assembly was wherever Pétion and Robespierre were. The rest," said he, "is but a rabble of priests, of nobles, of courtiers, adventurers, counter-revolutionists, or idiots. It is an anti-National Assembly. I do not know why Robespierre, Buzot, Pétion, Rœderer, and half-a-dozen others, do not send in their resignations at once, and retire from that senate of conspirators against the people, where it is impossible to do good."

Such words as these would not be read by Robespierre unmoved. In spite of his rising importance in the Assembly, he must have felt his comparative insignificance there when contrasted with his influence at the club.

The constitution was now completed, and on the 3d of September it was presented to the King, who, after several days' careful examination, declared his acceptance in the following terms: "I accept the constitution, and I engage to maintain it alike against civil discord and foreign aggression; and to enforce its execution to the utmost of my power."

This created immense enthusiasm; and Lafayette, taking advantage of the moment, procured a general amnesty for all who had been engaged in the flight of the King, or compromised by the events of the revolution.

Once more it seemed as if the revolution was completed, and the reign of peace was to return!

On the 30th, the King closed the Constituent Assembly. The president, Thouret, with a loud voice, exclaimed, "The Constituent Assembly declares that its mission is finished, and that at this moment it terminates its sittings."

When Robespierre and Pétion left the Assembly, the people crowned them with chaplets; and taking the horses from their carriage, dragged their defenders home in triumph. Magnificent fêtes were ordered by the King for the occasion, in spite of the already exhausted treasury. The palace and gardens of the Tuileries were superbly illuminated; and the King, Queen and royal family, drove through the long avenues of the Champs Elysées amidst the acclamations of the people.

The Constituent Assembly was no more; but, as Mr. Alison remarks, it had done great things for France and for Europe. Some of the greatest evils which afflicted France had been removed by its wise decrees. Liberty of worship was secured in its fullest extent. Torture, punishment of the rack, and all cruel corporeal inflictions, except death, were abolished; trial by jury was established; publicity of criminal proceedings, the examinations of witnesses before the accused, and counsel for his defence, were fixed by law; the ancient parliaments, though ennobled by great exertions in favor of freedom, were suppressed; and one uniform system of criminal jurisprudence was introduced. Lettres de cachet were abolished; exemptions from taxation, on the part of the nobles and the clergy, were extinguished; an equal system of finance was established throughout the whole kingdom; while the most oppressive taxes, those on salt and tobacco, taille and corvée, and tithes, were suppressed; the privileges of the nobility, and other feudal burdens were abolished. A national guard was established, and the highest ranks in the army were thrown open to every class.*

CHAPTER XV.

The Legislative Assembly—Robespierre retires to Arras—His reception there—Anecdotes—Returns to Paris—Some account of his private life—His betrothed Eléonore—His amability in society—Anecdote—His friends—Personal traits—Was he a man of no talent?—His power—His eloquence—Madame Roland.

THE work of the Constituent Assembly finished, nothing remained but to select a Legislative Assembly, which should legislate in conformity with the principles of the constitution. No set of legislators ever had a more difficult task. And yet this task was to be performed by deputies, who, for the most part, were mere boys. Almost all the white heads had disappeared from the benches: was this a symbol of France become young again? It was a legislative body formed from a new generation—from a generation which had discarded all the traditions as well as all the prejudices of the ancient régime. Much legislative wisdom was not to be expected from this body; but in default thereof, great patriotic fervor and considerable ability. In spite of their ability and patriotism, the history of France is now no more to be read in those columns of the *Moniteur* which report speeches and register decrees. The history of France is to be read elsewhere. So rash is the activity of this legislative body, that in the space of eleven months it is reckoned more than two thousand decrees are

---

* "C'est la plus illustre congrégation populaire," says Chateaubriand, in his Mémoires, "qui jamais ait paru chez les nations, tant par la grandeur de ses transactions que par l'immensité de leur resultats."

enacted! And with this activity in law-*making* on their side, we have to notice equal activity in law-*breaking* on the side of the people!

Robespierre was excluded from this Assembly by his own proposition, and while Pétion passed over to London, to be feasted at Constitutional Reform Clubs, to harangue and be harangued *more Britannico*, Robespierre retired for seven short weeks of quiet to his native Arras.

In the July previous he had published his "Addresse aux Français," in which he firmly, but not very eloquently, defends himself from the calumnies circulated against him, and explains the whole of his conduct as a deputy. The eulogies lavished on him by republican journals exasperated the other journalists, and calumny was flung upon his name almost as recklessly as praise. In the *Babillard* of the 19th July, I find him libeled as a member of a foreign faction! "It is said" (*on dit!* what will not *on dit* cover!) "that there are several agents of the English Minister at Paris, who, jealous of the advantages which France will derive from her new constitution, spare no expense and no trouble to overturn it. *On dit* that Robespierre, Pétion, Buzot," the three men most notorious for incorruptibility! "and others, are sold to this secret cabal," (O, potent and omnipotent gold of Pitt!) "and often dine with the English."

It was in the month of October, 1791, that Robespierre revisited his native town. His entry was an ovation. Some battalions of national guards were cantoned at Bapaume, a small town about five leagues from Arras, and two hundred of the officers and soldiers of these battalions came to the *auberge*, where he had put up, to compliment their patriot deputy. They insisted on being allowed to accompany him to Arras. It was an honor so vain a man was little likely to refuse. Two-and-twenty of the best mounted rode forward to announce his coming. They reached Arras about nine o'clock in the evening, and on the report spreading that Robespierre was on the way, patriots assembled in the streets, and ordered that every house should be illuminated. The windows of some citizens who refused thus to honor the patriot were smashed, and their names vilified.

The cortège arrived. It was composed of a group of old men bearing civic crowns, accompanied by women robed in white, and followed by a troop of children scattering flowers. The enthusiasm was immense. Verses and éloges were, it may be supposed, not wanting; all the execrable poets of *Les Rosatis* doubtless sprang upon their wooden Pegasus to pay a tribute to the Incorruptible; who, proud and bilious, rode into his natal city, thinking of the enormous progress he had made since last he left it an obscure provincial lawyer.

It is worth while to rescue from its surrounding rubbish a little *on dit* which was credited in credulous Paris, and to contrast it with the fact. The *on dit* circulated was that Robespierre had been ill-received in Arras, and that the mob had nearly hanged him! To turn an ovation into an escape from hanging was facile in those days of *on dits*. I have met with the probable origin of this, in the following epigram:—

> "D'être pendu le pauvre Robespierre
> Vient en Artois de courir le hazard;
> Or il le sera tôt ou tard:
> Dont mieux valoit se laisser faire."

Arras was proud of its deputy. In the seven short weeks he remained there his fellow-citizens in every way testified their admiration of his conduct. Of course there were many who regarded him with distrust and dislike; but the republicans looked upon him as a great and good man. He had gone there, as he said, to breathe the air of equality. His work as a legislator ended, he had returned once more into the ranks of his fellow-citizens. Had he chosen then to put his principles in practice, he might have settled down into private life, and thus escaped the infamy of his subsequent career. Up to this point his conduct had been irreproachable. But *could* he retire into privacy? Could he give up the excitement of a demagogue's career for the dull monotony of provincial life? He could not. Setting aside all personal ambition (of which he had an inordinate amount), the times were too stirring for any one to think of otiose retirement.

At Arras he lived secluded, only admitting into his society, as at Paris, a few chosen friends who shared his political views. Des Essarts reproaches him with preserving a supercilious silence whenever he was thrown among superior and intelligent men.* Surely the better explanation of this silence is his dislike to enter into discussion with those whom he knew to be opposed to him?

That so few anecdotes respecting this strange being should have been preserved, is really remarkable. Of his infancy we learn next to nothing; not even his own sister has remembered as much as is remembered of the most ordinary mortal in the most uneventful career. His townsmen are equally oblivious. That nothing should be recorded of his early years is easily to be accounted for; but now that he returns to Arras in triumph, bearing a name which is sounded all over France, no one seems to have been more solicitous about him than before,—at least, as far as regards the circulation and preservation of such anecdotes as usually delight the dinner tables and whist parties of a gossiping province. Here is one—the only one I have been able to rake up.

Robespierre was one day sitting in a café, next to an officer somewhat the worse for wine. The conversation turned of course upon the all-absorbing theme—politics. Robespierre, as usual, was silent; nor could he be prevailed upon to give his opinion. Suddenly the officer, who was of gigantic stature, seized him by the waist, and holding him up in the air, exclaimed, "Messieurs, I have a motion to make: it is that Robespierre be commanded to express his opinion. Those who agree hold up their hands!" All hands were raised, and Robespierre, confused and humiliated, stammered out a few words. The officer, uttering an oath, then said: "Buvons, mais ne buvons qu'aux francs et joyeux Français."

All I have further to relate of this Arras visit is, that he dis-

---

Crimes de Robespierre, vol. i. p. 16. This, by the way, is one of his *crimes!*

posed of the few small farms which had been left him as an heritage, and then returned to Paris, accompanied by his sister Charlotte and his brother Augustin, whom he took to live with him in his lodging in Duplay's house, where, since the night of the riot on the Champ de Mars, he had resided.

Let us, aided by Lamartine, glance into the interior of that house. It is No. 396, in the Rue St. Honoré.* The house is low. Its court, surrounded by sheds filled with timber and plants, gives it a rural appearance. In consists of a parlor opening into the court, and communicating with a salon which looks into a small garden. From this salon a door leads into a small study, where there is a piano. A winding staircase leads to the first floor, in which lives Duplay, and thence to the apartment of Robespierre. His private room is a low chamber, constructed garret-wise, over some cart sheds, the window opening upon the roof. The "look-out" is confined to the interior of the court, whence are constantly heard the sounds of workmen's hammers and saws, and across which Madame Duplay and her daughters pass to and fro in their domestic avocations. This chamber is also separated from that of Duplay by a small room, occupied in common by the family and Robespierre.

Robespierre's chamber contains only a wooden bedstead, covered with blue damask ornamented with white flowers, a table, and four straw-bottomed chairs. It is both study and dormitory. His papers, his manuscripts, written in a careful style, with perpetual erasures, are placed on deal shelves against the wall. On these shelves are a few chosen books. Busts and portraits of himself abound. On the table there is sure to be a volume of Rousseau or Racine lying open. Here he passes the greater part of the day.

At seven in the evening he goes to the Jacobin Club. His costume always precise, modest, and scrupulously clean; in striking contrast to the slovenliness of the demagogues, which they

---

* It was pulled down by order of Bonaparte; perhaps, according to the *Quarterly Review*, because he wished to obliterate even unimportant traces of the revolution. The Rue Duphot now passes over the site.

assumed in order to flatter the people. His powdered hair was turned up in clusters over his temples. He wore a bright blue coat buttoned over the hips and open at the chest, displaying a white waistcoat; short yellow breeches, with white stockings, and shoes with silver buckles, completed his invariable attire. It is supposed, that by never varying the style or color of his costume, he desired to make an impression of unswerving consistency.

The family of his landlord became a second family to him. It consisted of Duplay, his wife, one son, and four daughters, the eldest five-and-twenty, the youngest eighteen. In this small circle he was beloved. There, where toil, poverty, and retirement had fixed his life, he fixed his home and affections. Eléonore, the eldest daughter (who subsequently assumed the classic name of Cornelia), inspired him with a serious attachment. Not *love*, perhaps; not the love which ardent natures feel, and which he himself inspired, but a sort of protecting tenderness; a mixture of regard and passion which warmed without absorbing him. It was a gentle episode in his dark history. It was, to use Lamartine's happy expression, "The repose of the heart after mental weariness."

Eléonore loved him passionately. Does it seem strange? Strange indeed are the idols woman will adore! If Albertine could leave her husband to live in cellars with that mass of filth, rags, and fury, named Marat, surely a young girl in a republican family might worship a man whom France pronounced "incorruptible!"

Their mutual attachment was openly avowed, and commanded universal respect from its purity. They lived as affianced lovers, without forgetting that they were to be man and wife some day. His total want of fortune, and the uncertainty of the morrow, prevented their marrying until the destiny of France was fixed. But he only awaited the moment when the revolution should be concluded, to retire from the turmoil and strife, and take her with him to his native place, there to pass their days in obscure but untroubled happiness.

Of Eléonore's sisters, Robespierre preferred the youngest, who afterwards married his townsman Lebas. "This young woman," says Lamartine, "to whom the friendship of Robespierre cost the life of her husband eleven months after their marriage, has lived more than half a century beyond that day without having once diminished her devotion to Robespierre; and without having understood the maledictions of the world against this brother of her youth, who still appears in her memory so pure, so virtuous, and so gentle."

It has always, I confess, been a puzzle to me how any human being could love Robespierre; and yet the testimony of all those who knew him intimately concurs in establishing it as a fact, that his friends did really love him. I may be permitted to insert here an anecdote, the pleasantness of which, as a story, depends, however, less upon its relation to Robespierre than its exhibition of naïveté.

There is now living in Paris a certain M. Legrand, who boasts of his acquaintance with Robespierre, whom he regards as "the best abused man" of his acquaintance. To him Robespierre was a "very amiable man in society." He only thinks of him in that light. The reign of terror is a sort of nightmare—he no longer thinks of it. The "incorruptible" to him is no fierce demagogue hounding on the passions of an excited nation—no vain pedagogue striving by words of reason to calm those passions—but a pleasant, amiable, gentlemanly fellow enough, whom he delights to remember. There is one story he always tells; and I regret that I must spoil it in the telling, wherein so much depends upon the gesture, and the quiet senile tone of voice; but such as it is, it will, I think, amuse the reader:—"Je me rappelle qu'une fois étant chez la famille Lebas .... où il allait très souvent .... j'entends du bruit sur l'escalier. 'Tiens!' me suis-je écrié. 'Je parie que c'est ce farceur de Robespierre .... car il était très gai .... en société (this epithet of *farceur* is very piquant!) Effectivement c'était lui. Il entre dans le salon .... je m'approche de lui, et je lui dis: 'Citoyen, tu sais .... ou tu dois savoir .... que M. Legrand, un parent à moi—eh bien! il est *condamné*, et demain matin .... (here a very significant gesture imitative of the guillotine completes the sentence) .... Un homme, citoyen, dont l'innocence m'est prouvé! dont je réponds comme de moi-même

.... Et la vie d'un innocent, citoyen, c'est quelque chose—quoi!' Alors il me répond : 'Voyons, voyons, votre affaire' .... (car il était fort aimable en société—M. de Robespierre!) Je lui conte la chose; alors il me demande : 'A quelle heure ton ami doit-il mourir?' .... (car il était fort aimable en société—M. de Robespierre.) .... 'Citoyen,' que je lui réponds, 'c'est à neuf heures précises!'—'A neuf heures! c'est facheux.! car tu sais que je travaille tard; ainsi comme je me couche tard, je me lève tard. Je crains que je ne serais pas levé en temps de sauver votre ami .... mais nous verrons, nous verrons!' .... (car il était fort aimable en société—M. de Robespierre). After a short pause, he continues: 'Il parait .... que M. de Robespierre avait *beaucoup* travaillé cette nuit : car mon pauvre ami!' .... (Here again the guillotining gesture.) 'C'est égal! Je suis sur que s'il n'avait pas tant travaillé, il aurait sauvé mon pauvre ami .... car il était fort aimable en société—M. de Robespierre.' "

This man, " so amiable in society," was idolized by the family in which he lived. His evenings were not ungracefully spent in conversation, or in reading aloud one of the beautiful tragedies of Racine. Two or three times in the season he took Madame Duplay and her daughter to the theatre, but it was always to witness some "classical" tragedy, wherein long tirades reminded tyrants of their doom, and republican sentiments took the place of pathos, poetry, and action.

Robespierre retired early to his chamber, lay down, and rose again during the night to work. Innumerable discourses, delivered in the two National Assemblies and in the Jacobins; articles written for his journal, whilst he had one; and the still more numerous manuscripts of speeches which he prepared, but never delivered; the studied style, with its indefatigable corrections marked with his pen upon the manuscript, attest his labor and patient resolution.

One of his relaxations was a solitary walk in the Champs Elysées, or about the environs of Paris, in imitation of his model, Jean Jacques Rousseau. His sole companion in these walks was a large dog, to which he was much attached. This dog, named

Brount, was quite a character. He was well known in the district as Robespierre's constant companion and guard. He slept at the door of his master's chamber, and often by his winning ways solicited and won a few moments of play. It must have been a fine sight to see this lean, anxious, bilious, pedantic tribune, playing with his colossal, noble-spirited, and affectionate dog!

The dog was his only escort. In moments of extreme agitation, when the lives of the democrats were in danger, the printer Nicolas, the locksmith Didier, and other friends, followed Robespierre at a distance, but these precautions, taken without his knowledge, only irritated him.

"Let me leave your house, and go and live alone," said he to Duplay; "I compromise your family; and my enemies will construe your children's attachment to me into a crime."

"No, no, no," replied Duplay; "we will die together, or the people shall triumph."

Sometimes on a Sunday the whole family left Paris; and the democrat, withdrawn for a moment into the man, amused himself with them in the woods of Versailles or at Issy. A very few friends were admitted into his society. Lameth and Pétion, at first; Legendre, very seldom; Merlin De Thionville, Fouché, who loved Robespierre's sister, but whom Robespierre did not like, Taschereau, Coffinhal, Panis, Sergent, Piot; and every evening Lebas, St. Just, David, Gonchon, Buonarotti, Camille Desmoulins, Nicolas the printer, Didier; and lastly, Madame de Chalabre, a rich and noble lady, an enthusiast for Robespierre, "devoting herself to him, as the widows of Corinth or Rome to the apostles of the new creed;" offering her fortune to assist in the promulgation of his opinions, and winning the friendship of the wife and daughters of Duplay to merit one look from Robespierre. Among Robespierre's papers will be found some letters of hers; curious as indications of the idolatry he excited.

The features and expression of Robespierre's countenance betrayed a mind always at work; but these features sometimes relapsed into absolute gaiety when seated at table; or in the evening, when, seated around the wood fire, they chatted over the events of the day and the plans of the morrow; discussing the conspiracies of aristocrats, the dangers of the patriots, and the prospects of public felicity, when once the revolution was accomplished.

After dinner, winter and summer, there was always a pyramid of oranges placed before Robespierre, who ate them with extraordinary avidity. Fréron, from whom I get this detail, attributes this love of oranges to his biliousness: " He was perfectly insatiable in his appetite for them. No one ventured to touch the sacred fruit in his presence. No doubt the acidity acted on his bilious humors, and favored their circulation. It was always easy to detect the place at table which he had occupied, by the piles of orange-peel which covered the plate. It was remarked, that as he ate them his severity of countenance relaxed."

To these little personal traits let me also add, that he only drank water. While the natural sensuality of many of his rivals and colleagues, stimulated by the prevailing excitement of the epoch, exhibited itself in disgraceful orgies, Robespierre always retained the sobriety of a cynic.

His purity was his force. "Nature," as Charles Nodier justly says, "seems to have predestined him to anything rather than success as an orator. Imagine a little man, with a feeble frame, sharpened physiognomy, the brow compressed on both sides like that of a beast of prey; his mouth long, pale, and compressed; his voice hoarse in the lower, discordant in the higher tones, and which, during the exultation of rage, was converted into a sort of howl, like that of the hyæna; add to that a sort of heavy coquetry, and you have the man before you. There was an inexpressible sharpness sparkling from his savage eye, which seemed to wound in touching you. In the nervous trembling, which palpitated in all his limbs; in the habitual *tic*, which tormented the muscles of his face; in the trembling of his fingers, which played upon the tribune as upon the keys of a piano forte, you divined that the whole soul of this man was interested in the sentiment which he was about to communicate to you; and that, by identifying himself with the ruling passion of the moment, he could become, from time to time, great and imposing as that passion. It is a great mistake to call Bonaparte the 'revolution incarnate:' the 'revolution incarnate' was Robespierre, with his horrible good faith, his *naïveté de sang*, and his pure and cruel conscience."

Thibaudeau said of him, "There is in that man something of Mahomet and of Cromwell; he only wants their genius." It is very true: their genius he had not. He had not even geniality; but he almost supplied the place of genius by sincerity, by the force of his convictions, and the unalterable steadiness with which he labored to realize them. That is the answer to those who wonder at the ascendency he acquired. The Abbé de Montgaillard cannot explain this ascendency at all. "Rienzi, Massaniello," he says, "were endowed with qualities capable of acting on the imagination of the Italians. Beaufort, by his splendid appearance and singular eloquence, knew how to make himself beloved by the people; but what enthusiasm can such a man as Robespierre excite —a pusillanimous tribune, a demagogue wanting in every species of talent and every means of seduction? He had not the eloquence of Mirabeau, nor the force of Danton; and yet this poor advocate of Arras raised himself above the most famous authors of our revolution!"

Some quietly attribute this success to the effect of circumstances; to his "talent for hatred," and his intense desire to domineer. But why was *he* alone favored by circumstances? Why was his ambition alone crowned with such success? It is said that he usurped the powers of the national representation; but as Charles Nodier very properly remarks, how came it that his colleagues suffered him to usurp it? How came it that they gave to his will all the weight of their sanction? You say the Assembly was not free; they were afraid of the tyrant; but how is it that six hundred men had not force enough to put down one? What were his means of seduction, of intimidation? He had no money; he had no troops; he had no powerful friends; he had nothing but his principles, his discourses, and his popularity! He was powerful, because he personified power. He swayed the destinies of France, because he was the real tribune of the people. Had he for one moment placed himself in antagonism to the people, he would have been lost. He could not, like Mirabeau, defy them and then charm them. He could not by one speech, or one vote, excite their execrations; and then, by his mere presence at the theatre, turn those execrations into shouts of applause; or, by one burst of eloquence, regain the empire of that fluctuating mass. Robespierre's force was not in his genius, for he had none; but in his principles, and they were the principles of the revolution.

Too much has been said about Robespierre's intellectual mediocrity. A man of genius or of commanding abilities he was not, and yet he *did* exercise a sort of spiritual command over a nation peculiarly susceptible to the influence of talent. He had not what is usually called eloquence. Seldom, if ever, did he give utterance to those bursts of oratory in which the heart gives momentum and the imagination gives seductive beauty to an argument, and thus irresistibly carries away the listening multitude; he never reached the heights where a Mirabeau and a Danton seemed to revel in the plenitude of power. No lambent fire of fancy plays around his words; he has no graces of style beyond careful correctness. He modeled his style on that of Rousseau, but he could not imitate its color, its harmony, and its poetry. Notwithstanding all these drawbacks, his speeches are sometimes masterpieces. In their skill and oratorical art, they approach ancient models. More logical than poetical, they are better adapted to achieve their ends than almost any other modern speeches. Their force is the calm majestic force of reason. The only speeches that can be compared with them are those of Guizot, in whose style we perceive the same qualities and the same deficiencies as in that of Robespierre. There is nothing spontaneous in them, nothing generous, nothing grandiose. They betray the toilsome elaboration in which they were prepared, but they have all the excellencies of forethought, reflection, and artistic disposal of effects. When suddenly called upon, Robespierre could not find in the inspiration of the moment the burning words of eloquent reply; but let him retire to his room for a few days, and the concentrated energies of his mind on that one subject would produce a triumphant answer.

Carlyle, who never speaks of him but in terms of that measureless contempt with which he usually brands the objects of his dislike, describes him as "a poor seagreen atrabilia formula of a man; without head, without heart, or any grace or gift or even vice beyond the common; if it were not astucity, diseased rigor, as of a cramp; meant by nature for a methodist parson of the stricter sort, to doom men who departed from the written confession; to chop fruitless, shrill logic; to contend and suspect, and ineffectually wrestle and wriggle."

And elsewhere he says, "What spirit of patriotism dwelt in men in those times, this one fact, it seems to us, will evince, that 1500 human creatures, not bound to it, sat quiet under the oratory of Robespierre; nay, listened nightly, hour after hour, applausive, and gaped as for the word of life. More insupportable individual, one would say, seldom opened his mouth in any tribune; acrid, implacable—impotent, dull, drawling, barren as the Harmatten wind."

But the answer to all this is, that people listened to him because he *did* speak to them what they looked upon as the word of life, and what is more, he spoke to them better than any other man then living: not perhaps with the rhetoric of Vergniaud, the fierce sarcasms of Isnard, or the sort of grandiose brutality of Danton in his voice of thunder; but with more immediate effect. If he did not rouse multitudes to transports by glowing words or noble images, he did more: he carried the day—he made them vote as he voted!

Some of his speeches have really every quality of oratory except poetic beauty, and as it is impossible to deny the merit of this, some of his detractors have supposed that he had a prompter, who wrote his speeches for him.

"Robespierre," said Charles Nodier, "had for his secretary a feeble, little, lame man, named Duplay, with whom I was three or four times in prison, and whose mind was still more meagre than his body. Duplay was absolutely incapable of writing a passable letter. Yet this is the man supposed to have written for Robespierre! Moreover, it is from arguments, written entirely in the hand of Robespierre, and which had all the suddenness, a.. the *abandon*, all the disorder of a hasty composition, that his famous discourse of the 8th Thermidor was printed; and this discourse is certainly the most remarkable that Robespierre has left."

Charles Nodier, who was certainly one of the most exquisite judges in literary matters modern France has produced, without disguising his want of sympathy with Robespierre, does his talents full justice.

At the house of Madame Roland the nucleus of a great republican party was formed. There Robespierre, Pétion, Brissot, Buzot, Vergniaud, Guadet, Gensonné, Carra, Louvet, Ducos, Fonfrède, Duperret, Sillery Genlis, and many others, were to be met discussing with quiet earnestness the affairs of the nation.

"Every historian must feel a sinister curiosity in remarking the first impression made on Madame Roland by the man who, now conspiring with her, was one day to overthrow the power of her friends, destroy them as a body, and send her to the scaffold. No repulsive sentiment seems, at this epoch, to have warned her, that, in conspiring to advance Robespierre's fortune, she hastened her own death. If she had any vague fear, that fear is at once checked by a pity akin to contempt. Robespierre seemed to her an honest man; she forgave him his evil speaking, and pedantic utterance. Robespierre, like all men with one idea, was very tiresome. She remarked, however, that he was always very attentive in these meetings, that he never spoke freely, but listened to all other opinions before he delivered his own, and then never took the pains to explain his motives. Like all imperious men, his conviction always appeared to him a sufficing reason. The next day he mounted the tribune, and profiting by the discussions to which he had listened the previous evening, he anticipated the hour of action agreed upon with his allies, and thus divulged the plan concerted. Blamed for this at Madame Roland's, he excused himself carelessly. This was attributed to his youth, and the impatience of his *amour-propre*. Madame Roland, persuaded that he was passionately attached to liberty, mistook his reserve for timidity, and this conduct for independence. The common cause was a cover for all. Partiality transforms the most sinister indications into favor or indulgence. 'He defends his principles,' said she, 'with warmth and pertinacity—and there is courage in standing up singly in their defence at a time when the number of the people's champions is greatly reduced. The court hates him, therefore we should like him. I esteem Robespierre for this, and show him that I do; and even when he does not often attend the evening meetings, he comes occasionally and dines with me. I was much struck with the terror which agitated him on the day of the King's flight to Varennes. He said the same evening at Pétion's that the royal family had not taken such a step without preparing in Paris a Saint Bartholomew for the patriots, and that he expected death before he was twenty-four hours older. Pétion, Buzot, Roland, on the contrary, said that this flight of the King was his abdication, and it was necessary to profit by it in order to prepare men's minds for the republic. Robespierre, sneering, and biting his nails, as usual, asked what was a republic?'

"It was on this day that the plan of a journal, entitled the *Republican*, was conceived between Brissot, Condorcet, Dumont of Geneva, and Duchâtelet. One sees that the idea of a republic was born in the cradle of the Girondists before it was born in the soul of Robespierre, and that the 10th of August was not an accident, but a plot.

"At the same epoch, Madame Roland, in order to save Robespierre's life, had yielded to one of those impulses which exhibit a courageous friendship, and leave traces even in the memory of the ungrateful. After the massacre of the Champ-de-Mars, Robespierre, accused of having conspired with the instigators of the petition, and threatened as a rebel with vengeance by the national guard, was forced to conceal himself. Madame Roland, accompanied by her husband, went at eleven o'clock at night to his lodging in the Marais, to offer him a safer retreat in their own house. He had already fled from his domicile. Madame Roland then went to their mutual friend Buzot, and conjured him to go to the Feuillants, where he was still influential, and with all haste to exculpate Robespierre before any act of accusation could be issued against him.

"Buzot hesitated for a moment, then said—'I will do all to save this unfortunate young man, although I am far from sharing the opinion of certain persons respecting him. He thinks too much of himself to love liberty; but he serves it, and that is enough for me. I shall be there to defend him.' Thus, three of Robespierre's future victims combined that night, and unknown to him, for the safety of the man by whom they were eventually to die. Destiny is a mystery whence issue the strangest coincidences, and which tend no less to snare men through their virtues than through their crimes. Death is everywhere: but, whatever its fate, virtue alone never repents. Beneath the dungeons of the Conciergerie Madame Roland remembered that night with satisfaction. If Robespierre remembered it when in power, this remembrance must have fallen colder on his heart than the axe of the executioner."*

* Lamartine.

We must remember, that Madame Roland wrote the above sentences about Robespierre in prison, and they are therefore to be read *cum grano*. But Thiers has unwarrantably used them as an authority for his assertion that Robespierre was silent in society, in order that he might the next day proclaim at the tribune ideas which he heard expressed the night before. This is absurd. Robespierre borrowed his ideas from no one but Rousseau and Mably, and these he accommodated to the situation of the moment. He was too proud a man, too confident in the correctness of his own views, to borrow ideas from his friends.

CHAPTER XV.

Emigration of the nobles—The coalition—Patriots urgent for war: opposed by Robespierre—Quarrel between him and the Girondins—Accused of ambition, and of aspiring to a dictatorship—Robespierre avows his belief in a Providence—His Defenseur de la Constitution—Condemns the bonnet rouge—The mob enter the Tuileries; Louis puts on the bonnet rouge—Robespierre's attack on Lafayette—Arrival of the Marseillais—Plan of their attack—The 10th of August.

EMIGRATION was rapidly increasing, and nearly 100,000 of the most wealthy and influential families in France had joined it. "All the roads to the Rhine were covered by haughty fugitives, whose inability for action was only equaled by the presumption of their language."

Coblentz became a new Versailles, the centre of the counter-revolution. The European coalition was formed, and France was thus not only threatened from without, but the religious wars of La Vendée began to threaten it from within. France was in a most distracted state. "Yet," as Carlyle says, "overhead of all this there is the customary baking and brewing; labor hammers and grinds. Frilled promenaders saunter under the trees, white muslin promenadress, in green parasol, leaning on your arm. Dogs dance, and shoe-blacks polish on the Pont Neuf itself. The fatherland in danger; so much goes its course, and yet the course of all things is nigh altering and ending."

Never did France seem so near its destruction. Emigrants and foreign powers threatening it from without; La Vendée and the aristocrats from within; the King a vacillating do-nothing; the Queen corresponding with foreign powers, and bribing demagogues. Rivarol, with his "staff of genius," (as he calls his paragraph-writers,) which costs the King 10,000*l.* a month, all laboring to quell the spirit of the revolution.

Alarmed patriots loudly demand war. Brissot and his friends see in it the only hope of salvation. The Assembly, with M. de Narbonne at the head, votes 200,000 francs for war preparations. Luckner is made Marshal of France. One man alone of the Jacobins resisted the influence of this newly-awakened warlike enthusiasm: this man was Robespierre.

"Until now," Lamartine says, "he had been merely one who discussed ideas, a subaltern agitator, indefatigable and intrepid, but eclipsed by other and greater men. From this day he became a statesman. He felt his internal force. He knew this force reposed upon a principle; alone and unaided, he dared to combat for the truth. He devoted himself, regardless of the number of his adversaries."

For once, Robespierre seemed in antagonism with the people, and boldly maintained it, because he felt strongly and clearly that he was advocating the people's cause even against the people itself. All were in favor of war—Girondists, Aristocrats, Constitutionalists, and Jacobins. War was an appeal to destiny. Victory seemed to France the sole issue by which she could extricate herself from her difficulties. Yet Robespierre opposed France.

In one of his speeches at the Club he promulgated a strange maxim, a maxim upon which his whole career may be said to be a comment. In speaking of the suspicion with which the minister should be regarded, he said suspicion was to liberty what jealousy was to love: "La défiance est au sentiment intime de la liberté ce que la jalousie est à l'amour."

He needed great nerve and determination thus to confront his friends, his enemies, and public opinion itself. Great convictions are indefatigable; Robespierre, warmed by his conviction, stood out against France. His very enemies admired his firmness. He even rose to eloquence, and more than once startled and delighted the Assembly. "Carefully preserve the numbers that contain Robespierre's speeches," said the *Orateur du Peuple;* "they are masterpieces of eloquence, and should be preserved to teach future generations that Robespierre existed for the good of his country and for the preservation of liberty." Marat came over to Robespierre's side, and Camille Desmoulins followed.

There is something in this attitude of Robespierre singularly interesting to the biographer. It shows that he possessed the "courage of his conviction;" that he really had "faith in his ideas;" and that if he was a tribune, he was not wholly a demagogue; he spoke not merely to please the people, but to make the people triumph. He was a fanatic, but he was sincere. Having exhausted every argument that philosophy, policy, and patriotism could furnish against an offensive war, he mounted the tribune of the Jacobins for the last time against Brissot, on the night of the 13th of January, and made this admirable speech:—

"Well, then, I am vanquished; I pass over to you," he exclaimed, in a broken voice, "I also demand war. Nay more—I demand a war, more terrible, more implacable than you; I do not demand it as an act of prudence, an act of reason, an act of policy; I demand it as the resource of despair. I demand it on one condition, which doubtless we are already agreed upon, for I do not think that the advocates of war have wished to deceive us: I demand it to the death (*à mort*); I demand it heroic; I demand it such as the genius of Liberty would declare against every despotism, such as the people of the revolution under their own leaders would make it; and not such as cowardly intriguers would have it, or as the ambitious and traitorous ministers and generals would carry on.

"Well, then! Frenchmen! heroes of the 14th of July, who, without guide or leader, knew how to conquer liberty, come forth! Let us form that army which is destined to conquer the universe. But where is the general who, as the imperturbable defender of the people's rights, the born enemy of tyrants, has never breathed the poisonous atmosphere of courts, and whose virtue is attested by the hatred of the court; this general, whose hands, free from our blood, are worthy to bear before us the banner of liberty; where is he, this new Cato, this third Brutus, this unknown hero? let him who dares to claim the title present himself, and we will place him at our head. But where is he? Where are the soldiers of the 14th of July, who laid down in the presence of the people the arms given them by despotism. Soldiers of Châteauvieux, where are you? Come and guide our efforts. Alas! it is easier to rob death of its prey, than despotism of its victims. Citizens! Conquerors of the Bastille, come! Liberty calls you to the honor of the first rank. They answer not. Want, ingratitude, and the hatred of the aristocracy, have dispersed them. And you, citizens, massacred in the Champ de Mars in the very act of a patriotic confederation, will you neither be with us? Ah, what had these females, these massacred children done? God! how many victims! and all amongst the people—all amongst the patriots; whilst powerful conspirators live and triumph. Come to us, at least ye national guards, who have especially devoted yourselves to the defence of our frontiers in this war with which a perfidious court menaces us. Come!—But what!—you are not yet armed? For two years you have demanded arms, and yet have them not. What do I say? You have been refused even uniforms, and condemned to wander from department to department, objects of contempt to the ministers and of derision to the patricians, who look at you only to enjoy your distress. No matter. Come, we will combat naked, like the Americans.

"But shall we await the orders of the war-office to overturn thrones? Shall we await the signal of the court? Shall we be commanded by these same patricians, these eternal favorites of despotism, in a war against aristocrats and kings? No! Let us march forward alone. Let us be our own leaders. But see, the orators of war stop me! Here is Monsieur Brissot, who tells me that *Monsieur le Comte de Narbonne* must conduct the whole of this affair; that we must march under the orders of *Monsieur le Marquis de Lafayette*, and to the executive power alone belongs the right of leading the nation to victory and liberty. Ah, citizens, this word has broken the spell! Adieu victory and independence of the people! If the sceptres of Europe ever be broken, it must be by other hands. Spain will continue for some time the brutified slave of superstition and royalty. Leopold will continue to be the tyrant of Germany and Italy, and we shall not speedily behold Catos or Ciceros replace the pope and the cardinals in the conclave. I declare frankly, that war, as I understand the term—that war, such as I have proposed, is impracticable. And if we are to accept the war of the court, of the ministers, of the patricians who affect patriotism—oh, then, far from believing in the enfranchisement of the world, I no longer believe in your liberty. The wisest course left us is to defend it against the perfidy of those internal enemies who lull you with these heroic illusions.

"I sum up calmly and sorrowfully. I have proved that liberty has no more mortal enemy than war; I have proved that war counseled by men *suspects*, is, in the hands of the executive power, only a means of annihilating the constitution, a conspiracy against the revolution. To favor war, under any pretext, is to join in a conspiracy against the revolution. All the patriotism in the world, all the pretended political common-places, cannot change the nature of things. To preach, like M. Brissot and his friends, confidence in the executive power, and to enlist public favor for the generals, is to deprive the revolution of its last security, the vigilance and energy of the nation. In the horrible situation in which despotism, levity, intrigue, treachery, and the general short sightedness have placed us, I consult alone my heart and my conscience; I only care for truth, I only think of my country. I know that patriots blame the frankness with which I present this discouraging picture of our situation. I do not dissemble my fault from myself. Is not the truth already sufficiently culpable in being truth? Ah! so that our slumbers be soft, what matter if we awaken to the sound of our country in chains, and in the calmness of slavery? Let us no longer disturb the quietude of these happy patriots. No, but let them know that we can measure with a firm eye and steady heart the depth of the abyss. Let us adopt the device of the Palatine of Posnania—*I prefer the storms of liberty to the serenity of slavery.*'

"If the hour of emancipation be not yet arrived, at least we should have the patience to await it. If this generation was but destined to struggle in the depths of vice into which despotism had plunged it; if the theatre of our revolution was to present to the eyes of the universe nothing but a struggle between perfidy and weakness, between egotism and ambition—the rising generation would commence the task of purifying this earth so sullied by vice. It would bring, not the peace of despotism or the sterile agitations of intrigue, but fire and sword, thrones in flames, to exterminate oppressors. O, more fortunate posterity, thou art not alien to us! It is for thee that we brave the storms and the plots of tyranny. Often discouraged by the obstacles that environ us, we feel a yearning desire to attain thee. It is for thee to complete our work; but preserve in thy remembrance the names of the martyrs of liberty."

The separation between Brissot and Robespierre grew daily wider; they began to hate each other. Almost equal in popularity, it was evident they were afraid of each other in their attacks.

They affected mutual respect, but at times politeness was borne down in the vehemence of discussion.

Robespierre, on the 2d of April complained of the attacks upon him in the Girondist journals, and concluded his speech by saying: "If there is anybody who has any reproach to make to me, I await him here. If there is any one, let him present himself." M. Real exclaimed, "Yes, I." "Speak," said Robespierre, with stern brevity; and M. Real then brought forward a foolish accusation of stubbornness, and of exercising dominion over the society; a dominion which, as he admitted, was involuntary on the part of Robespierre; and which, therefore, amounted to nothing more than the empire of mind and will over weaker minds.

Brissot was more vehement. He spoke of the tribunes as the worst enemies of the people. "They flatter to enslave. They throw suspicions on all virtue which will not lower itself. Remember Aristides and Phocion; they were not always in the tribune;" and, as he darted this sarcasm, he looked towards Robespierre, who turned pale. "They did not always sit in the tribune," continued Brissot, "they were at their posts in the camp." Here a sneering laugh ran round the Girondist benches, for under that sarcasm there was an accusation couched against Robespierre's cowardice in abandoning his post at the moment of danger. "I will not imitate my adversaries," Brissot added; "I will not repeat rumors of their being paid from the civil list." This again was a sarcastic allusion to the report that Robespierre had been gained over to oppose the war.

When Brissot left the tribune, Guadet rushed to it, and told them to be on their guard "against empirical oracles, who have perpetually in their mouths the words liberty, tyranny, conspiracy; always mingle their own praises with the flatteries which they address to the people. Do justice to such men!" The allusion here was too plain; and Fréron exclaimed, "Order, order! no insult, no sarcasm!"

The gallery resounded with applause and hooting.

"I am called a villain," continued Guadet, "and yet I am not allowed to denounce a man who invariably thrusts his pride before the public welfare—a man who, incessantly talking of patriotism, abandons the post to which he was called. Yes, I denounce to you a man who has become the idol of the people." Here the voice of Guadet was drowned in the uproar.

Robespierre rose, and himself requested silence for his accuser. Guadet, frightened or softened by Robespierre's feigned generosity, said, "I denounce a man whose love of his country ought, perhaps, to impose upon him the law of ostracism; for to remove him from their idolatry, would be to serve the people." Peals of laughter followed these words.

Robespierre, with studied calmness, ascended the tribune; his brow grew bright at the smiles and applause of the Jacobins.

"I am invited," said he, "to ostracise myself. There would be some excess of vanity in me to condemn myself, for ostracism is the punishment of great men, and it is only for M. Brissot to name them. I am reproached for being incessantly in the tribune. Ah! let liberty be secured; let equality be confirmed; let the *intrigants* [a name invented by Robespierre to designate the Girondists] disappear; and you will see me as anxious to fly from this tribune as you now see me anxious to be in it. Then, indeed, my dearest wishes will be fulfilled. Happy in public felicity, I shall pass my peaceful days in the delights of a sweet and obscure privacy."

I believe this to have been no vain boast. I believe that Robespierre really meant to retire into privacy, though I do not believe he ever would have done so had the opportunity presented itself. His intense ambition would have prevented him; but we have no reason to suppose that he was not sincere in what he said.

He postponed his answer till a following sitting, when he thus spoke:—

" A pupil of Jean Jacques Rousseau, his doctrines have given me his own feelings towards the people. The spectacle of the great Assemblies in the first days of our revolution filled me with hope. Soon I understood the difference between limited Assemblies, composed of intriguers and egotists, and the nation itself. My voice was stifled there; but I would rather have excited murmurs from the enemies of truth, than have obtained disgraceful plaudits. I carried my glance beyond this Assembly, and my aim was to make myself heard by the nation and the whole human race. It is for this that I have so occupied the tribune. I have done more, I have given Brissot and Condorcet to France. These great philosophers have unquestionably ridiculed and combated the priests; but they have not less courted kings and nobles, out of whom they have made a pretty good thing. (Laughter.) You do not forget with what ferocity they persecuted the genius of liberty in Jean Jacques Rousseau, the only philosopher who, in my opinion, has deserved the public honors lavished on so many political charlatans and so many despicable heroes. Brissot, at any rate, ought to be grateful to me. Where was he when I was defending the Jacobins against the Constituent Assembly itself? But for what I did at that epoch, you would have not insulted me in this tribune; for it would not have existed. I the corrupter, the agitator, the tribune of the people! Nothing of the kind. *I am of the people myself.* You reproach me for having relinquished my place as Public Accuser. I relinquished it when I saw that it gave me only the right of accusing citizens for civil offences, and deprived me of the right of accusing political enemies. And it is for this that the people love me. And you wish me to condemn myself to ostracism, to withdraw myself from its confidence. Exile! How dare you propose it to me? Whither would you have me retire? What tyrant would give me a home?—Ah! we may abandon a happy, free, and triumphant country; but a country menaced, torn, oppressed, we do not fly from, we save, or die for it! Heaven, which gave me a soul burning for liberty, and gave me for birth-place a country under the dominion of tyrants—Heaven, which placed my life in the midst of the reign of factions and crimes, perhaps calls me to trace with my blood the road to happiness, and the liberty of mankind! Do you require from me any other sacrifice? *That of my reputation? Take it. I only wished for reputation to do good to my fellow-creatures; if, to preserve it, it be necessary to betray by a cowardly silence the cause of the truth and the cause of the people—take it, defile it. I will no longer defend it.* Having defended myself, I might attack you. I will not; I offer you peace. I forget your insults; I put up with your outrages; but on condition that you combat with me the factions which disturb our country, and, the most dangerous of all, that of Lafayette: this pseudo-hero, who, present at the revolution of the New World, has only exerted himself in arresting the progress of liberty in the Old World. You, Brissot, did not you agree with me that he was the assassin of the people, that the massacre of the Champ de Mars had caused the revolution to retrograde for twenty years? Is this man less redoubtable because he is at this time at the head of the army? No. Hasten then! *Let the sword of the laws move horizontally to strike at all the heads of great conspirators.* The news which arrives from the army is sinister. It already sows division amongst the national guards and the troops of the line; the blood of citizens has flowed at Metz; the best patriots are imprisoned at Strasbourg. I tell you, you are accused of all these evils: wipe out these suspicions by uniting with us, and let us be reconciled for the safety of the country."

This speech excited tremendous enthusiasm. The journals, according to their politics, took up the quarrel. The Quarterly Reviewer justly regards this quarrel as important in the history of Robespierre: "It proves that he could be no ordinary man, who, in a private station, was an object of alarm to the supreme authority, and was powerful enough to meet and to defeat single-handed the most eloquent and influential of the rulers of the state."

On the 26th of March previously, Guadet had attacked Robespierre for attributing their salvation to Providence. "I confess," he said, "that, attaching no sort of sense to this expression, I never should have thought that a man who has labored with such courage for three years to emancipate the people from the slavery of despotism, would ever have concurred in placing the people under the slavery of superstition."

It is to be remembered, that all religion, in those days, was stigmatized as superstition. "Superstition," replied Robespierre, "it is true, is one of the supports of despotism; but it is not leading mankind into superstition to pronounce the name of the divinity. I detest, as much as any one, all those impious sects who spread themselves abroad through the universe to favor ambition, fanaticism, and all the passions; clothing themselves in the sacred name of the Eternal who has created nature and humanity; but I am far from confounding religion with this. I maintain those eternal principles upon which human weakness rests itself as the basis of virtue. It is no vain language in my mouth, any more than in those of the most illustrious men who all believed in the existence of God." (Here many voices cried, "To the order of the day," and began shouting.) "No, messieurs," continued Robespierre, "you shall not stifle my voice; there is no order of the day that can stifle this truth. I shall continue to develop those principles which are rooted in my soul, and which are avowed by all defenders of liberty. I do not intend to enter here upon a religious discussion; but I must justify everything which is connected with the address presented to this society. To invoke Providence, as the expression of the idea of a supreme being who essentially influences the destiny of nations—who seems to me to watch with a peculiar love over the French revolution—that is not too bold, for it is the sentiment of my heart: a sentiment necessary to me, who, in the Constituent Assembly, surrounded by every passion and by vile intrigues—environed by so many enemies—have always sustained myself alone. How could I be equal to struggles which are above human strength if I had not elevated my soul to God? This divine sentiment has been a full compensation to me for all the advantages offered to those who have betrayed the people."

Surely this is very powerful!

"I name *Providence,*" he added, "that which others, perhaps, would prefer to call *chance;* but this word Providence accords better with my sentiments."

On the 30th, during the second reading of Robespierre's address, some one insulted him. A violent tumult ensued. Profiting by the first moment of tranquillity, Robespierre announced that he could not bear to see the Assembly so troubled on his account, and therefore he would withdraw his project; having in his hands, he said, other means of producing upon the public mind the good effect which he expected to result from it. He alluded to his *Defenseur de la Constitution;* a journal which he shortly afterwards published. From the prospectus of this journal I cannot resist selecting one passage. "It is not necessary for me to say that love of justice and of truth alone will direct my pen. It is only on this condition that, leaving the tribune of the French senate, I can mount that of the Universe, and speak, not to an assembly, which may be agitated by diverse interests, but to the human race." Tom Brown, Dr. Johnson's schoolmaster, published a spelling-book, which he dedicated to the Universe; and this idea of a man mounting the tribune of the

Universe, is not less ridiculous, and is a type of the rhodomontade every day then uttered.

Lafayette had for a long while entirely lost his popularity with the Jacobins. He was a chivalrous republican; but he never forgot that he was a noble. He wished for a republic; but he dreaded the mob.

Robespierre denounced him in a violent speech at the Jacobins, in which the perpetually recurring name of Lafayette had terrible effect. "Wherever there are enemies of liberty," he said, "Lafayette is the most dangerous of all; because he still preserves a mask of patriotism sufficient to retain under his banners a considerable number of citizens." And at the end of his speech, he demanded that the busts of Lafayette and Bailly should be destroyed.

We have seen Robespierre standing against the whole Jacobin Club on the question of war; we are now to see him boldly standing out against the Red Cap of Liberty, which, as a symbol of extreme opinion, was worn by the demagogues to flatter the people. From its first appearance it had been a subject of dispute amongst the Jacobins. Only the *Exaltés* wore it.

Robespierre had never worn this cap; and absolutely made a speech against it. "I respect every image of liberty, but we have a symbol which recalls our oath to live free or to die; here it is." He drew out the cockade. "Those citizens, who have worn the red cap out of a praiseworthy patriotism, will lose nothing by laying it aside. The friends of the revolution will continue to recognize each other by the tokens of virtue and reason; these emblems belong to us alone; all others may be imitated by aristocrats and traitors."

The *bonnet rouge* instantly disappeared from the Assembly; but not even the voice of Robespierre, nor the resolutions of the Jacobins, could arrest the enthusiasm which had placed this sign on every head; and the evening of the day on which it was rejected at the Jacobins, it was inaugurated at the theatres. The cap and pike became the symbol and weapon of the citizen soldier.

Robespierre rather strengthened than lessened his popularity by this opposition. The people felt that he was speaking on their side, and for their interests. In one of his speeches there is a very remarkable vindication of the people:—

"The mass of the nation," he says, " is good and worthy of liberty; its real wish is always the wish of justice and the expression of general interest. A particular corporation may be corrupted, however imposing the name which decorated it, as you may poison stagnant water; but you cannot corrupt the whole nation, for the same reason that you cannot poison the ocean. The people, that immense and laborious class, the people, I say, are not open to those causes of depravation which affect the so called superior classes. The interest of the weak is justice. It is for them that humane and impartial laws are a necessary safeguard. The people know neither idleness nor ambition, which are the two most fruitful sources of our evils and our vices. The people are nearer to nature and less depraved, precisely because they have not received that false education which, under despotic governments, is a perpetual lesson of falsehood, of baseness, and of servitude. Compare courtiers with artisans, who in this respect are found at the two extremes of the scale. Witness our whole revolution, every epoch of which is marked by the courage, by the disinterestedness, by the moderation, and by the generosity of the people; and by the cowardice, by the treachery, by the perjury, and by the venality of those who would raise themselves above them. Vile egotists and infamous conspirators feign to believe nothing of the kind. They obstinately continue to calumniate the people, and to degrade them. Not content with having enriched themselves by their spoils, they look upon that day as a fortunate one in which they may bathe themselves in the blood of the people. They assemble the satellites of foreign tyrants against the people; they render divine honors to assassins; they have on their side power, treasures, force, arms; the people has only its misery and celestial justice! It is this great cause we have to plead before the face of the universe!"

In the same speech he said, "Our enemies pretend that we

only agitate abstract questions and vain systems of politics; as if the first principles of morality and the dearest interests of the people were nothing but absurd chimeras, and frivolous subjects of dispute." A man who could speak in this way, and whose life did not belie his words, might brave the people with impunity.

On the 18th of June, a letter was read, addressed to the Assembly, by Lafayette, in which he calls upon the Assembly to put down the Jacobins. "Can you conceal from yourselves," he says, "that a faction, and to avoid all vague denominations, let me name it the Jacobin faction, has caused all the present disorders. It is that which I openly accuse. Organized as an empire apart in the metropolis, and in its affiliations blindly directed by some ambitious chiefs, this sect forms a distinct corporation in the midst of the French people; and usurps all the powers by the subjugation of the representatives of the people."

The letter produced great excitement in the Assembly; and at the very moment in which they were discussing it in the Assembly, in the clubs, and in the journals, Robespierre, in his *Defenseur de la Constitution*, published an article, in which he judged with greater bitterness and force than before, the political life of the general. This coincidence gave an extreme importance to the sixth number of his paper. In the seventh, Robespierre replied directly to the letter; discussing it phrase by phrase. It would occupy too much space to insert these articles, and they have now no other importance than that of showing the fierceness and bitterness with which he regarded Lafayette.

On the 20th of June, an enormous body organized by the Girondists came to overawe the Assembly, declaring they were resolved to avail themselves of the means of resistance in their power which were recognized in the declaration of rights. They presented a petition, which said, "The people are determined to resist oppression. Let the small minority of your body which does not participate in these sentiments retire to Coblentz. Examine the causes of our suffering; if they proceed from the royal authority, let it be annihilated. The executive power is at variance with you; the popular ministers have been dismissed. Does, then, the happiness of a people depend on the caprice of a sovereign? Should that sovereign have any other law than the will of the people? We complain of the inactivity of our armies; we call upon you to investigate its causes. If it arises from the executive power, let it be instantly annihilated." The Assembly, overawed, received the petition with indulgence, and permitted the mob to defile before them. Thirty thousand men, women, and children, in squalid attire, immediately passed through the hall, uttering various cries, and displaying seditious banners; shaking pikes and olive branches above their heads; dancing, and singing the "*Ca ira.*" They broke into the palace and into the royal apartments. The King appeared with a serene air, and those in front, overawed by the dignity of his presence, made an involuntary pause: there was still some divinity which hedged a King! The pause was not long; pressed on by the crowd behind, those in advance soon surrounded the Monarch. With difficulty his attendants withdrew him into the embrasure of a window; there, seated on a chair placed upon a table, surrounded by a few national guards, who kept off the unruly populace, he remained calm, while the crowd rolled on through the other rooms of the palace. Louis wanted moral courage, wanted decision; but he did not want firmness, or that sort of physical bravery which keeps men calm in the hour of danger. To the reiterated demand that he should give his assent to the decrees against the priests, and sanction the establishment of a camp near Paris, or die on the spot, he replied, "This is neither the time nor the way to obtain it of me:" an answer at once firm and mild. A drunken workman handed him the *bonnet rouge;* he quietly put on the revolutionary emblem and wore it as a crown for three hours. Another presented him with a cup of water: although he had long suspected an intention to poison him, he drank it off in the midst of the applause of the multitude. One of the national guard approached him to assure him of his devotion. "Feel," he said, placing the hand of the guard upon his bosom, "whether this is the beating of a heart agitated by fear."

At last the mob was persuaded to depart. By eight o'clock in the evening it had dispersed. Silence and astonishment reigned in the palace. The Queen suffered greatly throughout the day. The Princess Royal was weeping at the side of the Queen; but the infant Dauphin, in the innocence of childhood, smiled upon those who surrounded him, and willingly put on an enormous red cap handed to him by a ferocious pikeman.

France was very indignant. Lafayette urged the King to throw himself into the arms of the constitutional forces; the national guard offered to form a corps to defend his person; but the King declined all these offers. Expecting deliverance from the allied powers, he was unwilling openly to join the constitutional party.

It was time for the republicans to bestir themselves, and from this day, until the 14th of July, they did nothing but agitate. The cry of "The country is in danger!" everywhere resounded. The inaction of the armies, the alarm on the frontiers, and the more than equivocal attitude of Lafayette, deeply agitated the patriots.

Robespierre continued to hold himself at a distance. He was afraid of compromising himself. He confined himself to abstract views of public welfare. To watch and announce to the people every danger, was the object of his care. His popularity was high, but it was calm; he shunned the turbulent renown which might endanger his head. He seldom or never took the initiative; he was not the originator of violence, but always waited until violence had attained its object; he then came forward to profit by it, and to direct it. In his *Defenseur de la Constitution* of the 5th of July, he again attacked Lafayette. His style, usually heavy, is here so sharp and incisive, so unlike the verbiage of his early writings, that every one curious in such matters should carefully read the whole article. It will show what may be attained by force of study, even when nature has not gifted a writer with the qualities which at once lead to excellence in style; and will support Quintillian's remark, "*Neque solida atque robusta fuerit unquam eloquentia, nisi multo stilo vires acceperit.*" It will also give an idea of Robespierre's excellences when he was excellent. I cannot insert here the original, and to translate it would obviously be to frustrate the very object of citation, as the *style* alone merits attention.

Meanwhile, everything was preparing in the departments to send 20,000 troops to Paris. On the 17th of July a deputation from the *Fédérés* presented itself at the bar of the Assembly, and there read an energetic address, demanding signal punishment on the traitor Lafayette, demanding, also, that the executive power of the King should be provisionally suspended. This address was written by Robespierre, and is to be found in the tenth number of his *Defenseur*.

Barbaroux, at the instigation of Madame Roland, had summoned a troop of desperate Marseillais. In this body of 1200 or 1500 men were Genovese, Ligurians, Corsicans, and Piedmontese, banished from their country and recruited on the shores of the Mediterranean. The majority were sailors, soldiers, and brigands. They were commanded by Barbaroux and Isnard. These children of the south, rendered fanatic by the eloquence of the clubs, marched on through the population of central France, everywhere fêted, applauded, greeted with enthusiasm at the patriotic banquets which saluted them on their march. Their pretext was to fraternize at the federation of the 14th of July; their real motive was to intimidate the national guard, to arouse the courage of the faubourgs, and to be the vanguard of that army of 20,000 men which the Girondists had decreed as a means of controlling the Feuillants, the King, and the Assembly. Their bronzed faces, their warlike aspect, their garments covered with the dust of the roads, their Phrygian caps, their strange weapons, and the green branches which shaded their faces, all forcibly struck the imagination of the multitude. They sang, as they marched, that terrible song of the Marseillais—

> "Allons, enfants de la patrie,
> Le jour de gloire est arrivé!
> Contre nous, de la tyrannie
> L' étendard sanglant est levé!"

The regular tramp of thousands of men marching made the soil resound; mingled with this sound were the plaintive voices of women, the cries of children, the neighing of horses, and the tremendous chorus of

> "Aux armes, citoyens! formez vos bataillons!
> Marchons! qu'un sang impur abreuve nos sillons!"

The arrival of the Marseillais in Paris was to be the signal of action to both parties. These men were to form the central body of the insurrection. Madame Roland was the spirit, Pétion the instrument, Barbaroux, Danton, and Santerre, the ringleaders.

"Liberty is lost," said Roland, "if we do not strike the blow. In six weeks the Austrians will be at Paris."

On the 29th July the Marseillais arrived at Charenton; Barbaroux, Bourdon, Merlin, Santerre, went to join them at a fraternal banquet. At the conclusion of the banquet the conspirators retired to a house in the village. There were present Santerre, Danton, Fabre D'Eglantine, Panis, Gonchon, Marat, Camille Desmoulins L'Enfant, and Barbaroux. It was midnight when they reached this lonely house, their brains still excited by patriotic fervor and the fumes of wine. The day had been intensely hot. About ten a thunder-storm burst forth; the rain and hail poured down, and the lightning glared incessantly for some hours. It killed two sentries in their boxes. While the thunder roared, and the lightning flashed, the conspirators fiercely deliberated on the destruction of monarchy. It was felt that Robespierre was necessary to the scheme. His name would have been a watchword to so many of the conspirators, that we are not to be surprised if it was used by them even without his sanction. That he really had no share in the conspiracy is beyond a doubt. Barbaroux and Rebecqui allowed themselves to be taken to his lodgings. Panis and Fréron, two of his friends, were the introducers. They wished to see Robespierre at the head of the movement. But the austere and cautious Robespierre held back, and only uttered general reflections on the progress of the revolution. A crisis was at hand, he admitted, and he spoke of the necessity of some one chief in whom the control should be confided. The fiery Barbaroux and Rebecqui indignantly rejected such an idea; they saw in it the prompting of Robespierre's presumptuous ambition. "I want neither a King nor a dictator," said Rebecqui, with energy; and with this they departed. Panis followed them, and endeavored to explain: "You have misunderstood him. It is only a temporary and insurrectional authority he alludes to; a power to guide and save the people, not a dictatorship. Robespierre is the man of the people."

Here the overtures to Robespierre ended. He participated neither in the plans nor in the execution of the insurrection, which began on the 9th of August, at midnight, when the tocsin was sounded and the générale beaten in every quarter of the city.

On the 10th it broke out with terrible fury. The mob stormed the palace, and after a murderous combat, massacred the Swiss in the Place du Carrousel. The 10th of August became one more bloody day in the red annals of French history.

One curious anecdote recorded by Alison is worth repeating here. While the Swiss were being massacred, some of them climbed up the marble monuments which adorned the gardens of the Tuileries. The insurgents abstained from firing, lest they should injure the statuary, but pricked them with their bayonets till they fell down, and then murdered them. "An instance of taste for art," Alison remarks, "mingled with revolutionary cruelty, perhaps unparalleled in the history of the world."*

---

* The 10th of August was disgraced, not only by its massacre of the Swiss, but by horrible acts of individual cruelty. "Fiends, in the form of women, were here, as ever in the revolution," says Alison, "foremost in deeds of cruelty." In the fearful insurrection of June, 1848, the women also proved themselves to be the children of 1792.

CHAPTER XVI.

Robespierre after the 10th of August—His flattery of the mob—Appointed President of the Revolutionary Tribunal, but resigns—The Septembrizers: did Robespierre participate in these massacres?—Visit of St. Just to Robespierre on the night of the 2d of September—Robespierre's denial of any participation: his impudent hypocrisy—He is again accused of aspiring to the dictatorship—Marat defends him—Louvet's attack—Robespierre's reply—His Lettres à ses Commettans—His feeling towards the clergy and defence of their interests.

The 10th of August closed with the dethronement of the King, and the formation of the National Convention. Robespierre, who had kept aloof alike from friends and foes during the combat, now appeared at the council of the commune. He was there cheered by his disciples as the statesman of the crisis.

During the trying days which followed, the King displayed much firmness. On the 13th the royal family were conveyed to the Temple.

Robespierre wrote, in the twelfth and last number of his *Defenseur de la Constitution*, a long and violent article on the events of the 10th of August, in which he spoke of that day as one of the most glorious in the annals of the world. Lafayette, the King, the court, and the aristocrats, had, according to him, been guilty of a mass of crimes, of which the terrible commentary was that imposing formula proclaimed by the National Assembly, "The country is in danger." "The whole people of France," he says, "so long degraded and oppressed, felt that the moment was arrived to fulfil that sacred duty imposed by nature upon all living beings, and more especially upon all nations, that, namely, of providing for their own safety by a generous resistance to oppression. The formidable preparations of a new St. Bartholomew had for some time been made in Paris and in the Tuileries."

There is something quite ludicrous in thus characterizing the feeble efforts which the court made at resistance as preparations for a massacre of the people; but it is quite in the style of the writing and oratory of that day.

He does not impute the slaughter of the people to the Swiss; it was, he says, the execrable artifices of their chiefs, the aristocrats and courtiers, who urged them on! He speaks of the massacre of the Swiss in this style:—

"A great many of them were immolated to the manes of those defenders of liberty who had perished beneath the blows of tyranny." This is the way in which rhetoric gilds a frightful massacre! "Whose hand," he asks, "was it which plunged the poniard in the hearts of patriots? It was the hand of tyrants who have oppressed some, betrayed others, corrupted and misled the rest. In the miseries of mankind you may always see the crimes of despotism!"

He then welcomes the National Convention which is to set all right. He wishes, indeed, that the mode of election had been simpler, and more favorable to the rights of the people; but at any rate the National Convention will be a popular assembly, and he welcomes it.

"Thus," he says, "has commenced the most glorious revolution which has honored humanity. Let us go further and say, the only one which has had an object worthy of man: that of founding political societies on the immortal principles of equality, of justice, and of reason. What other objects could have united in one moment this immense people—these innumerable multitudes of citizens of all conditions—making them act in concert without chiefs, without watchwords? What other cause could have inspired that sublime and patient courage, and have given birth to miracles of heroism superior to all which history has related of Greece and of Rome?"

After this flattery, he thus apostrophizes his countrymen:—
"Frenchmen! do not forget that you *hold in your hands the destinies of the universe!*" After a narration of several touching incidents during the insurrection, incidents all redounding to the

honor and glory of the people, he concludes by saying: "How great were the people in all their actions! Those who had found furniture and money in the palace abstained from appropriating this booty taken from the enemy; they came and placed it at the feet of the National Assembly, and would have regarded as robbery any exercise of the right of conquest. They pushed that sentiment of delicacy even to excess. They immolated those among them who had thought themselves permitted to appropriate what had belonged to tyrants. They were cruel in believing themselves just.

"Great gods! the people punish amongst themselves even the appearance of crime; and all the tyrants who have caused their slaughter escape from punishment! Rich egotists, stupid vampires fattened by blood and rapine, dare you then again call the people brigands? Dare you affect insolent fears for your miserable goods purchased by baseness? Dare you remount to the source of your wealth, namely, the misery of your fellows? Behold on one side their disinterestedness and honorable poverty; and on the other your vices and your opulence, and say who are the brigands and wretches! Miserable hypocrites, keep your riches which stand in lieu of spirit and of virtue; but leave to others liberty and honor!

"No; they have sworn an immortal hatred to reason, to equality! When the people appear, they hide themselves. When the people retire, they conspire. Even now they renew their calumnies and their intrigues. Citizens, you will only have peace by keeping your eyes open to all their treacheries, and your hand raised against all traitors."

Not only in his paper did he assail the vanquished, but as the orator of a deputation from the commune he appeared before the Assembly to demand vengeance on the *culprits* of the 10th of August; among whom he designated Lafayette by name. He demanded that a tribunal should be formed to judge them. "The people," he said, "must have a government worthy of them. They must have new judges created for the circumstances; for if you restore the old judges, you will only re-establish the chaos which has nearly ruined the nation. The people environ you with their confidence; preserve that confidence, and do not repel the glory of saving liberty. The people repose, but they do not sleep; they demand the punishment of the guilty, and they are right!"

A tribunal was formed; the first model of the court afterwards so well known under the name of the Revolutionary Tribunal. It was appointed, constituted, and completed in a few days. The forty sections of Paris met and chose the judges, accusers, and juries. Robespierre was appointed one of the judges. He was also named president; but the papers, at the same time that they announced his appointment, announced also his resignation. This gave rise to a great deal of discussion; whereupon Robespierre addressed the following letter to the *Moniteur*, which was inserted in the number of the 28th of August:—

"Certain persons having thrown some doubts upon my refusal of the presidency of the tribunal destined to judge the conspirators, I owe the public an explanation of my motives.

"From the beginning of the revolution I have combated the greater portion of these criminals of *Lèse-nation;* I have denounced the greater part of them; I have predicted all their attempts, even when the people believed in their patriotism. I could not be the judge of those of whom I had been the adversary; and I was forced to recollect, that if they had been the enemies of my country, they had also declared themselves the enemies of my person. One maxim, good under all circumstances, is peculiarly applicable to the present, that the justice of the people ought to bear a character worthy of it: it should be as imposing as it is prompt and terrible.

"The exercise of these new functions, being incompatible with those of a representative of the commune, which had been confided to me, I was forced to take a choice. I remained at the post where I was, convinced that it was there I could best serve my country."

The revolutionary tribunal displayed extraordinary activity. The first victim was D'Angremont, who was accused of being an agent of the court, and was executed on the Place du Carrousel on the 24th. He was the first of the many victims who suffered by the guillotine. Daily executions of royalists delighted the people; but the guillotine, though active, was too slow; and Danton and the municipality of Paris conceived a more wholesale method.

"My advice," said Danton, "is, that, to paralyze our enemies, we must strike terror into the royalists." The *Comité* but too well understood these ominous words. He wished to impress the enemy with a sense of the energy of the Republic, and to engage the multitude in such sanguinary measures as, by rendering retreat impossible, gave them no chance of safety but in victory; and in September the massacres were organized!

I need not narrate that ghastly and too famous episode of the French Revolution. It has written itself in terrible characters of blood on the page of history, to the ineffaceable disgrace of France. But as Robespierre has constantly been accused of having participated in it, I feel bound to rescue him from that infamy.

His conduct was the same as on the 10th of August; he did not *act*, he *remonstrated;* and when once accomplished, he accepted it as a new step taken by the revolution, impossible to be retracted.

Up to the 2d of September, the day of the massacre, he was associated with the directors of the commune, and the directors of Paris at the Hôtel de Ville; but the day on which Danton and Marat organized their scheme, Robespierre, either from timidity, or perhaps from horror, ceased to appear at the commune, and from that day no longer attended there.

On the day of the first meeting of the Convention he was still the "incorruptible." The commune itself, not altogether implicated in the September massacres, gloried in Robespierre, and his authority there was supreme. It seems to me that when Daunou,[*] speaking of the September massacres, says that Robespierre sought with a smile on his face among the list of victims for the names of his personal enemies, he is merely writing from a general feeling of prejudice and hatred. He has no shadow of authority for that frightful phrase.

The editors of the "Histoire Parliamentaire," who have ex-

---

[*] Fragment of his *Hist. de la Convention.*

amined this subject with their usual care and impartiality, declare, that "The historians have almost unanimously, and as a matter of habit, always written at the same time the names of Danton, Robespierre, and Marat, with respect to all revolutionary measures, and have inculpated Robespierre without any proof." The editors themselves completely absolve him. "We would observe," they say, "in the first place, that he had before refused to become a member of the tribunal of the 17th of August, and that he had exposed himself to strange calumnies simply from the respect for that principle of right which says that the same man ought not to be a denouncer, an accuser, and a judge. We will add that, with his immense reputation for integrity, it is not doubtful that he would have been a member of the *comité de surveillance* if he had wished it, if he had not testified his repugnance to enter it. Now his name is never amongst those who successively composed that tribunal. He remained one of the two hundred and eighty-eight members of the commune without title, and without exercising any other functions than those of orator at the bar of the Assembly. These reasons are more than sufficient.

"It is true that in the month of August the *Moniteur* announces that Panis, Collot-d'Herbois, Barrière, and Robespierre, formed the council of the ministry of justice; but it does not appear that that council was ever assembled, nor that Danton consulted it upon anything. Thus, when Danton came to the legislative assembly, and to the commune, to provoke those great measures, he presented himself alone; he spoke in his own name, and never, in his subsequent discourses, did he attempt to diminish the responsibility which fell entirely upon himself."

A fact, also, recently revealed by a mutual friend of Robespierre and Saint Just, entirely exonerates the former. Robespierre and Saint Just lived together in the intimacy of master and disciple. On the 2d of September, at eleven o'clock at night, they left the Jacobins together, exhausted by the fatigue of the day. Saint Just resided in a furnished apartment in the Rue St. Anne, not far from the house of Duplay. The two friends arrived at the lodging, discussing the events of the day, and the menacing aspect of the morrow. Robespierre accompanied Saint Just to his chamber, there to prolong the conversation. Saint Just, however, took off his clothes and prepared for bed.

"What are you doing?" asked Robespierre.

"Going to bed," replied Saint Just.

"What! can you sleep on a night like this? Do you not hear the tocsin? Know you not that to-night will perhaps be the last of thousands, who, living men at the moment you fall asleep, will be lifeless corpses ere you awake?"

"Alas," replied Saint Just, "I know there will be massacres to-night: I deplore it: would that I were powerful enough to moderate these convulsions of a society, struggling between life and death; but what am I? And after all, *those who perish to-night are not the friends of our ideas.* Adieu." And with these words the young fanatic turned aside to sleep. The men who were to fall were not the friends of his ideas! That removed them from the sphere of pity; that shut his heart against them. He could sleep calmly, knowing men were to be massacred because they held opinions different from himself! Robespierre was not quite so fierce a fanatic as this. He passed the night in gloom and agitation. The next morning, as day dawned, Saint Just awoke, and beheld him pacing with hasty steps up and down the room, occasionally stopping to look out of the window, or to listen to the various noises in the streets.

"And what has brought you back so early?" said Saint Just.

"What brings me back?" replied Robespierre; "do you think, then, that I have *returned?*"

"What! have you been to sleep?" asked Saint Just.

"Sleep!" exclaimed Robespierre, "sleep! whilst hundreds massacre thousands; whilst the pure or impure blood of victims runs like water down the streets? Oh, no," he added with a sardonic smile, "I have not gone to bed; I have watched like a remorse or a crime. I have had the weakness not to sleep; *but, Danton, he has slept.*"*

The author of the article Robespierre in the " Biographie des

Contemporains," relates from personal knowledge, that on first hearing the blood was flowing in torrents in the prisons, Robespierre hastened to Danton, accompanied by Pétion and a third person, from whom the writer gets his information, and there, with the accent of consternation and terror, he loudly urged Danton to employ his authority with the Parisian populace, and to arrest the course of murder, with which a few wretches were to disgrace the name of patriots. Danton at first pretended his incapability of restraining them, and afterwards, showing his true feeling, and his indifference to any responsibility, "Perish my memory," he exclaimed, "and let France be saved!"

Robespierre returned home very sad, only saying, with an accent of terror and disgust, "*Qu'on est heureux d'être Danton!*"

The reader will by this time have been assured enough of my impartiality with respect to Robespierre, not to suppose that my desire to extricate him from any complicity in the September affair arises from the ordinary biographical tendency to white-wash a hero. I have looked into the matter with great care, and with a mind perfectly unbiased by any predilection for Robespierre, and my conviction is that he was innocent. The utmost that can be charged against him is, that he used none of his enormous influence with the people to arrest that horrible riot of blood and vengeance. But he was a timid man, and never ventured to oppose a riot, however he might venture to oppose an idea.

In defending himself from the charge of having participated in it, in his reply to Louvet, on the 5th of November, he says—

"Those who say that I took the slightest part in those events, are men either excessively credulous, or excessively perverse. If you demand why I did not endeavor to stay them, I will tell you." He then proceeds to explain the causes of this outbreak. They were: The fall of Longwy and Verdun, Brunswick advancing towards Paris, and the terror of the populace venting its rage upon those it considered as its worst enemies, the aristocrats! "I have been calmly told by people that the municipality should have proclaimed martial law. Martial law, indeed, on the 2d of September! Martial law at the approach of the enemy! Martial law after the 10th of August! What could magistrates oppose against the will of a determined and indignant people?" I pause to remark here on the characteristic and wilful misrepresentation which this speech exhibits; he speaks of the massacre being the act of a determined and indignant *people*. He knew very well—none better—that the people took no share in it whatever, but that a band of 200 hired ruffians did the whole work. Had martial law been proclaimed, the slaughter must have ceased at once.

There is something truly odious in the impudent hypocrisy with which he proceeds to say:

"I am assured that one innocent man perished. It has pleased some people to exaggerate the number, but even one innocent man, that, doubtless, is too much! Citizens, weep over that cruel mistake! I have wept long over it. The victim was a good citizen; he was one, therefore, of our friends. Weep, indeed, over the culpable victims who have fallen beneath the sword of popular justice; but let your grief have an end, like all human things. Let us keep some tears for calamities more touching. Weep for the hundred thousand patriots immolated by tyranny; weep for our fellow-citizens expiring beneath their burning roofs, and the sons of our fellow-citizens massacred in the cradle, or in the arms of their mothers! Have you not also brothers, children, wives, to avenge? The family of French legislators is the country; it is the whole human race—with the exception of tyrants and their accomplices."

He was loudly applauded!

No doubt, much may be said in extenuation of the horrors of September. We have need of a great effort of imagination to throw ourselves back into that period of terrible excitement, before we can in any shape pretend to judge of those events. The tocsin was sounding its dreadful boom; the tramp of an advancing army was heard within the walls of Paris. Paris and France seemed about to fall beneath a foreign yoke; and the exasperated patriots saw no other means of escape than by striking terror into the souls of their enemies.

Danton was minister of justice, carried there, as he said in one of his gigantic figures, through the breach made by the cannon, and in the midst of the terror he arose, and in a voice of thunder said :—

"Legislators, it is not the alarm cannon that you hear, it is the *pas de charge* against our enemies! To conquer them, to hurl them back, what do we need? To dare, and again to dare, and without end to dare!" (*il nous faut de l'audace, et encore de l'audace, et toujours de l'audace.*)

In moments of extremity like these, actions are not to be judged as peaceful times.*

The National Convention began its sitting, and attempts were made to crush Robespierre, by denouncing him as aspiring to the dictatorship.

On the 25th of September Barbaroux accused him by name. He narrated his interview with Robespierre, when the Marseillais came to Paris; adding, that Paris had designated Robespierre as the virtuous man who ought to be dictator.

The reports of a dictatorship had been spread partly by Robespierre's enemies, and partly by his partisans; and Marat had not only credited these reports, but really desired to place the power in one man's hands, that he might destroy all his enemies at once.

The *Moniteur*, in reporting the sitting of the 29th of October, gives an extract of a letter, addressed by Merodière to the vice-president of the second section of the Criminal Tribunal of Paris.

"I was with a member of the section of the Cordeliers Club. He said, that the revolution was not yet complete, and that the 2d of September had not done all its work, but that a new bleeding was necessary. 'We have,' he added, 'the cabal of Roland and Brissot, which we must crush.' I think it is time that we

---

* It is perfectly gratuitous in the *Quarterly Review* to assert—"We have not the slightest doubt that the massacres in September—the most atrocious crime that stains the annals of mankind—were perpetrated for the chief if not the only purpose of securing the election of Robespierre and his partisans for the city of Paris." No election could have been more secure than that of Robespierre, unaided by other engines than his own popularity.

should arrest this evil in its source, by taking severe measures against the violent. Vergniaud, Guadet, Lasource, Barbaroux, Brissot, are those who compose the Roland cabal. The Cordeliers only talk of Robespierre, and pretend that he is the only man capable of saving the country."

Robespierre replied to this; and Louvet demanded *la parole* to accuse Robespierre. Rebecqui and Barbaroux also demanded it.

"Citizens," said Robespierre, "in mounting this tribune to reply to the accusation raised against me, it is not my cause, but the public cause I come to defend. When I justify myself you will not believe that I care for self, but for the country. Citizen," continued he, apostrophizing Rebecqui— "citizen, you have had the courage to accuse me of desiring to enslave my country, in the face of the representatives of the people, in the very place where I have defended it—I thank you! I see in this the civism which characterizes the city (Marseilles) for which you are a deputy. I thank you! for we shall all gain by this accusation. I have been called the chief of a party which is held up to the hatred of all France as aspiring to tyranny. There are men who would sink under the weight of such an accusation. I do not fear such a misfortune—thanks to what I have been able to effect for liberty: it is I who for three years have combated every faction in the assembly; it is I who have combated the court, disdained its presents, despised the caresses of a more seductive party, which at a later period rose to oppress liberty."

The Assembly, annoyed by this panegyric of himself, interrupted him several times, and called him to the question. Robespierre implored silence, and recalled his services in the revolution. "But there," he added, "commenced my crimes, for a man who has wrestled long against all parties, with inflexible courage, without assuring any party to himself, must become an object of hatred and persecution to all the ambitious."

"Robespierre," they cried out from all sides, "tell us simply if you have aspired to the dictatorship or the triumvirate."

Robespierre was indignant at the narrow limits prescribed to him. The Convention murmured, and exhibited its weariness in inattention. "Be brief, be brief," they shouted from every seat.

"I will not abridge," he replied; "I recall you to your dignity."

Marat, in his turn, demanded to be heard. Cries of "Down

with Marat," and murmurs of disgust for some time closed his mouth.

"In this Assembly I have a great number of enemies," said Marat, commencing.

"All, all," exclaimed almost the whole Convention, rising from the benches.

"I have in this Assembly a great number of enemies," continued Marat. "I recall them to a sense of shame. Let them not overpower with insults and menaces a man who devotes himself to his country and their safety! Let them hear me in silence. I will not abuse their patience. This accusation can only apply to me, and I declare that my colleagues, especially Robespierre and Danton, have constantly disapproved the idea of a triumvirate, or of a dictatorship. If any one be guilty of having thrown out this idea, it is I. I call down the vengeance of the nation upon myself, but before I cause opprobrium or the sword to fall upon my head, hear me."

He then justified his life. "Am I accused of ambition? Behold and judge." He pointed to the dirty handkerchief which enveloped his head, and shook the tattered waistcoat which covered his naked breast. "Had I wished," continued he, "to affix a price on my silence, had I wished for a place, I might have been the object of court favors. Well, what has been my life? I have been shut up in subterraneous cellars. I have condemned myself to penury and every danger. The steel of twenty thousand assassins was suspended above me, and I preached truth with my head upon the block. Let those who have revived the phantom of dictatorship unite with me, and with all true patriots, in those great measures which are alone capable of assuring the happiness of the people, and for which I would sacrifice my life."

A sort of stupor succeeded this speech. On that day, Marat had outdone in audacity even Danton himself.

Such was the result of the first demonstration of the Girondins; a demonstration which had only the effect of increasing the hatred of the Jacobins, and of rendering Robespierre still more popular.

Although they failed this time, they were not discouraged; and on the 29th of October, Louvet brought forward his formidable accusation. In an energetic and eloquent speech he traced the character and actions of the man whom he denounced. He followed him to the club of the Jacobins, to the municipality, and to the electoral assembly, exhibiting him as eternally calumniating his adversaries and flattering the mob; taking advantage of the passions of a blind multitude to urge it to every excess; insulting, in its name, the majesty of the legislature, and compelling the sovereign power to issue the decrees *he* commanded, under pain of rebellion; directing, though unseen, the massacres of September, to support the usurpation of the municipality by means of terror; sending emissaries through all France to instigate the commission of similar crimes, and to induce the provinces to follow the example of Paris; incessantly occupied with his own praise, and magnifying the grandeur and power of the people, from whom he sprang.

"The glory of the 10th of August," he added, "is the work of us all; but that of the 2d of September belongs to you. Ye barbarous conspirators, it is yours, and yours only! (*A sensation of horror.*) The people of Paris knew how to fight, but not how to assassinate. They were seen in a body before the Tuileries on the glorious 10th of August; but only a few hundred assassins perpetrated the massacres of September. How many murderers were there in the prison? Not two hundred. How many spectators outside? Not twice the number. Ask Pétion, he will witness it himself. Why were they not prevented? Because Roland spoke in vain; because Danton did not speak; because Santerre, who commanded the sections, waited for orders; because the municipal officers, with their scarfs, presided at these executions; and because the Legislative Assembly was domineered over, and an insolent demagogue appeared at the bar to control its decrees."

Here a general murmur of indignation spread through the Assembly. Many members pointed with their fingers at Robespierre. Cambon stretched out his arm towards the Mountain, and exclaimed, "Wretches! behold the sentence of death to the dictator!" Voices from every side exclaimed, "Robespierre to the bar! let Robespierre be accused!" but the president restored order, and Louvet continued. Turning with sudden energy towards his enemy, he said—

"Robespierre, I accuse you of having ceaselessly calumniated the purest patriots! I accuse you of having circulated calumny during the first week of September; that is to say, at a time when calumny was death. I accuse you of having, to the best of your power, debased the character and the authority of the representatives. I accuse you of having constantly put yourself forward as an object of idolatry; of having suffered yourself to be designated, in your own presence, as the only virtuous man in France who could save the people; and of having said so yourself! I accuse you of having aspired to supreme power, as is demonstrated by the facts which I have indicated, and by your whole conduct, which will accuse you louder than I can."

During the whole of this tremendous philippic, Robespierre sat pale and agitated, his features convulsed with anger, as he saw himself abandoned even by his own colleagues. Nevertheless, the very fierceness of the attack, and the greatness of the charges brought against him, were flattering to his vanity. It was something to be so feared, it was something to be thought capable of being a dictator!

Louvet descended from the tribune amidst thunders of applause.

Had Danton or Mirabeau been in Robespierre's place, they would have risen, and by some speech of power, at once turned back the tide of reprobation upon the accuser; but Robespierre was not equal to such a task. Warned by his first defeat of the inadequacy of an extempore speech, he asked a week to prepare his defence; a delay which the Assembly granted with an indulgence too like contempt.

On the following day, Barbaroux followed up Louvet's accusation, enlarging upon the conspiracies of Robespierre. The Jacobins became alarmed for their idol, and the people assembled every evening about Robespierre's dwelling. The Girondins and aristocrats gave vent to their rejoicings, and men were heard singing in the streets—

> "La tête de Marat, Robespierre, et Danton,
> Et de tous ceux qui les défendront,
> O gué!"

On the 3d of November he was to reply. The galleries of the Convention were surrounded by members of both parties, whose gestures and language formed an exciting prelude to the combat. The president at length ordered Robespierre to the tribune. He was very pale, and whilst waiting for silence to be established, his trembling fingers struck the table of the tribune like one carelessly striking the notes of a piano forte. There was little encouragement in the Assembly. No affectionate smiles, no gestures of support: almost every look was hostile. Silence being obtained, his shrill piercing voice was heard uttering these words:

"Citizens! of what am I accused?" said he, after a brief appeal to the justice of his colleagues. "Of having aspired to the dictatorship, to the tribuneship, or the triumvirate? Such a project, it must be confessed, is more daring even than criminal; for to execute it, it was necessary first to overthrow the throne, to annihilate the legislature, and above all to prevent the formation of a National Convention. But how comes it that I was the first, in my speeches and in my writings, who called a National Convention as the only remedy for the evils of the country? To gain the dictatorship, it would be necessary first to conquer Paris and enslave the departments. Where are my treasures? Where are my armies? What are the great places with which I was provided? It rests with my accusers to show this. To make their charge in the least degree probable, they must prove me to have been completely insane. But if I was insane, how have so many men employed such eloquence and such stratagem to prove me the most dangerous of conspirators? Let us come to facts. With what am I reproached?—the friendship of Marat? But I will not betray my thoughts to flatter the reigning opinion. I had in 1792 a single interview with Marat. I reproached him with the exaggeration and violence which prejudiced the cause which he espoused. He declared, on parting from me, that he did not find in me *either the views or the audacity of a statesman.* This refutes the calumny of those who confound me with this man. I was named on the 10th of August. I am far from pretending to wrest the honor of the combat and the victory from those who sat in the commune before me on that terrible night, who armed the citizens, controlled their movements, baffled treason, and arrested Mandat, the bearer of the perfidious orders of the court. It is said there were intriguers in the council; who knows it better than I? They are amongst my enemies. When the Consul of Rome had stifled the conspiracy of Catiline, Clodius accused him of violating the laws. I have known such citizens, not like Clodius, but who, some time previous to the 10th of August, had the prudence to seek refuge out of Paris, and who, after the commune of Paris had triumphed, denounced it. Acts which are illegal! Does one save a nation by the general code? Yes, our acts were illegal; as the taking of the Bastille was illegal, as Liberty itself was illegal! Citizens, do you desire a revolution without a revolution? What is the spirit of persecution which seeks to revise, so to speak, that which has broken our fetters? And who can assign the precise point where the waves of the popular insurrection are to stop? What people at this price would ever destroy despotism?"

He then adverted to the affair of the 2d and 3d of September; but I have already given the substance of what he said on that point.

"To these terrible pictures," he continued, "my accuser has added a project, which he supposed I had, of degrading the legislative body, which was continually tormented and outraged, he says, by an insolent demagogue, who came to its bar to *control* its decrees: a figure of oratory, by which Louvet has travestied two petitions which I was charged to present to the Legislative Assembly in the name of the *Conseil Générale de la Commune*, relative to the resurrection of the department of Paris."

In replying to Louvet on the subject of his denunciation, he says: "What, then, is this horrible doctrine, which declares that to denounce a man, is the same thing as to assassinate him? Under what republic do we live, if the magistrate, who, in the municipal assembly, explains himself freely upon the authors of a dangerous plot, is only regarded as an instigator of murder?"

"Let us bury," said he, in conclusion, "these miserable machinations in eternal oblivion. Let us conceal from the sight of posterity these shameful days of our history, wherein the representatives of the people, misled by wretched intrigues, seem to have forgotten the great destinies to which they have been called. For myself, I have renounced the easy advantage of replying to the calumnies of my adversaries by denunciations still more redoubtable. I have suppressed the offensive part of my justification; I renounce the just vengeance which I should have the right of exercising upon my calumniators. I wish only for the return of peace and liberty. (*Applause.*) Citizens! advance in your brilliant career with a firm and rapid step, and may I, at the expense of my life, aye! and even of my reputation, concur with you in effecting the glory and happiness of our country."

This defence gained the victory. Loud applause followed his speech, and the Assembly decreed it should be printed. Louvet and Barbaroux, irritated at the applause, both sought to speak, but in vain. Barbaroux quitted his seat in the centre, and descended to the bar to claim that right of speech as a citizen which was denied him as a deputy. "I demand," said he, "to denounce Robespierre, and to sign my denunciation. If you will not hear me, I shall be reputed a calumniator. I will descend to the bar. I will engrave my denunciation upon marble—" but murmurs, sarcasms, and laughter drowned his voice.

The news of Robespierre's triumph was rapturously received among the crowd which had congregated around the Tuileries. On going that evening to the Jacobins, his entrance was saluted with riotous enthusiasm.

Camille Desmoulins published a journal to defend the cause of Robespierre. "I do not know," said he, "whether Robespierre should not tremble at the success he has obtained over his cowardly accusers. *What is virtue if Robespierre be not its image?* What are eloquence and talent if the speech of Robespierre be not their *chef d'œuvre?* In this speech I find all the irony of Socrates, with all the keenness of Pascal, and two or three passages equal to the finest bursts of Demosthenes."

As the charges against Robespierre are really of the vaguest kind, it may be assumed, that whatever might have been passing in the depth of his own soul, Robespierre had not, as yet, made any efforts towards dictatorship; though probably these very discussions helped to foster the idea. In defending himself against the accusation, he might well say to himself, I have not aspired to the dictatorship, but why should I not aspire? Am I not the only virtuous man in France? The only sincere Republican? The only great man? The only man worthy to be a dictator? To give greater publicity to his views, he commenced a newspaper entitled *Lettres de Maximilien Robespierre à ses Commettans*, which appeared every Friday. Characteristically enough, he says, that by his "commettans" he designated *all* Frenchmen, thus making himself the representative of France. In a long introduction, he says : " It is not enough to have overturned the throne ; we must raise upon its ruins sacred equality and the imprescriptible rights of man. A republic is not to be constituted by a vain word, but by the character of its citizens. The soul of the republic is virtue ; that is to say, love of our country : that magnanimous devotion which confounds all private interests in the general interest."

This was adroit flattery of himself, his own universal reputation of incorruptibility making the application so obvious!

In one of the sittings of the Jacobins, he indignantly repelled the idea which had been proposed, of withdrawing the government salary from the priests. It is strange that Lamartine, who, on the whole, takes so favorable a view of Robespierre's character, should charge him with cowardice and inconsistency in standing by the priests. We have seen that he has done so throughout his career. We have seen that, in the first place, he had very strong religious convictions, though not perhaps of the most orthodox kind; and we have seen him in the Assembly always advocating the real interests of the priesthood. In one of his *Lettres à ses Commettans*, he thus explains himself :

"God created all men for equality and happiness. It is He who protects the oppressed and exterminates tyrants. My religion is that of justice and humanity. I do not particularly love the power of priests. It is another chain on humanity, but it is an invisible chain, and fetters the mind. The legislator may assist reason to free itself from this chain, but not to break it. Our situation, in this respect, appears to me favorable. The empire of superstition is almost destroyed. The priest is no longer the object of veneration, but the idea of that religion which he personifies. The torch of philosophy, penetrating even to the lowest classes, has dispelled all those ridiculous phantoms which the ambition of priests and the policy of kings bade us adore. Little now remains save those eternal dogmas which are the support of all our morality, the touching and sublime doctrines of charity and equality which the son of Mary formerly taught mankind. Soon doubtless the gospel of reason and liberty will be the gospel of the universe. Belief in the Divinity is implanted in every mind; the people connect it with the religion they have hitherto professed; and to attack this belief would be to attack the morality of the nation. But remember that our revolution is based upon justice, and everything which tends to weaken morality is anti-revolutionary. Remember how careful ancient lawgivers were to preserve this element of morality. Let us throw no fresh element of discord among the people by making them believe we attack religion in attacking priests. Do not say that is not a question as to whether we shall abolish this religion, but only of not paying it; for those who believe in it, think that not to pay for it, or to suffer it to perish, is the same thing. Besides, do you not perceive that by leaving each man to find a religion for himself, you kindle the signal of discord in every town and every village? Some would wish for a religion, others would wish for none, and would thus become mutual objects of contempt and hatred."

It was well for the infidel journalists of that period to accuse Robespierre of inconsistency and cowardice; but Lamartine should not have called this " masking his weakness under a sophism." It was well for the Girondists to affect a pity for Robespierre's superstition; it served their turn to accuse him of aspiring to be the pontiff of a new religion.

"It is asked," said they, " why there are so many females at Robespierre's house, at the tribune of the Jacobins, at the Cordeliers, at the Convention? The reason is, the French revolution is a religion, and Robespierre hopes to make a sect. He is a kind of priest who has his devotees, his Marys, and his Magdalens. All his power is in a distaff. Robespierre preaches, Robespierre censures; he is furious, grave, melancholy; he thunders against the rich and great. He lives on a trifle. He has but one mission—to speak, and he talks unceasingly. He has all the characteristics of a founder of religion. He has a reputation for sanctity. He talks of God and Providence, and calls himself the support of the poor and oppressed; he is followed by women and men of weak intellect. Robespierre is a priest, and will never be anything else."

To the same effect we read a passage in Vilate's " Mystères de Dieu Dévoilés." On the occasion of Robespierre's defence, he says: "The galleries were filled with women who applauded him with transports of devotional fervor. At the conclusion of the séance, I met Rabaut de St. Etienne, who exclaimed, 'What a man is that Robespierre with all those women! He is a priest who wishes to become a god!'" Rabaut then agreed with Manuel that they should write an article against Robespierre in *La Chronique*, in which he should be painted as a priest—a designation then thought equivalent to that of charlatan!

CHAPTER XVII.

The captive king—Robespierre demands that the king be tried—The trial—The execution—Robespierre's reflections on this deed—His self-glorification—Verses against him.

FROM neighboring windows curious spectators might see, not without a touch of pity, at a certain hour Louis Capet, the dethroned king, taking his daily walk in the Temple Garden, with his queen, his sister, and his two children. "Imprisoned in that temple, he has heard strange things; the yells of September massacres; the distant war-thunders of Brunswick, dying off in disaster and discomfiture. Quietly he walks and waits, that irresolute man; his daily meals, his lessons to his son, his daily walk in the garden, his game at ombre, or draughts, fill up the day. Outside the wall there is famine, and an infuriated people lay the scarcity of grain upon his head; outside the walls there is distracted agitation, and the excited people attribute all their agitation to him. Poor discrowned king, he is looked upon as the source of all the evils which fill France with dismay; and France loudly demands that he be tried." The trial of Charles I. of England is printed, sold, and read everywhere; an "example how the people judge a tyrant, and become the first of free people, which France thinks it would be well if she were to imitate."

And Robespierre demands that the last tyrant of France, the rallying-point of all conspirators, the cause of all the troubles of the republic, should be promptly sentenced.

Gamain, the locksmith, who had worked for the king, and had constructed in the wall of a dark passage leading to his cabinet a secret closet, revealed the existence of that closet, where the king's secret papers were concealed. These papers, except the treaty of the Court with Mirabeau and others, were for the most part little but vague plans for the king's escape, and the resumption of his power. They were enough, however, to condemn him. Indeed he would have been condemned without them; so we may say no more of that matter. Robespierre's speech, demanding that the king should be tried, is remarkable for its frankness, no less than for its vehemence.

"You wander from the question," he said; "there is no *procès* here! Louis is not an accused, nor are you judges. You have no sentence to pass, but a measure of public safety—an act of national providence to exercise. (*Applause.*) What is the conduct prescribed by sound policy to cement the republic? It is to engrave deeply into all hearts a contempt for royalty, and to strike terror into the partisans of the King. To place his crime before the world as a problem, his cause as the object of the most imposing discussion that ever existed, to place an immeasurable space between the memory of what he was and the title of a citizen, is the very way to make him most dangerous to liberty. Louis XVI. was king, and the republic is established. The question is solved by this single fact. Louis is dethroned by his crimes, he conspired against the republic; either he is condemned, or the public is not acquitted. (*Applause.*) To propose the trial of Louis XVI. is to question the revolution. If he may be tried, he may be acquitted; if he may be acquitted, he may be innocent. But, if he be innocent, what becomes of the revolution? If he be innocent, what are we but his calumniators! The coalition is just; his imprisonment is a crime; all the patriots are guilty; and the great cause which for so many centuries has been debated between Crime and Virtue, between Liberty and Tyranny, is finally decided in favor of Crime and Despotism!

"Citizens, beware! you are misled by false notions. The majestic movements of a great people, the sublime impulses of virtue, present themselves as the eruption of a volcano, and as the overthrow of political society. When a nation is forced to recur to the right of insurrection, it returns to its original state. How can the tyrant appeal to the social compact? He has destroyed it! What laws replace it? Those of nature: the people's safety. The right to punish the tyrant or to dethrone him is the same thing. Insurrection is the trial of the tyrant—his sentence is his fall from power; his punishment is exacted by the liberty of the people. The people dart their thunderbolts, that is, their sentence: they do not condemn kings, they suppress them—thrust them back again into nothingness. In what republic was the right of punishing a tyrant ever deemed a question? Was Tarquin tried? What would have been said in Rome if any one had undertaken his defence? Yet we demand advocates for Louis! They hope to gain the cause; otherwise we are only acting an absurd farce in the face of Europe. (*Applause.*) And we dare to talk of a republic! Ah! we are so pitiful for oppressors because we are pitiless towards the oppressed!

"Two months since, and who would have imagined there could be a question here of the inviolability of Kings? Yet to-day a member of the National Convention, citizen Pétion, brings the question before you as though it were one for serious deliberation! O crime! O shame! The tribune of the French people has echoed the panegyric of Louis XVI. Louis combats us from the depths of his prison, and you ask if he be guilty, and if he may be treated as an enemy? Will you allow the Constitution to be invoked in his favor? If so, the Constitution condemns you; it forbids you to overturn it. Go then to the feet of the tyrant, and implore his pardon and clemency.

"But there is another difficulty—to what punishment shall we condemn him? The punishment of death is too cruel, says one. No, says another, life is more cruel still, and we must condemn him to live. Advocates! is it from pity or from cruelty, you wish to annul the punishment of crimes? *For myself I abhor the penalty of death;* I neither love nor hate Louis; I hate nothing but his crimes. I demanded the abolition of capital punishment in the Constituent Assembly, and it is not my fault if the first principles of reason have appeared moral and judicial heresies. But you who never thought this mercy should be exercised in favor of those whose offences are pardonable, by what fatality are you reminded of your humanity, to plead the cause of the greatest of criminals? You ask an exception from the punishment of death for him who alone could render it legitimate! A dethroned king in the very heart of a republic not yet cemented! A king whose very name draws foreign wars on the nation! Neither prison nor exile can make his an innocent existence. It is with regret I pronounce the fatal truth: Louis must perish rather than a hundred thousand virtuous citizens! Louis must perish, because our country must live!"

The doctrine here put forth with respect to the right of insurrection, is that used to justify our own revolution. There are times, indeed, when it would seem as if there were a law above all law; Gordian knots in human history which can only be cut with a sword, for human reason fails to unravel them. The executions of Charles I. and of Louis XVI. can be justified by no law; they were, at the best, only terrible expediencies. Clemency, no less than political philosophy, teaches us that it was a mistaken act— that, having dethroned the king, they were only staining their cause with needless blood by executing him; but in times of revolution, men are not so calm; their fears get the better of their reason; and nothing is so cruel as cowardice.

On Tuesday, the 11th of December, through drizzling rain, the king is carried to the Convention Hall. The procession wends on in silence, or amid growlings of the Marseillaise hymn; and Santerre, holding Louis's arm with his hand, leads him before the Convention. The King looks round with a composed air to see what kind of convention and parliament it is. "Strange sight for those royal eyes! It is but two years since the Constituent Assembly spread fleur-de-lys velvet for him when he came over to speak kindly to them, and they all started up, swearing fidelity; all France started up swearing, and made a glorious feast of pikes."

And Louis's trial begins. The accusation consists of fifty-seven questions, the substance of which, says Carlyle, is this:—"Louis, who wert king, art thou not guilty to a certain extent, by act and written documents, of trying to continue king?" To every question he replies with clearness and precision; denying some of the alleged crimes; showing that others were the work of his ministers; and justifying all by the powers conferred on him by the constitution. After three hours, Barrère says, "Louis, I invite you to withdraw."

On the 26th of December, he was tried. After hearing his defence, a stormy discussion arose in the Assembly.

It was all in vain. The appeal to the people was rejected by a majority of 423 to 281; and the question then arose as to what punishment should be inflicted.

"Long night," says Carlyle, "wears itself into day, morning's paleness is spread over all faces; and again the wintry shadows sink, and the dim lamps are lit; but, through day and night and the vicissitudes of hours, member after member is mounting continually those tribune-steps; pausing aloft there, in the clearer upper light, to speak his fate-word; then diving down into the dusk and throng again. Like phantoms in the hour of midnight; most spectral, pandemonical! Never did President Vergniaud, or any terrestrial president, superintend the like. A king's life, and so much else that depends thereon, hangs trembling in the balance. Man after man mounts; the buzz hushes itself till he have spoken: Death; banishment; imprisonment till the peace. Many say, death; with what cautious, well-studied phrases and paragraphs they could devise of explanation, of enforcement, of faint recommendation to mercy. Many, too, say, banishment: something short of death. The balance trembles, none can yet guess whitherward. Whereat anxious patriotism bellows, irrepressible by ushers."

Robespierre ascends the tribune, and says:

"I do not like long discourses upon obvious questions; they are a sinister presage for liberty; and they cannot supply the place of love of truth and patriotism, which render them superfluous. I cannot flatter myself that I understand the subtle distinctions, imagined for the sake of eluding the consequences of a recognized principle. All that I know is, that we are the representatives of the people, sent here to cement public liberty by the condemnation of a tyrant; and that suffices me.

"I know not how to outrage reason and justice, by regarding the life of a despot as more valuable than that of the simplest citizen; nor in torturing my mind to shield great culprits from that punishment of the law which has already been inflicted upon their accomplices. I am inflexible for oppressors, because I compassionate the oppressed. I do not understand that humanity which slaughters people, and which pardons despots. The sentiment which has made me vainly demand from the Constituent Assembly the abolition of the punishment of death, is the same which forces me to-day to demand that it should be applied to the tyrant of my country, and to royalty itself in his person. I cannot predict or imagine future or unknown tyrants, to dispense with my striking the one whom I have declared convicted. I vote for death." Others followed him; death, with or without conditions, was on most of their tongues. It was a fearful spectacle, and yet, as Carlyle says,

"If the reader fancy it of a funereal, sorrowful, or even grave character, he is far mistaken : 'the ushers in the Mountain quarter,' says Mercier, 'had become as box-keepers at the Opera;' opening and shutting of galleries for privileged persons, for 'D'Orleans Egalité's mistresses,' or other high-dizened women of condition, rustling with laces and tricolor. Gallant deputies pass and repass thitherward, treating them with ices, refreshments, and small-talk; the high-dizened heads beck responsive; some have their card and pin, pricking down the ayes and noes, as at a game of *rouge-et-noir*. Further aloft reigns Mère Duchesne, with her unrouged Amazons; she cannot be prevented making long *hahas*, when the vote is not *La Mort*. In these galleries there is refection, drinking of wine and brandy, 'as in open tavern, *en pleine tabagie.*' Betting goes on in all coffee-houses of the neighborhood. But, within doors, fatigue, impatience, uttermost weariness sits now on all visages; lighted up only from time to time by turns of the game. Members have fallen asleep; ushers come and awaken them to vote. Other members calculate whether they shall not have time to run and dine. Figures rise, like phantoms, pale in the dusky lamp-light, utter from this tribune only one word: Death. '*Tout est optique,*' says Mercier, 'the world is all an optical shadow.' Deep in the Thursday night, when the voting is done, and secretaries are summing it up, sick Duchâtel, more spectral than another, comes borne on a chair, wrapt in blankets, in 'night-gown and night-cap,' to vote for mercy: one vote, it is thought, may turn the scale.

"Ah, no! In profoundest silence, President Vergniaud, with

a voice full of sorrow, has to say: 'I declare, in the name of the Convention, that the punishment it pronounces on Louis Capet is that of death.' Death, by a small majority of fifty-three. Nay, if we deduct from the one side, and add to the other, a certain twenty-six, who said death, but coupled some faintest ineffectual surmise of mercy with it, the majority will be but *one*.

"To this conclusion hast thou come, oh hapless Louis! The son of sixty kings is to die on the scaffold by form of law.

Royalty is not only abolished, but the symbol of royalty, in the person of this unhappy Louis, is also to be abolished.

It is Monday, the 21st of January, 1793. In the Tower, through the iron bars, the day begins to dawn; there is heard the noise of drums beating in all quarters, the trampling of gendarmes' horses, and the rolling of wheels of cannon and tumbrils arriving at their stations. The poor King, calm and resigned, listens to these sounds with indifference. He yesterday took leave of his family, promising to see them to-day, but he spares them the anguish of parting. At eight o'clock the municipals enter. The King gives them his will, and prepares to depart. The carriage awaits him at the entrance of the second court; two gendarmes stand by the steps; one of these mounts first, and seats himself in front, the King gets in, followed by his confessor, the second gendarme then enters, fastens the door, and the vehicle moves on. Sixty drums are beating at the heads of the horses; a moving army, consisting of national guards, troops of the line, cavalry, and artillery, march before, behind, and on each side of the carriage. An order of the day has forbidden any citizens, not forming a portion of the armed militia, to cross the streets which lead to the Boulevards, or to show themselves at the windows on the line of the procession. The very markets are empty. The weather is foggy and chilly. Under a lowering sky in the Place de la Revolution, there is a forest of bayonets and pikes; at intervals, this double row of steel is reinforced by the detachments of infantry from the camp around Paris, with their knapsacks on their backs; cannon loaded with grape, the matches lighted, guard the main streets on the line of road; a fearful stillness reigns over the city; no man even utters his thoughts to his neighbor; the King leans back in the carriage, and is scarcely perceived; he is talking to the Abbé Edgeworth, or seeking in the Psalms such passages as are peculiarly suited to his situation. The priest prays beside him. At the Temple gate are heard some faint cries, perhaps from voices of pitiful women, exclaiming, "Grâce! grâce!" but for the rest, all is silent. As the clock strikes ten, they reach the Place de la Revolution, once called Place de Louis Quinze; there stands the guillotine. The terraces of the Tuileries, the parapets on the borders of the river, the roofs of the houses in the Rue Royale, even the leafless branches of the trees in the Champs Elysées, are filled with the countless multitude. The King descends from his carriage, and enjoining those around him to take care of the Abbé Edgeworth, he mounts the scaffold, though with some hesitation. He is dressed in a puce coat, gray breeches, and white stockings; his hair turned up beneath his hat. He strips off his coat, and the executioners approach to bind him. "Bind me!" he indignantly replies, "no, no, I will never consent. Do your business, but you shall not bind me; don't think of such a thing." The executioners insisting, raise their voices and call for help. A personal struggle is about to sully the victim, at the foot of the scaffold, when the Abbé Edgeworth says to him, "Sire, submit to this insult as the last trait of resemblance between yourself and the God who is about to recompense you."

The King raises his eyes to heaven, with an expression of resignation. "There needed nothing less than such an example to make me submit to such an indignity." Then turning round, he extends his arms towards the executioners—"Do as you will, I will drink the cup to the dregs." Turning towards the palace, where the greatest number of the populace could see and hear him, "People," he exclaims, "I die innocent of all the crimes imputed to me. I pardon those who have sentenced me, and pray to God that the blood you are about to shed may not fall on France."

A shudder runs through the crowd. The principal officer of the staff, Beaufranchet, Comte d'Ozet, son of Louis Quinze, fearing the effect of this speech, orders the drums to beat. A long loud roll drowns the voice of the King, and the murmur of the multitude. In another instant, he is fastened to the plank, and the Abbé Edgeworth, stooping, says, " Son of Saint Louis, ascend to heaven!" The axe clanks down, and a king's life is shorn away.

Samson, the executioner, raises the head, and then arises a fierce shout of "*Vive la République!*" caps are waved on the tops of bayonets, handkerchiefs are dipped in the blood; locks of the king's hair, and fractions of the puce coat, are sold; and in about an hour afterwards the whole multitude has departed. " Pastrycooks, coffee-sellers," says Carlyle, " milkmen sing out their trivial quotidian cries; the world wags on as if this were a common day. In the coffee-houses that evening, says Prudhomme, patriot shook hands with patriot in a more cordial manner than usual. Not till some days after, according to Mercier, did public men see what a grave thing it was."

Strange to say, men are not yet agreed on this murder of a king. While some look on it with unmitigated horror, and some with sad pity, there are many who can justify it on the ground of expediency. Certain it is that the republicans had no misgivings whatever; amidst the horror and consternation it inspired throughout Europe, the republicans never once reproached themselves, even in secret. " The coalized kings threaten us," said Danton, in one of his gigantic figures; " we hurl at their feet as a gage of battle the head of a king." This indeed was not altogether a figure of speech, but expresses, in its terrific energy, a thought which was in the minds of the executioners. It was the bold act with which they terrified all Europe, and committed France to a republic. After such an act, there was no alternative but a republic or a despotism.

It is curious to read Robespierre's reflections on this event, published in his "*Lettres à ses Commettans:*" " Citizens, the tyrant has fallen beneath the sword of the law; this grand act of justice has terrified the aristocracy, annihilated the superstition of royalty, and created the Republic: it gives a great character to the National Convention, and renders it worthy of the confidence of

Frenchmen. If we recall the arts which active intrigue has put in motion to save the ex-monarch, the league of all the internal enemies of our liberty, and the conspiracy of all the Courts of Europe, to intimidate, or corrupt the representatives of the French people, we shall see that the probity and *civism* of the National Convention could not have been proved in a more decided manner. The Convention has remained firm to its principles, and the genius of intrigue has succumbed before the genius of liberty and the ascendency of virtue. The imposing and majestic attitude which the Convention has exhibited must alarm all the tyrants of the earth, more than even the scaffold.

"A profound silence reigned till the moment when the head of Louis fell beneath the sword of the law; at that instant the air resounded with that unanimous and imposing cry bursting from a hundred thousand citizens, '*Vive la République;*' and it was not the barbarous curiosity of men who came to satisfy themselves at the execution of another man; it was the powerful interest of a people burning for liberty, to assure themselves that they heard the last sighs of royalty. Formerly when a king died at Versailles, the reign of his successor was immediately announced by this cry, 'The king is dead, long live the king,' as if to make the nation understand that despotism was immortal. Here a whole people, moved by sublime instinct, exclaimed '*Vive la République,*' to teach the universe that tyranny was dead with the tyrant."

I cannot without a revulsion of feeling read this word "tyrant," so uniformly coupled with the name of Louis—poor, weak, indolent, well-meaning, vacillating Louis, whose great fault really was, that he had not enough of the tyrant in him to preserve his own head, and secure the continuance of his dynasty. But it was the cant of those days to speak of every king as a tyrant, as it is the cant of our days, among a certain set of writers, to look upon all aristocrats as pampered, heartless egotists, whose greatest object in life is to oppress and degrade the people.

If there were no other doubts of Robespierre's incorruptibility —I mean moral incorruptibility—it would suffice to convict him in the eyes of any impartial judge, that he uniformly, vehemently, incessantly, and ferociously wrote and declaimed against kings, princes, nobles, and royalists, as if they were abstract ideas, not men—incarnate vices, not human beings; and he did this at a time when he was the associate and leader of such ruffians as Collot d'Herbois, Billaud Varennes, Barrère, Marat, Hébert, Momoro, *et id omne genus.* The man who, with his experience of patriots, could talk in his dithyrambic style of the virtue of patriots, and the calculated villany of the aristocracy, or indeed of every one opposed to Jacobins, must, to use a favorite phrase of his, forever remain *suspect.* We may allow some license to the language of opposition, we may allow some exaggeration in the heat of political discussion; but, as it is impossible that any man, not a madman, could ever have entertained the opinions of Robespierre, at least in that uncompromising form, we can only regard his fulminations as the unscrupulous language of polemical virulence, and the speaker as a contemptible demagogue. There can be no question that his envious soul detested superiority of all kinds; superiority of genius, of character, of virtue, no less than of rank and station. There is a curious speech of his at the Jacobins, on the 5th of December, in which he demands that Mirabeau's bust should disappear from the Temple of Liberty, and in which, in the most undisguised manner, he points himself as the only idol for a people to worship.

"We must, at the same time," he said, "consecrate a great principle too often forgotten; we must disabuse the people of their facility of offering incense to culpable idleness; we must declare that we will record honors and public esteem only to the real friends of the people, *not to those who have developed the greatest talents, but to those who have terminated their career in showing an unalterable zeal for the defence of humanity;*" in other words, they were not to worship Mirabeau, they were not to worship genius, they were to worship political consistency, they were to worship the incorruptible Maximilien Robespierre!

I will conclude this chapter with a verse from a satirical poem, published about this time by J. M. Girez, in which Robespierre's rabid denunciations, and perpetual self-glorification, are happily hit off.

> "Suivi de ses dévotes,
> De sa cour entouré,
> Le dieu des sans-culottes,
> Robespierre, est entré.
> Je vous dénonce tous! cria l'orateur blême;
> Jésus, ce sont des intrigans,
> Ils se prodiguent un encens
> Qui n'est dû qu'à moi-même."

CHAPTER XVIII.

Dissension between the Gironde and the Mountain—The date of Robespierre's election into the Revolutionary Tribunal—Meeting of Robespierre and Danton—Robespierre's doctrines—Accusation and triumph of Marat—Robespierre openly attacks the Girondins—Fall of the Gironde—Charlotte Corday: Assassination of Marat—Garat's interview with Robespierre to save the Girondins—Robespierre elected into the Comité de Salut Public—Interview with Danton, whom he promises to defend: his defence—Robespierre as a minister.

The King was dead, and Europe was in arms.

Nothing could be more perilous than the situation of the Republic. The coalition without was not more terrible than the dissension within. The Mountain had conquered the Gironde in the struggle for the King's life; and now was to commence the long struggle which ended in the ruin of the Gironde, ruined by the accusation of Moderatism. To be a Moderate was then as perilous as formerly to be a Royalist. A Republic, cost what it might, France *would* have. But the defection of Dumouriez spread alarm throughout the republican camp; and unhappily for them, the Girondins seemed to be implicated in that defection. Robespierre, in the name of the Jacobins, addressed a proclamation to the people, in which he ascribed all the reverses of the army to the Girondists. He accused them of being the instigators of pillage, which might dishonor popular doctrines, and force the wealthy proprietors and commercialists to the side of the counter-revolution. He demanded a rampart of heads between the nation and its enemies; and *first*, the heads of the Girondins.

It should be observed, with reference to this struggle, that, as far as Robespierre is concerned, the Girondins were the aggressors; they commenced the attack; and he knew that it was a struggle of life and death. If he had not taken their heads, they would have taken his. But although he played a part in the accusation of the Girondins, it was by no means a prominent part. Marat, Hébert, the Jacobin Club, the Cordeliers, were the most furious against the Girondins. Marat, in one of his fearful outbursts, exclaimed, "They call us blood-drinkers! well, let us deserve the name by drinking the blood of our enemies! The death of tyrants is the last resource of slaves. Cæsar was assassinated in the public senate; let us treat traitors in the same manner; let us stab them upon their benches, the theatre of their crimes." Another proposed that the Girondins should be assassinated in their own homes. The beastly Hébert approved of this proposal. "Death, dealt noiselessly in the night," he said, "will avenge the country, and will show the hand of the people suspended at all hours over the head of the conspirators." A plan was formed to put this proposal into execution, but it was frustrated.

Robespierre proposed the concentration of the Executive power in a Committee of Public Safety; that is to say, a Dictatorship above the Convention. Thus the Revolutionary Tribunal was decreed. Five judges, a jury, named by the Convention, and a public accuser, Fouquier Tinville, formed this terrible tribunal, which was to save France from anarchy, from counter-revolution, and from Europe. It is often asserted, on the authority of Montjoye and others, that Robespierre was one of the first members of the Committee of Public Safety. There is great confusion here in writers on this subject. We must bear in mind that there were two great committees, the Committee of Public Safety, which was charged with the highest political functions, and the Committee of General Safety, which conducted the more ordinary details of administration and police; and it was into the latter that Robespierre was elected on the 26th of March. I extract from the *Quarterly Review* the following particulars.

"Montjoye, who was an eye-witness of much that he relates, and who began his poor and prejudiced history of Robespierre while he was still alive, and published it soon after his fall, gives us to understand that Robespierre was a member of the Committee of Public Safety as early as its first formation, soon after the death of the King.

"Papon, in his history, also states that Robespierre was an original member of the Committee of Public Safety, and he, too, seems to place its creation shortly after the death of the King, and, at latest, before the 21st of March, 1793.

"Mignet says that he was elected to it on its first *renouvellement*, after the 31st of May, 1793.

"Messieurs Beaulieu and Michand, in their article in the *Biographie Universelle*, state that he was a member of the Committee of General Defence, before the fall of the Girondists (31st of May, 1793), and that *immediately* after that event, he assiduously attended the Committee of Public Safety.

"M. Thiers, on the contrary, states that it was not till the resignation of Gasparin, in August, 1793, that the *Convention, which had hitherto declined to elect Robespierre on any committee*, was now reluctantly subdued into naming him into the Committee of Public Safety.

"Durand de Maillane, a member of the Convention, and a party to all these proceedings, says, that the Committee of General Defence was organized on the 25th of March, 1793, with great powers; which, however, he adds, were restricted by the *subsequent* appointment of a Committee of Public Safety, *into which Robespierre did not obtain* early admission, but where he was dreaded before he was admitted.

"And finally the *Moniteur*, the *dernier ressort* in all such cases, sets the appointment of the Committee of General Defence on the

25th of March, 1793, and gives a list of its members, including all the leading men of the convocation, Vergniaud and *Robespierre*, Sièyes and Danton, &c., to the number of twenty-five. This Committee of General Defence is, however, in the very next *Moniteur*, called the Committee of General Safety, but it appears that, on the 6th of April, the formation of a Committee of Public Safety of nine members, was decreed on the motion of Isnard, a Girondin, and to *this* committee—the celebrated Committee of Public Safety —Robespierre did not belong till the 26th of July, when he was elected in the room of Gasparin, resigned."

The statements of the *Moniteur*, though imperfect, must be, as far as they go, correct, and they contradict, in one point or another, every one of the former statements, except that of Durand.

Although the Jacobins had succeeded in obtaining their Committee of Public Safety, they did not at once turn it against their enemies the Girondins. They whetted the edge of the axe upon the necks of Emigrés, and Aristocrats; waiting till they should bring the Girondins also to the block. The Girondins were not idle; and in the departments, especially by means of newspapers, increased their party.

Danton, who was suspected of complicity in the treason of Dumouriez, was deserted by Robespierre. Le Gendre undertook to reconcile them. They met at his table. Danton, with that frankness and placability which characterized him, advanced openly towards Robespierre, holding out his hand. Robespierre declined, and remained silent till the end of dinner, when he let fall a few phrases which, without directly indicating Danton, yet expressed his mistrust for those who only looked upon a revolution as a bloody path to fortune. This was an unmistakeable allusion to the suspicions circulated against Danton; and he retorted sarcastically on men " who put forward their pride as virtue, their cowardice as moderation."

The two great demagogues separated; from rivals they had become foes. Danton turned to the Girondins. But avoided by Robespierre on account of his corruption, he was also avoided by the Girondins on account of his violence. The terror he inspired alone protected him, and that terror enabled him to carry haughtily his infamous reputation. He had recently married a beautiful girl of sixteen, and he retired from the tumult of the revolution to his country house, on the banks of the Sèvres, for a moment to forget the contests of party in the delights of conjugal happiness.

On the 26th, as we saw, Robespierre was elected into the Committee of General Safety. On the 27th, he made a long speech in his usual style, declaring that the moment was arrived, either to save the state, or let it perish forever. He ended by proposing the following decree:—

That all the Capet family should, within a week, quit the French territory, and all the countries occupied by the Republican army; that Marie Antoinette, of Austria, should be brought before the revolutionary tribunal, and immediately judged, as having participated in the attempts against the liberty and the surety of the state; that the son of Capet should be detained in the Temple.

But this proposition was set aside for the present.

The Convention was forced for a moment to forget its dissensions, and turn all its energies against Europe. Robespierre continued to develop every evening, in the Jacobins, his social philosophy. The Jacobin Club thus became, through him, a powerful engine to coerce the Convention. The declaration of rights, says Lamartine, in enlarging itself in the hands of Robespierre, became the basis of a new constitution. It was the popular decalogue, which contained every social axiom, the application of which was the creation of institutions. Not only did Robespierre endeavor to frame democracy into a government, but with respect to popular education, he demanded that it should be obligatory on all families; thus forming in the same mould an entire generation, he established a community of children, and a community of ideas. Labor should form part of education; the schools should be workshops. The cultivation of the soil was to be the first of those labors. Herein he followed the example of ancient legislators, considering agriculture as the most moral and social of all employments, because it most directly nourishes the laborer, excites the least cupidity, and creates less vices and miseries than the labor of the manufacturer. The child was to learn reading, writing, arithmetic, and principles of universal morality. He was to learn the laws of his country, and to develop his mind by the recitation of the most striking passages which poetry, eloquence, and philosophy had bequeathed to mankind. He was to choose his own religion when education had sufficiently matured his reason, so that the religion of the man should not be the thoughtlessness of infancy, but the deliberate choice of an intelligent being.

Robespierre, moreover, proposed a tax to defray the expenses of these establishments, which he called the Children's Tax. He also demanded a tax for the poor, the aged, and the infirm. Thus the rich gradually stripped of their superfluous wealth, the poor gratuitously educated, everything in this scheme tended to community of property and equality of condition.

On the 26th of April he delivered a remarkable speech, in which he showed that, however anxious he might be to relieve the poor, he was not, like his modern imitators, the advocate of spoliation.

"I propose," he said, "certain articles necessary to complete your theory of property. Let the word alarm no one. Degraded wretches! (*âmes de boue!*) who only prize gold, I do not wish to touch your treasures, however impure their source may be. You ought to know that the Agrarian law, of which you have spoken so much, is but a phantom created by scoundrels to frighten idiots. There was no need of a revolution to teach the Universe that the extreme disproportion of fortune is the source of many evils and of many crimes; but we are also not the less convinced that community of goods is a chimera. As for me, I think it still less necessary to private happiness than to public felicity. We had better render poverty honorable than proscribe wealth. The cottage of Fabricius need not envy the palace of Crassus. For my part, I would sooner be the son of Aristides, brought up at the expense of the Republic, than the presumptive heir of Xerxes, born in the corruption of courts, to occupy a throne adorned from the degradation of the people, glittering with public misery."

He then defined property to be "the right which every citizen has of enjoying and disposing of that portion of goods which is guaranteed him by the law. The right of property is limited, as are all other rights, by the obligation of respecting the rights of other people. It should neither be prejudicial to the safety, nor to the liberty, nor to the existence, nor to the property of our fellow-men. All property which violates this principle, is illicit and immoral."

With respect to taxes, he proposed that all citizens whose revenue did not exceed that which was necessary to their subsistence, should be dispensed from contributing to public expenses; the others should pay progressively in proportion to their fortune.*

Whilst the Convention was occupied by philosophical discussions, the Commune, the Jacobins, and the Cordeliers, were exciting the Faubourgs against the Girondins, as the great obstacle to the happiness of the people, and the safety of the country. To compel the provinces to submit to Paris, to subdue the Convention itself by terror—to govern the Commune by the sections, and the sections by a few agitators, under the orders of two or three demagogues: such was the plan of these blood-thirsty wretches. Robespierre and Danton, to their shame, be it said, adopted this plan, though they adopted it with repugnance. In fact they dared not oppose Marat, who had grown and grown in violence and audacity, until he had raised himself to the very pinnacle of popularity. They despised, but dreaded him.

On the 24th of April he had appeared before the Revolutionary Tribunal. But he alarmed his judges by the audacity of his attitude. Backed as he was by the crowd which escorted him, he insolently demanded that his innocence should be recognized. It was proclaimed; and Marat, raised upon the arms of four men, was carried above their heads to be shown to the crowd. Women encircled his head with crowns of laurels, and the ragged army of sans-culottes bore him over Paris in triumph. At the windows were women showering ribbons and crowns of flowers on the conqueror. He was finally carried into the Convention, where Danton,

---

* See this proposition reproduced in the luminous and masterly "Principles of Political Economy," by J. S. Mill. Book V. ch. 2, § 3.

pretending to be carried away by the enthusiasm of the mob, demanded that the cortège of Marat should receive the honors of the Assembly. Marat, holding the crown in his hand, went and seated himself upon the highest bench of the Mountain. "Now," said he, in a loud tone of congratulation, "I have the Girondists! they shall go in triumph also, but it shall be to the guillotine." Then addressing himself to the deputies, who had issued the decree of accusation against him, he apostrophized them in language which only excited a smile of contempt in the hall. Robespierre himself shrugged his shoulders in scorn. Marat, with a glance of defiance, called him *lâche scélérat!* Robespierre pretended not to hear. Marat, giddy at the height to which he had been raised, had the insolence to demand before Robespierre's face that all informations against the ministers, should be sent to him to be judged; thus boldly personifying the people in himself. Robespierre scarcely dared to murmur!

Marat continued his denunciations against the Girondins, and fiercely demanded their heads. Robespierre held back. He did not desire their death, but preserved a sort of mysterious silence, neither instigating nor restraining the people. But on the eve of the insurrection, when victory was certain, Robespierre assumed his menacing attitude against the Commission of Twelve. One may suspect, indeed, that, seeing the popularity of Marat, Robespierre might have feared lest the fall of the Gironde should only be the triumph of his rival; and, however he might hate the Girondins, he could not calmly contemplate the triumph of Marat. But his assistance was not needed. The alarming news which arrived from La Vendée, from the frontiers, and from the south, drove the people to desperation. The disasters of the Pyrenean army, the retreat of the northern army, Valenciennes and Cambray blockaded without hopes of receiving succor, the Republican troops defeated at Fontenay, Marseilles on fire, Bourdeaux and Lyons in insurrection; all these calamities, bursting at once upon the republic, exasperated the people, who, not knowing whom to accuse, accused the Girondins. When this cry of "The country is in danger" was at its height, Robespierre adroitly hinted at a dictatorship.

"It is necessary that the executive," he said in the Jacobins, "should be placed in popular and incorruptible hands, in the hands of those pure men who merge their happiness in the general happiness."—A significant allusion to himself, which does not, however, seem to have taken.

Forced to side against the Girondins, he did so, at last, with energy:—

"I told you," he said in the Jacobins, "that the people ought to repose upon their force, but when they are oppressed, when they have only themselves to look to, he is a coward who would not tell them to rise. It is when all laws are violated, when despotism is at its height, when good faith and modesty are trampled under foot, that the people ought to rise in insurrection. That moment has arrived. Our enemies openly oppress patriots; they wish in the name of the law to plunge the people once more in misery and slavery! Such corrupt men shall never call me friend. They may offer me treasures; I prefer dying with republicans to triumphing with wretches. I exhort every citizen, therefore, to preserve the sense of his rights. I urge him to reckon on his force, and on that of the whole nation. I urge the people to place themselves in insurrection against the corrupt deputies; I declare that, having received from the people the right of defending their rights, I regard him as my oppressor who interrupts me, who refuses me speech; and I declare that I alone, I, place myself in insurrection against the President, against all the members who sit in the Convention. When they affect a contempt for the sans-culottes, I declare that I place myself in insurrection against all the corrupt deputies; and I invite all the deputies of the Mountain to rally round me, and combat the aristocracy, and I say that there is for them but one alternative, either to resist with all their force the efforts of intrigue, or to give in their resignation."

In the midst of the applause which followed this speech, the whole society rose, and declared itself in insurrection. And yet, it was not death, but riddance, which he wished, and in conjunction with Pache, he applied himself to give the insurrection the character of an irresistible demonstration of the people's will. Their objects were, to suppress the Commission of Twelve, to expel twenty-two members from the Convention, to give the majority to the Mountain, to deliver the revolutionary government over to the Commune of Paris, and to establish a legal terror, in the name of an intimidated and subjected national representation. Danton, and even Marat himself, at last agreed in this project; the insurrection was organized, and the Convention was surrounded. Vergniaud, rising, said :—

"'The Convention cannot deliberate at present; let us join the armed force, and place ourselves under the protection of the people;" and he went out, accompanied by some friends, but returned soon afterwards, and found Robespierre in the Tribune, reproaching the Assembly with its hesitation. Vergniaud demanded leave to speak, but Robespierre, looking down upon him from the tribune with intense disdain, fulminated in his most violent style against the whole of the Gironde. His peroration produced immense effect. Vergniaud impatiently exclaimed, "Conclude! conclude!"

"Yes, I will conclude," said Robespierre, "and it shall be against *you!* Against you who, after the 10th August, wished to send to the scaffold those who effected it! Against you who have incessantly invoked the destruction of Paris! Against you who wished to save the tyrant! Against you who conspired with Dumouriez! Against you who have unrelentingly persecuted those who demanded the head of Dumouriez! My conclusion is the decree of accusation against the accomplices of Dumouriez, and against all those designated in the petition."

The Gironde fell; the Commission of Twelve was abolished; and the Committee of Public Salvation was established. Opinions were divided in this Committee, with respect to the punishment of the Girondins. Pache, Bouchotte, and Garat, declared that the arrest of the twenty-two was the only measure which could calm the excitement of Paris; but the cruelty of this was repugnant even to Barrère. "We must see," said he, "who represents the nation, the National Convention, or the Commune of Paris." Garat lamented the peril, and the consequences of such a sacrifice made to the mob. Danton generously said, "The unity of the Republic shall triumph, if necessary, over our corpses; an equal number of our party and of our enemies must exile ourselves from the Convention, in order to restore it to strength and peace. I will propose this to our noble friends of the Mountain, and will myself offer to go to Bordeaux."

The Committee, carried away by the generosity of the plan, adopted it. It left the honor of the sacrifice to the Mountain, saved the Girondins, and gave the victory to patriotism. But Danton found only a few of his friends equally generous; the rest wished time for consideration. Robespierre was sounded, but he was not the man to be influenced by any act of generous heroism; he was more politic, more calm; "his reason would not permit him, he said, to abdicate—not his power, for he had none—but the mandate of the people, which had assigned to him the post where he would die. It is not a question of persons, but of ideas. My ideas are those of the people, and I have no right to abdicate. Let them take my head if they will. Besides, this gulf of Aristides is only a sublime sophism. Either Aristides believes that he is noxious to his country, and in that case he ought to precipitate himself into the gulf; or he believes that he can save it, and in that case he ought to precipitate his enemies. That is logic. The heroism of Danton is only the tenderness of a weak heart, which yields the revolution to a tear."

Danton and his friends were compelled to abandon their project, and saw no chance of safety for the Convention but in the voluntary abdication of the Girondins, whom they vainly strove to convince of the necessity of sacrificing themselves to the Republic. Barbaroux exclaimed, "If the Convention deems my suspension necessary, I will obey its decree, but I never will myself lay down the authority with which I have been invested by the people. Expect no resignation from me. I have sworn to die at my post, and I will keep my oath." Many others imitated him; but the struggle was useless. Perceiving that their defeat was inevitable, many of the Girondins fled into their departments, there to rouse the people against Paris. Robespierre, Danton, and the Committee of Public Salvation, shut their eyes to this flight. They had scotched the snake, and did not wish to kill it.

To the terror of the coalition and internal dissension, a new terror was now added, by the assassination of Marat, who fell beneath the hand of Charlotte Corday.

The rage and fury of the mob, at this immolation of their idol, exceed description. Robespierre and Danton were happy at being freed from a rival whom they feared. The night after his murder, the people hung garlands at his door, and the Convention inaugurated his bust in their hall. It was decreed that he should be buried in the Pantheon, and some proposed that an empty tomb should be erected to him beneath every tree of Liberty.

"If I speak to-day," said Robespierre, "it is because I am bound to do so. Doubtless the honors of the poniard are reserved for me also. Priority has been established by hazard, and my fall is near at hand: hazard alone made it light on that great patriot. Think no longer, therefore, of vain declamations on the pomp of burial. The best way to avenge Marat is to prosecute his enemies with relentless vigor. The vengeance which is satisfied with funereal honors, is soon past, and loses itself in useless pomp; renounce, then, these useless discussions, and avenge him in the manner alone worthy of his name."

Among these enemies were of course the Girondins. Garat made a feeble effort to save them, and he thus describes his interview with Robespierre:

"Of the two very different species of generosity," he says, "which the human heart is capable of, one having its source in the affections, and the other in pride, the latter, I was sure, was the only one which could affect Robespierre. I therefore endeavored to seduce him through his pride, but I saw in an instant that he placed his pride, his triumph, and his grandeur, in pitilessly crushing his enemies. I endeavored to touch his soul in another way—*by fear*. I represented to him that if they commenced killing some deputies, we should all be soon menaced with the same fate, and that those who sent others to the scaffold, would soon be sent there themselves. I saw at once that he fancied he was only safe in the destruction of all those who inspired him with fear. Thus repulsed, I said, 'But will the Convention suffer them to be judged by that tribunal which was erected contrary to all their declarations?' 'It is good enough for them,' he said. What a sentence!"

The Committee of Public Salvation was now invested with every power. Its members were Saint Just, Couthon, Barrère, Gasparin, Thuriot, Hérault, De Séchelles, Lindet, St. André, Carnot, Prieur, Billaud Varennes, and Collot-d'Herbois. Gasparin having retired, Robespierre was elected in his place. This was the decemvirate which bore, during fourteen months, all the dangers, all the power, all the glory; and has borne all the maledictions of posterity.

From this period may be said to commence Robespierre's personal responsibility. He ceased to be a mere member of an opposition, to become a minister. Royalty abolished, the Girondists vanquished, and Danton departed, there was nothing apparently to interfere with the healthy action of the Republic.

Before his departure, Danton had a secret conference with Robespierre, in which he confided to him his discouragement at the state of affairs. He requested Robespierre to defend him during his absence. Robespierre, pleased with this deference, and with the retirement of his great rival, was careful not to detain him; and they separated, swearing mutual esteem and constant support. Danton retired to Arcis-sur-Aube, where he spent a few happy weeks with his wife and children. He there spoke of Robespierre as a dreamer; sometimes cruel, sometimes virtuous, but always chimerical. He relied on Robespierre's defence; and not without cause, for Robespierre had undertaken to protect him against his denunciators in the Convention. "New men," he said, "patriots of a day, endeavor to ruin the reputation of the oldest friends of the people. I cite, for example, Danton, who is calumniated; Danton, on whom no one has the right to lay the slightest reproach. Let them prove that they have more energy, more talent, or more love of the country than he! They praise Marat, that they may rail against living patriots. What avails it to praise the dead, provided one may calumniate the living?" This defence will be worth remembering when we come to Robespierre's accusations against Danton.

Robespierre, as we have said, was now Minister. He had favored anarchy only so far as he believed necessary to the triumph of the revolution. It now seemed time to take a stand against the instigators of the disorder. He allowed himself no repose. Though ill and exhausted by mental labors which would have destroyed most men, he devoted himself with greater ardor to the pursuit of his ideal government. His attitude and language were completely changed. He strove to rally public opinion in the Convention, through the Jacobins; to resist the anarchical encroachments of the Commune; in a word, he strove to establish harmony and unity of action. In the organization of the committee of government he was more assiduous than ever. At the meetings of the Jacobins, he turned all the thoughts of this society towards the great problems of social organization.

Among the papers found in Robespierre's lodgings, there were two notes in his handwriting, without date, but which from internal evidence belong to this period. They are too significant to be omitted:—

"There must be but one will (*il faut une volonté, une*).

"And this must be republican or royalist.

"If it be republican, it is necessary to have republican ministers, republican papers, republican deputies, and a republican government.

"The foreign war is a mortal disease, whereas the malady of political society is revolution, and the division among the people.

"*Our internal dangers come from the bourgeois; to conquer the bourgeois we must rally the people.*

"Everything was disposed to place the people under the yoke of the bourgeois, and to make the defenders of the republic perish on the scaffold.

"They have triumphed at Marseilles, at Bourdeaux, and at Lyons. They would have triumphed at Paris, had it not been for the present insurrection. It is necessary that the insurrection should continue, until the necessary measures are taken to save the republic. It is necessary that the people should ally themselves with the Convention, and that the Convention should make use of the people.

"It is necessary that the insurrection should extend step by step, on the same plan; that the sans-culottes should be paid, and should remain in the towns; they must have arms given them, and be enlightened. The republican enthusiasm must be excited by all possible means. If the deputies are dismissed, the republic is lost; they will continue to mislead the departments; while their substitutes would not be any better."

This is the second:—

"What is our aim?

"The execution of the Constitution in favor of the people.

"Who are our enemies?

"The vicious and the rich.

"What are the means they employ?

"Calumny and hypocrisy.

"What causes favor the employment of these means?

"The ignorance of the sans-culottes. It is necessary, therefore, to enlighten the people. Mercenary writers mislead them by impudent daily impostures.

"What do we conclude from this?

"First, that these writers must be proscribed, as the most dangerous enemies of the country; second, that we must distribute good writings with profusion.

"What are the other obstacles to the establishment of liberty?

"Foreign war and civil war.

"What are the means of terminating foreign war?

"Placing republican generals at the head of our armies, and punishing those who have betrayed us.

"What are the means of terminating civil war?

"The punishment of traitors and conspirators: above all the culpable deputies and administrators; to send patriotic troops, under patriotic chiefs, to crush the aristocrats of Lyons, of Marseilles, of Toulon, of La Vendée, of the Jura, and of all the other countries, where the standard of rebellion and of royalism has been raised; and to make terrible examples of all those wretches who have outraged liberty, and spilled the blood of patriots.

"First: proscription of perfidious and counter-revolutionary writers; propagation of patriotic writings. Second: punishment of traitors and conspirators, above all, the culpable deputies and administrators. Third: nomination of patriotic generals; destitution and punishment of others; and Fourth: subsistence and popular laws."

It is worthy of remark, how Robespierre here insists upon the proscription of opinion; he who had so eloquently argued for liberty of the press!* But it is only the difference between a speaker in opposition and a minister. His proscription is paralleled by the energetic decision of Cavaignac, who, immediately on receiving the dictatorship of June, 1848, arrested Emile Girardin, and forbade the appearance of all such newspapers as he considered anarchical in their tendency.

Paris had now to contend not only against Europe and against faction, it had also to contend against the terrible pressure of famine. A maximum had been decreed, an arbitrary price, below which no bread, meat, fish, wine, coals, &c., could be sold. There was likewise fixed a maximum of weights. The effect of this was only to cramp commerce and increase the famine. Crowds of workmen, of beggars, and of women collected round the Hotel de Ville shrieking for bread. Hébert and Chaumette encouraged these assemblies. Lamartine says that Robespierre one while appeared indignant at the success of anarchy, at another feigned to comprehend its necessity, to pardon it—to instigate, that he might rule it. I doubt this. Whatever discrepancy may be observed in his views is owing, I think, to the vacillation of his mind as he stood face to face with the awful mob, which he had

* "La liberté de publier ses pensées étant le premier boulevard de la liberté, *ne peut être limitée en aucune manière si ce n'est dans les états despotiques*. . . . Il n'y a réellement que les hommes dont la vertu est nulle ou équivoque qui puissent redouter la plus grande liberté de la censure de leurs concitoyens."

so powerfully aided in evoking, and which now, as a minister, he had the awful problem of ruling. Remember that his was no longer the office of instigating and exciting the masses to rebellion. He was no longer in opposition. The Republic, if ever, was now to be formed, and he had the terrible task of forming it. But republics, and other forms of government which act so smoothly upon paper, become very different things when we attempt to realize them, having as our instruments ferocious and ignorant masses of hungry men! Certain it is, that he essayed many times to restrain these petitioners; essayed in vain. His popularity, great as it was, scarcely survived this resistance to the popular will; and he often entered his dwelling alone, forsaken, and despondent.

Pache came one night to confer secretly with him upon the means of calming these ebullitions. "All is over with the Revolution," said Robespierre, "if it be abandoned to these idiots. The people must be defended by terrible institutions, or they will destroy themselves with the weapons with which they think to defend themselves. The Convention has but one method of wresting the sword from their hands. That method is to take the sword in its own hands, and strike its enemy without pity. If we permit these children of the Revolution to sport with the thunder of the people, it will burst and destroy us." Ominous words; full of sad meanings soon to be disclosed!

CHAPTER XIX.

Robespierre's task as minister—The Terror—Trial of Marie Antoinette—Trial of the Girondins—The Feast of Reason—Robespierre's opposition to it—His reports on the Principles of Government and on Political Morality—His desire for the cessation of the Revolution—His share in the bloodshed exaggerated—Hébert—Robespierre's struggle against the Anarchists—Defence of Danton and Camille—Fall of Hébert—Danton threatened—Robespierre's hypocrisy—Fall of Danton and Camille.

THE fifth act of this long and dismal tragedy now opens, and the moral of the story begins to glimmer through its horrible events. Robespierre has gained his ambitious object: what use will he make of it? We have traced him step by step along his troubled path; we have seen him an obscure honest reformer, wishing to have abuses removed, but never contemplating the abolition of a constitutional monarchy. From that early stage, we have seen him gradually pass onwards to republicanism. We have seen him borne upon the tide of popularity, instigating insurrection, approving massacres, exasperating the minds of a furious people by fierce declamations and rabble-rousing words, denouncing every man whose power seemed an obstacle to the realization of his ideas—doing all this evil that good might come of it : *that* good being nothing less than a pure Republic. He has now nearly attained the culminating point of power. He is almost a dictator. Now commences the fearful task of realizing ideas—of passing from the easy office of criticism to the perilous office of action. He who so fiercely upbraided the acts of others, has now to act himself; he who was pitiless towards those who fell short of his ideal, taking no heed of obstacles, giving no credit for intentions, is now to be himself the butt of that opposition which he has hitherto directed against others. Patriotism, vague declamations about love of one's country and republican virtue will avail him no longer; powerful in opposition, these phrases are powerless in office. His business is to act, not to declaim. He has to govern a nation—and what a nation! Phrases will not govern it. It can only be governed by institutions, and those must be based upon ideas. What social ideas has Robespierre! None. He has nothing but aspirations. He *desires* a Republic; but he has not *thought out* even the most elementary plans of institutions necessary for a Republic. Face to face with the great problem of social misery—face to face with the terrible problem of government for an anarchical nation—he is powerless to solve it; powerless to shape that chaos into order.

There is something to my mind infinitely tragic in such a situation. Let any man pause awhile amidst the contention of daily debate, and conceive himself, or the most illustrious man of his party, suddenly placed in such a position, with the terrible complexity of the great social problem harassing him on all sides, and ask: how is this anarchy to be stilled? How are the *wants* of these millions to be reconciled to their *wills?* The crushing responsibility, and the feebleness of any one mind, or set of minds, in such a situation, will then be imagined. As long as society is at peace, and the great machine works with only a little creaking here and there, particular measures may remedy particular evils, and a change of rulers only means the entrance into power of men who will carry through some particular change. But when society is troubled to its depths, when the whole machine has fallen to pieces and needs reconstruction, then particular measures are but trivial acts, and change of rulers is only a change of incapacities. To create institutions on paper is no difficult task; and facile theories easily demonstrate how, *if* certain changes were adopted, happiness would be the universal result. Unhappily for theorists, men are not so easily persuaded. They are not simple units in a calculation; they are complex beings, having many wants, many passions, and much foolishness; they do not, they will not act as you tell them, and your republic, which went so smoothly upon paper, cannot live a day.

Maximilien Robespierre was one of these theorists. He sincerely believed that if France were once rid of the Royalists and the Gironde—"the tyrants" as he called them, he could establish a republic which should be a model to the civilized world. He has now arrived at the threshold of his desires, and he is now to learn by sad experience the difference between theory and practice. We shall see the incompetence of the demagogue—

"Qui n'a que ses fureurs pour maximes d'état."

His first great act was, in conjunction with the Committee of Public Safety, the institution of *La Terreur!* An army of 6000 men, and 1200 artillery, was decreed for the purpose of everywhere executing revolutionary laws. Two francs a day were paid to workmen who left their shops to assist in the assemblies of the section; and three francs a day to the members of revolutionary committees. The law against the suspected (*loi des suspects*) was decreed. The meaning of which was that any one could be arrested at the will of the committee. The revolution, said St. Just is like thunder, it must strike.

The Terror was the despair of a Revolution which felt its aim frustrated. The *folly* of it, politically speaking, was as great as its *cruelty*. It is, however, needless here to argue against that which is universally execrated.

The fearful activity of the Terror may be estimated in a very few sentences. On the fall of the Girondins, the number of prisoners in the different jails of Paris was about 1150: three months reign of Terror had raised the number to an average of six, seven, and eight thousand, in the metropolis alone. Had these been all political enemies, one might have applauded at least the energy of the Committee, but the prisoners were for the most part perfectly harmless.

And now the clamor was raised for vengeance on Marie Antoinette. The Committee of Public Safety ordered Fouquier Tinville to press sentence against her. Some of the Committee were very loth to have her tried; even Robespierre himself, incensed as he was against the King, would have preserved her. "Revolutions are very cruel," said he; "neither sex nor age is anything before them! Ideas are pitiless, but the people ought to have mercy. If my head were not necessary to the Revolution, there are moments when I would offer that head to the people, in exchange for one of those which they demand of us." Does any one believe this?

Marie Antoinette was condemned and executed amidst the execrations of the mob. To this had she fallen! She, who, so few years back, in the triumph of her youth and beauty, had been idolized by that very mob, she now fell upon the scaffold amidst the exultation of that mob!

> ὥστε θνητὸν ὄντ' ἐκείνην τὴν τελευταίαν ἰδεῖν
> ἡμέραν ἐπισκοποῦνται, μηδὲν ὀλβίζειν, πρὶν ἂν
> τέρμα τοῦ βίου περάσῃ, μηδέν ἀλγεινόν ταθων.
>
> Œdip. Tyran. 1528.*

Vilate relates the following scene:

"The day after the judgment of Marie Antoinette, Barrère ordered a dinner at the Restaurant Venua, to which he invited Robespierre, Saint Just, and me. Saint Just kept us waiting; they sent me after him. I found him at the committee, writing. On mentioning the name of Robespierre, he followed me. On the way he seemed surprised. 'Robespierre dine with Barrère!' he said; 'he is the only one Robespierre has pardoned.' In a private apartment they asked me to describe to them the debates on the trial of the 'Austrian woman.' I did not forget that burst of outraged nature, when, on Hébert's accusing Antoinette of obscenities with her son eleven years old, she turned with dignity towards the people, and said, 'I appeal to all mothers present. I appeal to their consciences to declare if there is one who does not shudder at such horrors.'†

---

* "Call no mortal happy till thou hast seen the last day of his life, and he has brought his wanderings to a close without having suffered some great woe."

† This is Vilate's account, but Marie Antoinette's real reply was this. A juryman asked her why she had not replied to Hébert's accusation. "I have not replied to it," she said, "because there are accusations to which

"Robespierre, struck with this reply as by an electric shock, shattered his plate with his fork, exclaiming, 'That idiot Hébert! It is not enough that she is really a Messalina, but he must also make her an Agrippina, and secure her in her last moments this triumph of public interest.' Every one was at first stupefied. Saint Just broke silence saying, ' *Les mœurs gagneront à cet acte de justice nationale,*' and Barrère exclaimed that the guillotine had cut a great knot in European diplomacy. This was, however, but a slight prelude to the great political conversation we had. Robespierre did not dissemble his fears respecting the great number of the enemies of the revolution. Barrère comprehended under this class, all the nobles, all the priests, and all *les hommes de Palais,* without excepting the physicians. Saint Just then gave us the outlines of his discourse on the confiscation of the property of the *suspects.* Barrère, impatient to show his ardor for principles, exclaimed, 'The vessel of the revolution will only arrive in port on a sea reddened with waves of blood.' Saint Just replied, 'That is true; a nation only regenerates itself upon heaps of corpses.' Robespierre saw two dangers: the excessive effusion of blood, which would revolt humanity, and the insufficiency which would arise from that false sensibility towards a small number, and be prejudicial to the happiness of all.

The Girondins who had been imprisoned since the 31st of May were now to be brought to a trial, which was tantamount to death.

"I cannot save them," replied Robespierre, when he was implored to interpose; "there are periods in revolutions when to live is a crime, and when men must know how to yield their heads if demanded. Mine also will perhaps be demanded," added he, seizing it in both hands; "you shall then see if I dispute it."

The *Acte d'Accusation* of Fouquier Tinville, concocted, it is said, by Robespierre and Saint Just, was little more than a bitter reproduction of the pamphlet of Camille Desmoulins, called the "Histoire de la Faction de la Gironde." In this pamphlet

nature refuses to reply. I appeal against it to all the mothers here present."

Camille, always careless of truth, had amassed a fearful amount of injustice, but he probably satisfied his conscience as a politician with the morality of Orestes:—

δοκῶ μὲν οὐδὲν ῥῆμα σὺν κέρδει κακον.*

It was, as Lamartine said, the history of calumny received as evidence by the executioner. Their sentence was death; which Valazé anticipated by stabbing himself in open court. The rest returned to their dungeon singing the "Marseillaise." There are few scenes more ghastly or more impressive than the last supper of the Girondins. They spent the evening in singing, in sallies of gaiety, and in discourses on the happiness of mankind. Valazé, with bloody breast, slept cold in death, hearing not their singing. Vergniaud, who had his dose of poison, flung it away from him, because there was only enough for himself, and he would die with his friends. In reading the graphic account given by Lamartine of this last supper, and of Vergniaud's discourse on the immortality of the soul, the scholar will naturally recall that other, greater and far more solemn scene in Plato's "Phædon," where Socrates, about to die, also proclaims to his friends the immortality of the soul—a scene whose solemnity was not disturbed by the snatches of song and sallies of gaiety which rendered that of the Girondins so ghastly.

It was Philippe Egalité's turn next. *Apropos* of his execution, Mr. Alison gives currency to an atrocious slander against Robespierre, for which he has adduced no authority and which is contradicted by the whole evidence of Robespierre's life. "He (Philippe) was detained," says Mr. Alison, "above a quarter of an hour in front of the Palais Royal, by order of Robespierre, who had asked in vain the hand of his daughter in marriage, and had promised, if he would relent in that extremity, to excite a tumult which would save his life."

Mr. Alison also subsequently quotes, without the slightest mis-

---

* "I think no speech evil that results in gain." This line occurs either in the Chœphoræ of Æschylus or in the Electra of Sophocles; I am not certain which.

giving, the slander of Les Deux Amis de la Liberté, who in their fourteenth volume declare that the Duchesse d'Angoûleme owed her life solely to a project which Robespierre had formed of marrying her, "thus uniting in his person the revolutionary and royalist parties." It is unnecessary for me to do more than allude to these slanders.

The execution of Bailly followed that of Egalité. On hearing of it, Robespierre lamented it. He said to Duplay, "It is thus we ourselves shall be martyrized." Duplay, who was one of the judges of the tribunal, having desired to explain to Robespierre why he had not absolved Bailly, "Do not speak of it," replied Robespierre; "I do not call you to account for your sentence; the Republic will ask that of your conscience." That evening he remained gloomily shut up in his room, and received none of his friends. The axe which spared neither rank nor age, neither talent nor virtue, how long would it spare him?

Republican energy triumphed abroad, and became as terrible to Europe as it was to faction. I must not pause to recount its history; but pass on to the infamous Feast of Reason, which was decreed in the Convention by the most furious of the Jacobins, and which excited almost as much disgust in Robespierre's mind as in the mind of all Europe. No such buffoonery had the world seen as that of jubilant atheism rejoicing in being freed from the fetters of superstition, while worshiping a prostitute.*

"The inauguration of this religion," says Lamartine, "took place in the Convention on the 9th of November. Chaumette, with some members of the Commune, and escorted by a vast crowd, entered to sounds of music and the chorus of patriotic hymns. He led by the hand one of the most beautiful courtesans of Paris. A long blue veil half covered her form. A group of prostitutes, her companions, followed. Some of the seditious escorted them. This corrupt band entered the hall confusedly, and seated themselves on the benches of the deputies. Lequinio presided. Chaumette, advancing towards him, raised the veil which covered the courtesan, and exhibited her beauty to the multitude. 'Mortals! recognize no other

* "Mrs. Momoro," says Carlyle, in his quaint way, "made, it is admitted, one of the best Goddesses of Reason, *though her teeth were a little defective.*"

divinity than Reason, of which I present to you the loveliest and purest image.' At these words Chaumette bowed, and made a semblance of adoration. The president, the Convention, and the people pretended to imitate this worship. A *fête* in honor of Reason was decreed in the cathedral of Paris. Songs and dances welcomed this decree. Some members of the Convention—Armonville, Drouet, and Lecarpentier—joined in these dances. The majority of the Assembly, however, appeared cold and disdainful. Satisfied with having voted these saturnalia, they abandoned them to the people, and blushed at participating in them. Robespierre, seated beside St. Just, simulated inattention and indifference. His severe countenance never relaxed; glancing at the disorder in the Chamber, he took notes, and then conversed with his neighbor. The degradation of the Revolution appeared to him the greatest of crimes. At the moment when the popular orgie was most applauded, he rose with ill suppressed indignation, and retired with St. Just. He would not by his presence sanction these profanations. Robespierre's departure disconcerted Chaumette. The president raised the sitting, and restored the temple of the laws to decency."

Robespierre was so incensed that he afterwards declared Chaumette deserved death for his share in the transaction. The Feast of Reason may be taken as the extreme point of revolutionary madness; from that moment the reaction began. In a vigorous speech made in the Jacobin Club by Robespierre on the 21st of November, we read:—

"Let men, animated by pure zeal, lay on the altar of their country the useless and pompous monuments of superstition. Let others renounce such ceremonies, and adopt on all matters the opinion which seems to them most conformable with true reason. Philosophy can only applaud their conduct. But by what title does hypocrisy come here to mingle with that of *civism* and virtue? What right have men, hitherto unknown in the revolution, to come into the midst of you, to seek in passing events false popularity, to hurry on patriots to fatal measures, and to throw among them the seeds of trouble and discord? By what right do they disturb the existing worship in the name of Liberty, *and attack fanaticism by fanaticism of another kind?* By what right will they degrade the solemn homage rendered to truth into an eternal and ridiculous farce? One would suppose the Convention had proscribed the Catholic faith: it has done no such thing. It has, on the contrary, by a solemn decree, established the liberty of worship. It will alike proscribe the ministers of religion who disturb, and protect those who respect the public peace. It is the royalist, not the Catholic priesthood whom it has with justice persecuted. We have heard of priests being denounced for having said mass; they will only say it the more for being disturbed: whoso would prevent them is a greater fanatic than he who says the mass. There are men who would go further; who, under the guise of destroying superstition, would establish atheism itself. Every philosopher, every individual, is at liberty to adopt whatever opinion he pleases, but the legislator would be a thousand times blameable who adopted such a system. The Convention abhors all such attempts; it is no maker of metaphysical theories; it is a popular body, whose mission is to cause not only the rights, but the character of the French people to be respected. Not in vain has it proclaimed the rights of man in the presence of the Supreme Being.

"They will say, perhaps, that I am prejudiced, that I am a man of narrow mind; that I am a fanatic. I have already said that I do not here speak as an individual, nor as a systematic philosopher, but a representative of the people. Atheism is aristocratic. The idea of a supreme being, who watches over oppressed innocence, and punishes triumphant crime, is altogether popular (*loud applause*). The people, the unfortunate, will always applaud me; I shall find detractors only among the rich and the guilty. I have from my youth upwards been but an indifferent Catholic, but I have never been a cold friend, or a faithless defender of humanity. I am even more strongly attached to moral than political truth. If God did not exist, it would be necessary to invent him. I speak here in a tribune where the impudent Guadet dared to accuse me of having pronounced the word 'Providence,' as if that were a crime. And when? When my heart, ulcerated with all the crimes' of which we were the witnesses and the victims, when shedding bitter, powerless tears on the misery of the people, eternally betrayed, eternally oppressed, I endeavored to raise myself above the crowd of impure conspirators who environed me, and invoked against them celestial vengeance, in default of the thunder of the people! And if ever tyranny should reappear amongst us, where is the energetic and virtuous soul that would not appeal in secret to that eternal justice which seems to have been written in all hearts? It seems to me that the last martyr of liberty would exhale his soul with a more tender sentiment, relying on that consoling idea. This sentiment is the sentiment of Europe, of the universe; it is that of the French people! The people is not attached either to priests or to superstitions; it is only attached to the idea of an incomprehensible power, the terror of crime, the support of virtue, to whom it is pleased to render those homages which are due to it, and which are so many anathemas against injustice, and triumphant crime!

"If the philosopher is able to erect his morality upon another basis, let us, nevertheless, be careful not to wound that first instinct, that universal sentiment of nations! Where is the genius who could replace, by any invention of his, that grand idea, the protector of social order, and of all private virtues?"

In the same spirit he read, on the 25th of December, a report on the principles of the revolutionary government, some passages of which are worth preserving.

"The function of government," he says, "is to direct the moral and physical forces of the nation. For this purpose, the aim of a constitutional government is the republic. The aim of a revolutionary government is to found it. The revolution is the war of liberty against its enemies: the Constitution of the *régime* of liberty, victorious and at peace. The revolutionary government has need of an immense activity, precisely because it is at war: it is subject to rules less uniform, and less rigorous, because the circumstances in which it finds itself are stormy and changeable; and above all, because it is forced incessantly to use new and rapid resources in new and pressing dangers.

"A constitutional government occupies itself principally with civil liberty; the revolutionary government with public liberty. Under the constitutional *régime*, it is almost enough to protect individuals against the abuse of public power; under the revolutionary *régime* public power is obliged to defend itself against all the factions which attack it. The revolutionary government owes national protection to all good citizens; it owes to the enemies of the people nothing but death.

"These opinions suffice to explain the nature and origin of those laws which we call revolutionary. Those who name them arbitrary, or tyrannical, are stupid sophists, who seek to confound contrary ideas. They wish to subject to the same *régime* both peace and war, health and disease; or rather, they only wish for the resurrection of tyranny, and the death of the country. If the revolutionary government needs to be more active in its march, and more free in its movements than ordinary governments, is it for that less just or less legitimate? No. It reposes on the most sacred of all laws, the safety of the people; on the most irrefragable of all titles, necessity. Its rules are taken from justice and order: it has nothing in common with anarchy, nor with disorder. Its aim, on the contrary, is to repress them; to bring about, and consolidate, the reign of law. It has nothing in common with what is arbitrary. It must sail between two rocks, weakness, and temerity; moderatism, and excess. Moderatism, which is to moderation that which impotency is to chastity; and excess, which resembles energy, as dropsy does health."

In the same *rapport*, there is also a curious defence of the *errors*, as he politely calls them, of patriots.

"Patriotism," he says, "is ardent in its nature. Who can coldly love his country? Patriotism is the characteristic of simple men, little capable of calculating the political consequences of an action, whose motive is altogether civic. Where is the patriot, even the enlightened patriot, who has never been deceived? Well, if we admit that there exist moderates and cowards of good faith, wherefore should there not exist patriots of good faith, whom a praiseworthy sentiment sometimes carries too far? If, then, we were to regard as criminal all those who in the revolutionary movement have passed the line traced by cautious prudence, we should envelop in a common proscription with bad citizens, all the real friends of liberty, your friends, and all the supporters of the Republic."

Were it worth while to dissect Robespierre's arguments, or to pause and comment upon his contradictions, one might reasonably here demand of his *honesty*, how he could believe in the good faith of mistaken and misguided patriotism, and yet be so pitiless towards the errors of those who differed from him? But in truth a fanatic's reasons are seldom remarkable for consistency, and tolerance of the mistakes of others never yet bore any proportion to the tolerance of the mistakes of our own party.

On the 5th of February, he read a second and still more remarkable report on the Principles of Political Morality, for the guidance of the Convention. In it he says:—

"After having marched for a long time at hazard, and, as it were, carried away by the movement of contrary factions, the representatives of the people have at last formed a government. A sudden change in the nation's fortune announced to Europe the regeneration which had been operated in the national representation; but up to this moment, we must admit that *we have been rather guided in these stormy circumstances by the love of good, and by a sense of the country's wants, than by any exact theory, or precise rules of conduct.*

"It is time to distinguish clearly the aim of the revolution, and the term to which we would arrive. It is time for us to render account to ourselves, both of the obstacles which still keep us from that aim, and of the means which we ought to take to attain it.

"What is the aim to which we tend?

"The peaceful enjoyment of liberty and equality; the reign of that eternal justice, of which the laws have been engraved, not upon marble, but upon the hearts of all mankind; even in the hearts of the slaves who forget them, or of the tyrants who have denied them! We desire a state of things wherein all base and cruel passions shall be enchained; all generous and beneficent passions awakened by the laws; wherein ambition should be the desire of glory, and glory the desire of serving the country; wherein distinctions should arise but from equality itself; wherein the citizen should submit to the magistrate, the magistrate to the people, and the people to justice; wherein the country assures the welfare of every individual; wherein every individual enjoys with pride the prosperity and the glory of his country; wherein all minds are enlarged by the continual communication of republican sentiments, and by the desire of meriting the esteem of a great people; wherein arts should be the decorations of that liberty which they ennoble, and commerce the source of public wealth, and not the monstrous opulence of some few houses. We desire to substitute morality for egotism, probity for honor, principles for usages, duties for functions, the empire of reason for the tyranny of fashion, the scorn of vice for the scorn of misfortune, pride for insolence, greatness of soul for vanity, the love of glory for the love of money, good citizens for good society, merit for intrigue, genius for cleverness, truth for splendor, the charm of happiness for the *ennui* of voluptuousness, the grandeur of man for the pettiness of the great, a magnanimous people, powerful, happy, for a people amiable, frivolous, and miserable; that is to say, all the virtues and all the miracles of a republic, for all the vices and all the follies of a monarchy.

What is the nature of the government which can realize these prodigies? The democratic or republican government.

"Democracy is that state in which the people, guided by laws which are its own work, executes for itself all that it can well do, and, by its delegates, all that it cannot do itself. But to found and consolidate democracy, we must first end the war of liberty against tyranny, and traverse the storm of the revolution. Such is the aim of the revolutionary system which you have organized; you ought, therefore, to regulate your conduct by the circumstances in which the republic finds itself; and the plan of your administration ought to be the result of the spirit of revolutionary government, combined with the general principles of democracy.

"The great purity of the French revolution, the sublimity even of its object, is precisely that which makes our force and our weakness. Our force, because it gives us the ascendency of truth over imposture, and the rights of public interest over private interest. Our weakness, because it rallies against us all the vicious; all those who in their heart meditate the robbery of the people; all those who, having robbed them, seek impunity; and all those who have rejected liberty as a personal calamity, and those who have embraced the revolution as a trade, and the republic as a prey. Hence the defection of so many ambitious men, who have abandoned us on our route, because they did not commence the journey to arrive at the same object as we did. We must crush both the interior and exterior enemies of the republic, or perish with her. And in this situation, the first maxim of your policy should be to conduct the people by reason, and the enemies of the people by terror. If the spring of popular government during peace is virtue, the spring of popular government in rebellion is at once both virtue and terror; virtue, without which terror is fatal! terror, without which virtue is powerless! Terror is nothing else than justice, prompt, secure, and inflexible! It is, therefore, an emanation of virtue; it is less a particular principle, than a consequence of the general principles of democracy, applied to the most urgent wants of the country.

"It has been said that terror is the instrument of a despotic government. Does yours then resemble despotism? Yes, as the sword which glitters in the hand of a hero of liberty, resembles that with which the satellites of tyranny are armed! The *government of a revolution is the despotism of liberty against tyranny.* Is force then only made to protect crime? Is it not also made to strike those haughty heads which the lightning has doomed? Nature has imposed upon every being the law of self-preservation. Crime massacres innocence to reign, and innocence struggles with all its force in the hands of crime. Let tyranny but reign one day, and on the morrow there would not remain a single patriot. Until when will the fury of tyranny continue to be called justice, and the justice of the people barbarity and rebellion? How tender they are to oppressors: how inexorable to the oppressed! Nevertheless, it is necessary that one or the other should succumb. Indulgence for the Royalist! exclaimed certain people. Pardon for wretches! No! Pardon for innocence, pardon for the weak, pardon for the unhappy, pardon for humanity!"

This, it must be confessed, is very powerful writing. Amidst all the revolutionary jargon, however, one perceives the reactionary tendency of his thoughts. He sincerely wished for the reign of peace and justice. And now, when it seemed within human reach, there arose between him and it the fearful figures of the Anarchists, Hébert and his set. Opposing them, he incurred the accusation of Moderatism. What a charge: Robespierre a moderate! But such is the moral of revolutions: the vehement are easily surpassed in vehemence by those who make a trade of their fury.

Robespierre's popularity was too wide and too firmly fixed to be shaken by such a charge; and I find, in this very month of February, that, on the occasion of a slight illness, the popular societies were constantly sending deputations to inquire after his state of convalescence.

It should be observed that Robespierre was in decided antagonism to the Committee of Public Safety, of which he was a member; and his policy was far from prevailing in it. Because Robespierre best personifies the revolution, it has long been the custom to attribute to him the whole, or greater part of the responsibility of the acts of the Committee. But in truth he merited

"Ni cet excès d'honneur, ni cette indignité."

M. Louis Blanc told me of a curious fact relative to Robespierre's share in the executions which decimated France at that period. "If," said he, "there is one name of those belonging to the Committee which by almost universal consent has been allowed to escape infamy, it is that of Carnot; and if there is a name which has been execrated, it is that of Robespierre. Well; the records of that period show us Carnot's signature affixed to almost every sentence, while the signature of Robespierre is excessively rare!" This curious fact is the best answer to the formidable array of figures which the "Quarterly Review" brings forward to show how the number of executions increased after Robespierre's entry into the tribunal. The editors of the *Histoire Parlementaire* remark that Robespierre's real predominance commenced on the 7th of May, 1794, and finished on the 23d of June; but it was during the first six months which *preceded his reign,* and during the forty days which *elapsed after* his participation in the government, that the greatest number of heads fell. This does not appear to be quite accurate. The executions in 1794 were:

January	83	
February	75	
March	123	
April	263	
May	324	Robespierre's predominance.
June	672	His attendance ceased.
July	835	

From the 672, in June, must be deducted 199 executed after the 23d, leaving 473 for that portion of the month during which Robespierre was an attendant on the Committee.

These figures show a very rapid increase; but that was only the action of a political engine—the Terror. It must not wholly be laid at Robespierre's door; nor do we think the "Quarterly Review" correct in assuming that he ought to bear the onus, because, although he absented himself from the Committee, Saint Just and Couthon, his instruments, were there. The absence of his signature is very significant. If he was the blood-thirsty wretch he is usually depicted, how is the rarity of his signature to be explained, in a time when patriotism meant energy, when slaughter was a proof of civism?

Let no one imagine I wish to absolve Robespierre from the horrible responsibility of the Terror. If he did not sign the orders, he inflamed the minds of the people who instigated and permitted the slaughter. The Terror was his doctrine; let the responsibility fall upon his head. For *his* purposes he preached that doctrine; for *their* purposes shameless ruffians used it. While *he* thought of decimating enemies of the republic, *they* were reckless whom they decimated. Had the fanatic been pure—had he only sought the lives of formidable enemies, it would be unjust to charge him with the excesses committed in the name of his doctrine; but when did he ever raise his powerful voice to save the feeble, to save women, boys, and innocent men? Never. Yet there are men who not only vindicate his conduct, but who venerate him as a great, good man! Because he was not the monster which popular prejudice has figured him, there are men who, in the vehemence of reaction, proclaim him pure and noble!

Let me confess how much it has astonished me in wading through the voluminous memoirs and pamphlets of this period, to observe such universal virulence against Robespierre, coupled with such a total absence of any definite charges supported by facts. Men declare their intention of exposing his tyranny, and do nothing more than recount the acts of other members of the Comité. Hate must have an object: and Robespierre has borne the execration roused by the whole Comité. This is unjust. But justice forces me, after long and patient examination, to declare that if Robespierre is not to be charged with participation in many acts of bloodshed, he *is* to be charged with a most execrable indifference to bloodshed. Cold, pitiless, inhuman, reckless of human life when it opposed his ideas, his very consistency becomes a vice, because it is the rigid consistency of a logical proposition, not the steadiness of a truth-loving heart.

To return to our narrative. The struggle between Robespierre and the Anarchists was violent but brief. Camille Desmoulins started his *Vieux Cordelier*—the best written journal which appeared during the whole revolution—and he took the first number to Robespierre, knowing its attacks on Hébert would please him. But he neither approved nor blamed. He defended Camille, however, against the attacks of the Anarchists, and again defended Danton.

Hébert's friends were alarmed, and endeavored to move Robespierre by flattery. Hébert had a charming wife, who was intimate with the Duplays; and Robespierre felt for her that respect and esteem which he refused to her husband. She endeavored to reconcile them. At a dinner given by Duplay, she tried to dissipate the suspicions which Robespierre cherished against the Cordeliers. In the evening, Robespierre, unbending himself a little, insinuated that a concentration of power in a triumvirate, composed of himself, Hébert, and Danton, might perchance secure the Republic. Hébert replied that he was incapable of playing any other part than that of Aristophanes of the people. Robespierre turned from him with disgust. Hébert's wife, on their leaving, said, "Hébert, such an insinuation as the one you have repulsed is a mortal danger." "Reassure yourself," replied Hébert, "I fear Robespierre no more than Danton. Let them come, if they dare, to seek me in my commune." Robespierre did dare, and crushed him!

Danton was the next victim. Yes, Danton, his old rival, his friend, the man whom he had defended; the man with whom he had vainly tried to act! An intense anxiety agitated him during the days and weeks preceding his attack. He was often heard hypocritically exclaiming, "Oh, if Danton were but honest! If he were but a true republican!" "What would I not give for the lantern of Diogenes, to read the heart of Danton, and learn if he be the friend or the enemy of the Republic!" This was mere cant, it is to be feared.

The Mountain became aware of the pending struggle. Compelled to choose between these two men, their heart, as Lamartine says, was for Danton; their head for Robespierre. They adored the first, whose voice had so often electrified them; the second they dreaded more than they loved. His concentrated character, his repulsive manner, and his imperious language, repelled all familiarity. But they felt that if Danton were their favorite patriot, Robespierre was the legislator of their views; and that without Robespierre, the Republic would be a hurricane without a course.

Danton was warned, but with his usual audacity he said he was stronger than his enemies, and that they dared not attack him. They did attack him, however, and Saint Just made a detail of his crimes, and demanded his arrest, together with that of his principal accomplices, Lacroix, Philippeaux, and Camille Desmoulins.

All eyes were turned on Robespierre; but he who had risen indignantly when first Billaud Varennes proposed Danton's arrest; he who had then so energetically defended Danton, now was silent. This silence made them understand that Saint Just had spoken for both. Danton was arrested.

In those days, accusation was synonymous with condemnation; and Danton fell. His last moments were full of audacity and ostentation, the very bravado of infamy. As he passed beneath Robespierre's windows, the mob which accompanied the cart roared its execrations. The shutters were closed, but the shouts made Robespierre turn pale, and he turned into an inner apartment. He had destroyed his rival, and trembled at his work. "Poor Camille," said he; "and I could not save him!" "As to Danton," he added, "he only clears the path for me. Innocent, or guilty, we must all give our heads to the Republic."

The death of Hébert made Robespierre master of the Commune; the death of Danton, master of the Convention; while at the Jacobins his influence had never been disputed.

CHAPTER XX.

The Comité—Robespierre at the height of power—Speaks against the Atheists—Attempt to assassinate him—Festival of the Supreme Being, and Robespierre's discourse—Robespierre weary of the Terror—The law of the 22d Prairial—Robespierre's cowardice—His struggle against his enemies—Catherine Théot—Charlotte Robespierre's letter to Maximilien.

THE republicans had destroyed their King, their Queen, their nobles, their virtuous and their illustrious leaders; they now turned against each other. Danton—Camille—Hébert—these popular idols had fallen; how long could Robespierre survive?

He was now seemingly arrived at the height of his power; but in effect he was less powerful than before. The opinion of France decreed him the dictatorship, and his colleagues feigned to believe in it. His name reigned, but he was powerless. He had not the courage to organize his dictatorship. Lamartine says that he refused the supreme power, because he knew not what revolutionary institutions to give the Republic. A man of thought rather than a man of action, he possessed the sentiment of the revolution rather than its political formulæ. His theories were brilliant, but vague. He believed that the words Liberty, Equality, Disinterestedness, Devotedness, and Virtue, were sufficient for a government. He was irritated at his want of success in establishing order, and attributed to others the failure of his plans. He tried to cut through difficulties by the guillotine; then, irritated at the very excess of bloodshed, he returned to ideas of justice and humanity. "Death—always death!" he frequently exclaimed in private, "and the scoundrels throw it all upon me! What a memory shall I leave behind me if this lasts! Life is a burden to me."

One phrase escaped him which seems to me to be singularly significant of his whole career. "No, I was not made to rule; I was made to combat the enemies of the people." He was not made to govern, for he had not a doctrine wherewith to govern, he had not even the practical mind, he had not the necessary energy which could have made him adopt and execute the plan of another. While thus vacillating, he was an object of hatred and terror to the Convention. Hitherto, his disinterestedness had been universally believed, but suspicions now arose of his ambition.

He had obtained a brilliant success against the Atheists. He caused the liberty of worship to be decreed; but his speeches remained mere *speeches:* they did not become *acts*. The parliamentary and administrative acts continued to be dictated by the spirit which he had combated, and to serve the passions which he had endeavored to enchain. The pro-consuls sent into the departments were in no degree influenced by him. The Convention, as the "Histoire Parlementaire" very truly says, judged that it was politic to oppose to the manifestoes of the coalition the moral and religious apologies of Robespierre, but as for adopting them as its profession of faith and the rule of its actions, it did nothing of the kind. On all the serious occasions which followed his discourses against the Atheists, every time that Robespierre endeavored to make his personal influence prevail, he failed completely. Camille Desmoulins, in his " Vieux Cordelier," had demanded a Committee of Clemency. Robespierre proposed and caused to be decreed a Committee of Justice. This committee was to examine the accusation of *les suspects*, to revise arrests, and to watch with care that the precipitation commanded by public safety should fall on no innocent victim. But the Committee of General Safety, and the Committee of Public Safety, to whom this decree was sent to form into a law, found it dangerous, and modified it in such a manner as completely to change its nature; and in spite of the representations of Robespierre, they declared it impossible to execute. In the Committee of Public Safety, according to the excellent testimony of Senart, there were three parties: the politicians, Robespierre, Couthon, and Saint Just; the revolutionists, Billaud Varennes, Barrère, and Collot D'Herbois; and the administrators, Carnot, Lindet, and Prieur. Between Robespierre's party and that of Billaud Varennes there was little concord.

When Robespierre was absent, they muttered the word " tyrant." They accused him of domineering, or else of remaining silent, and of leaving to the Committee the responsibility of the acts which he had inspired. He often blamed at the Jacobins what he had consented to at the Tuileries. He arrived late, entered with a negligent air, seated himself without speaking, cast his eyes upon the table, leaned his face upon his hands, expressed neither praise nor blame; and habitually feigned absence of mind—sometimes sleep, to show his indifference. Of this and more they accused him. It was certainly not the way to be popular in the Committee. They looked on him not only as a tyrant, but as one who knew, and despised them. And still greater crime !—he was now wearied of the Terror. He wished to found a republic of virtue. What place could Billaud and his associates hope to have in such a republic?

Robespierre, although he had no precise doctrine, had, in an extraordinary degree, what Lamartine calls the *sentiment* of the revolution. He felt—no one more strongly—the necessity of a doctrine: and that religious tendency which I have been careful to point out as characteristic of his mind, now suggested to him his famous festival "de l'Etre Suprême." A republic, he thought, should have no other sovereignty than that of morality; it should have for its basis a divine idea.

In the beginning of April, he passed some days in the forest of Montmorency. There he often visited the hut in which Jean Jacques Rousseau had lived. It was in this house, in this garden, where his master had so eloquently written of God, that he finished his famous report.

On the 18th of Floréal (7th of May, 1794) he ascended the tribune to read his report on the relation between religious and moral ideas, and republican principles.

"The only basis of civilized society," said he, "is morality. To what, then, is this mysterious science of politics and legislation reduced? To the introduction into our laws and administration of those moral truths which are found in the books of philosophers, and the application to the conduct of those trivial notions of probity which every one is forced to adopt for his own private conduct; that is to say, to employ as much ability in establishing the reign of justice, as governments have hitherto employed for injustice.

"Citizens," he continues, "every doctrine which consoles and elevates the mind ought to be received; reject all those which tend to degrade it and corrupt it. Reanimate—exalt—every generous sentiment and those great moral truths which some have attempted to extinguish. Who has commissioned thee to announce to the people that the Divinity exists not, O thou who art impassioned for this arid doctrine, and who hast no passion for thy country? What advantage is there in persuading man that a blind force presides over his destiny, and strikes, at hazard, both crime and virtue? that his soul is but a breath, which is dissipated at the portal of the tomb?

"Will the idea of his annihilation inspire him with purer or more elevated sentiments than that of his immortality? Will it inspire him with greater respect for mankind or for himself; more devotion for his country;

more boldness against tyranny; or more contempt for death? You who regret a virtuous friend, you love to think that his soul has escaped death! You who weep over the coffin of a son or of a wife, are you consoled by him who tells you that nothing more remains of them than the vile dust? Ye unfortunate, who perish by the blade of an assassin—your last sigh is an appeal to eternal justice. Innocence upon the scaffold makes the tyrant in his triumphal chariot turn pale. Would it have this power if the grave leveled the oppressor and the oppressed? The more sensibility and genius a man has, the more he attaches himself to ideas which elevate him; and the doctrine of such men becomes that of the world.

"The idea of the Supreme Being and of the immortality of the soul is a continual appeal to justice; this idea is then social and republican. (*Applause.*) I know of no legislator who ever attempted to nationalize atheism. I know that the wisest among them have mingled some fiction with truth, to strike the imaginations of the ignorant, or to attach them more firmly to their institutions. Lycurgus and Solon had recourse to the authority of oracles: and Socrates himself, to accredit truth amongst his fellow-citizens, was obliged to persuade them that he was inspired by a familiar demon.

"You will not thence conclude that it is necessary to deceive men to instruct them; but only that you are fortunate in living in an age and in a country whose enlightenment leaves us no other task to fulfil than to recall men to nature and to truth.

"Be very cautious not to sever the sacred bond which unites men to the author of their being.

"And what has been substituted in place of what has been destroyed? Nothing—if it be not chaos and violence. They despised the people too much to take the trouble of persuading them; in lieu of enlightening them, they desired only to irritate and deprave them.

"If the principles which I have developed so far are errors, I err, at least with all whom the world reveres. Let us learn the lessons of history. Remark how men who have influenced the destiny of states were determined towards one or the other of two opposite systems by their personal character, and even by the nature of their political views. See with what profound art Cæsar, pleading in the Roman senate in favor of the accomplices of Catiline, wanders into a digression against the dogma of the immortality of the soul; so much did these ideas appear to him calculated to extinguish in the hearts of the judges the energy of virtue; so closely did the cause of vice appear to him allied to atheism. Cicero, on the contrary, invoked against traitors both the sword of the law and the thunder of the gods. Socrates, when dying, conversed with his friends on the immortality of the soul. Leonidas, at Thermopylæ, supping with his companions in arms on the eve of one of the most heroic designs that human virtue ever conceived, invited them on the morrow to a banquet in another world. There is some distance between Socrates and Chaumette, between Leonidas and Père Duchêne! (*Loud applause.*)

"A great man, a veritable hero, esteems himself too highly to delight in the idea of his annihilation. A wretch, contemptible in his own eyes, horrible in those of others, feels that nature cannot bestow upon him a better gift than annihilation. (*Applause.*)

"A sect propagated with great zeal the materialism which prevailed amongst the nobles and the *beaux esprits*; to it is owing, in great part, that practical philosophy which, reducing egotism to a system, regards human society as a war of cunning, success as the rule of the just and of the unjust, honesty as an affair of taste and convenience, and the world as the patrimony of adroit rogues. Amongst those who, at the time of which I speak, signalized themselves in the career of letters and of philosophy, one man, Rousseau, by the elevation of his mind and the grandeur of his character, showed himself worthy of being the preceptor of the human race. He openly attacked tyranny. He spoke with the enthusiasm of the Divinity; his masculine and virtuous eloquence painted in glowing colors the charms of virtue; it defended those consolatory dogmas with which reason supports the human heart. The purity of his doctrine, drawn from nature, and in profound hatred of vice, no less than his invincible contempt for the intriguing sophists who usurped the name of philosophers, drew upon him the hatred and persecution of his rivals and of his false friends. Ah, if he had witnessed this Revolution, of which he was the precursor, and which has carried him to the Pantheon, who can doubt that his generous soul would have embraced with transport the cause of justice and equality? But what have his cowardly adversaries done for it? They have fought against the Revolution from the moment they feared that it would raise the people above them.

"The traitor Guadet denounced a citizen for having pronounced the name of Providence! We heard, some time afterwards, Hébert accuse another for having written against Atheism! Was it not Vergniaud and Gensonné, who, in your presence, wished to banish from the preamble of the constitution the name of the Supreme Being, which you had placed therein? Danton, who smiled with pity at the words of virtue, glory, and posterity; Danton, whose system was to debase all that could elevate the mind; Danton, who was cold and dumb during the greatest dangers of liberty, supported them. Fanatics, hope nothing from us! To recall men to the pure worship of the Supreme Being is to give a mortal blow to fanaticism. All fiction disappears before truth, and every folly falls before reason. Without constraint, without persecution, every sect ought to amalgamate itself with the universal religion of nature. (*Applause.*) Ambitious priests, do not expect, then, that we shall re-establish your empire! Such an enterprise would be even above our power. (*Applause.*) You have destroyed yourselves. And, besides, what is there in common between the priests and God! How different is the God of nature from the God of Priests. (*Continued applause.*) I know of nothing so resembling atheism as the religions they have made. They have so disfigured the Supreme Being that they have done their best to destroy the idea; they have made him sometimes a globe of fire, sometimes an ox, sometimes a tree, sometimes a man, and sometimes a king. Priests created a God in their own image,—they made him jealous, capricious, covetous, cruel, and implacable. They have treated him as the mayors of the palace treated the descendants of Clovis, to reign in his name, and to put themselves in his place; they have exiled him to heaven, and have only called him upon earth, to serve him in their demand for wealth, honors, pleasures, and power. (*Loud applause.*) The true priest of the Supreme Being is Nature; His temple the universe; His religion virtue; His *fêtes* the joy of a great people assembled under his eyes, to draw closer the sweet bonds of universal fraternity, and to present to him the homage of pure and sensitive hearts.

"Let us leave the priests and return to the Divinity. (*Applause.*) Let us establish morality upon an eternal and sacred basis; let us inspire in man that religious aspect for man, that profound sentiment of his duties, which is the sole guarantee of social happiness.

"Woe on him who seeks to extinguish this sublime enthusiasm, and to stifle by desolating doctrines this moral instinct of the people, which is the principle of all great actions! It belongs to you, representatives of the people, to cause the truths we have developed to triumph. Brave the wild clamor of presumptuous ignorance, of hypocritical perversity! Will posterity believe that the vanquished factions carried their audacity so far as to accuse us of moderation and of aristocracy, because we recalled the ideas of the Divinity and morality? Will it believe that in this hall it was said that we had thus thrown human reason back several centuries? Let us not be surprised if all the wretches combined against us prepare hemlock for us, but before we drink it, let us save the country. (*Applause.*) The vessel which bears the fortune of the republic is not destined to be wrecked, she sails under your auspices, and the storm itself will be compelled to respect her. (*Applause.*)

"The enemies of the Republic are all corrupt men. (*Applause.*) The patriot is in every sense an honest and magnanimous man. (*Applause.*) It is little to annihilate kings; we must make every nation respect the character of the French people. It is useless to bear to the end of the universe the renown of our arms, if every passion tears with impunity the bosom of our own country. Let us beware of the intoxication of success! Let us be terrible in reverses, modest in triumph (*applause*), and let us secure peace and happiness by wisdom and morality. That is the true aim of our labors—that our heroic and difficult task. We believe we shall achieve this aim by proposing the following decree:—

"Art. 1st. The French people recognize the existence of the Supreme Being, and the immortality of the soul.

"Art. 2d. They acknowledge that the worship worthy of the Supreme Being is one of the duties of man."

All France resounded with his praises. Petitions flowed in from the departments urging him to continue in that high moral strain, and the Republic would be saved. The most immoral of the revolutionists adopted probity and virtue as watch-words; but in the midst of all the applause which his discourses excited, Robespierre could easily discover that the majority of the Convention was decidedly hostile to his dogmas—that they only thought they were fulfilling a simple formality in decreeing his propositions; and while they applauded all the violent accusations against priests, superstitions, fanaticism, and hypocrisy, they listened with incredulity and silence to the enunciation of his religious views.*

Charlotte Corday now found her imitator. In the second article of the Declaration of Rights, these words occur: "The tyrant of a country may be put to death by a free man." Men who called themselves free had put to death the King they called a tyrant, but it is surprising how few attempts were made to assassinate the tyrants of the Convention. Marat had fallen, yet no one had imitated Charlotte Corday until now.

* I have often paused to make comparisons between the Revolution and that which is going on in France at the time I write this; and I may therefore throw into a note the following paragraph:—

"At Rodez, the chief town of the department of Aveiron, there is a club of women, and the first question discussed in it was on the existence of God. The debate was very animated, and the two parties were so nearly equal that a solution was for a long time in suspense. It was finally decided in favor of the existence of a God, by a majority of twelve votes."—*Daily News*, 10th June, 1848.

Curiously enough, two distinct attempts at assassination were made in one day. The first was by a man called Ladmiral, who came to Paris with the intention of killing Robespierre. It so happened, that he lodged in the same house with Collot d'Herbois. He laid in wait for Robespierre several days in vain. At length, wearied with seeking him, he deemed that fate had pointed out another, and one night, meeting Collot d'Herbois on the stairs, he snapped a pistol at him. It flashed in the pan. He snapped a second; it hung fire. The ball passed close by Collot's head. Collot grappling with the assassin, both rolled down the stairs. The report of the pistol alarmed the house. Ladmiral shut himself in his room, and threatened to fire on the first man who approached him. A locksmith ventured and was instantly shot, but Ladmiral, after a desperate struggle, was seized and brought before Fouquier Tinville. There he declared he sought to deliver his country from a tyrant.

At the very same moment a young girl of seventeen went to Robespierre's house, and asked to see him. Her youth and innocent appearance lulled all suspicion, and she was shown into the ante-room. There she remained some time, till her pertinacity exciting attention, she was told to withdraw. She declined. "A public man," she said, "should be accessible to all who wished to see him." A guard was called in; she was searched. They found in her basket some clothes and two small knives. She was carried before the Tribunal of the Rue des Piques, and there examined. "What was the object of your visit to Robespierre?" "I wanted," she replied, "to see what a tyrant was like."

Her name was Cécile Renault. She was the daughter of a paper maker. On being asked why she provided herself with the clothes, she said, "Because I expected to be sent to prison." "Explain the presence of the two knives? Did you intend to stab Robespierre?" "No, I never wished to hurt any one in my life." "What made you wish to see Robespierre?" "To satisfy myself if he was like the man I had imagined." "Why are you a royalist?" "Because I prefer one king to sixty tyrants."

The news of these two attempts caused great fury against the Royalists, and increased the idolatry for Robespierre.

At the sitting of the Convention on the next day, Barrère exaggerated the dangers. He accused Mr. Pitt (of course the gold of Pitt!) of having instigated Ladmiral and Cécile. Robespierre also spoke in the same strain.

The 8th of June arrived. It was the day fixed for the festival *de l'Etre Suprême.* Robespierre had awaited it with feverish impatience; for of all missions, the highest and most holy in his eyes was the regeneration of the religious sentiment of the people.

His private friends were surprised at his unusual serenity. As he wandered with them in the garden of Mosseaux, his heart beat with joy, and he talked of nothing but the 8th of June, when he hoped to close the Terror and to open the era of fraternity and clemency. The fête had been organized under the directions of the painter David, and Cuvellier, a well known writer of pantomimes and spectacles; of course, under the direction of Robespierre himself, who was anxious that this ceremony should be very impressive. "But why," said he to Souberville on the previous evening, "why must there be one scaffold left in France! Life alone ought to-morrow to appear before the Source of all life," and he insisted that punishments should be suspended on that day.

Barrère and Collot D'Herbois had agreed to breakfast with Vilate. On calling, they found him out. He encountered them in the street, in company with Prieur and Carnot, who wanted him to breakfast with him at a restaurant. "I quitted them," says Vilate, "and in passing through the Salle de la Liberté I met Robespierre, attired in the costume of a Representative, holding in his hand a bouquet of flowers. For the first time his face was lit up with joy. He had not breakfasted. With a heart full of the sentiment which this superb day inspired, I invited him to come home with me and breakfast. He accepted without hesitation. He was astonished at the immense concourse of people which crowded in the gardens of the Tuileries, hope and gaiety beaming upon every face; the women all in their gayest dresses. He scarcely ate anything. His eyes wandered constantly towards this magnificent spectacle, and he seemed plunged in the intoxication of enthusiasm. 'Behold,' said he, 'the most interesting portion of humanity! the Universe is here collected together. Oh, Nature! how sublime and delicious is thy power! How tyrants ought to turn pale at the idea of this fête!' That was all he said."

The Convention, as an honor, nominated Robespierre their President, in order that the author of the decree might also be the principal actor therein. As he rose to place himself at the head of the procession, which was already moving, a young woman residing at Vilate's house, entered with a child in her arms. The name of Robespierre at first frightened the stranger, but he, reassuring her, began playing with the child; the young mother playfully obtained from him his bouquet.

It was past twelve o'clock, and Robespierre forgot that he was keeping his colleagues waiting. They murmured at his delay; he enjoyed it as a proof of their inferiority.

The day was magnificent; the sky of an eastern purity. Robespierre, attired in a coat of pale blue, a white waistcoat, yellow leather breeches, top boots, and a round hat, with a quantity of *tri-color* ribbons in it, fixed universal attention. In his hand was an enormous bouquet of flowers and wheat-ears. Garlands of oak foliage, and wheat-sheaves, were hung from every window, and thrown across the street on the ropes of the night lamps.

Paris on that day was a splendid spectacle. An immense amphitheatre, resembling an ancient circus, was erected behind the Tuileries. In the centre of this amphitheatre an elevated tribune, somewhat resembling a throne, was reserved for Robespierre. In front of this was a colossal group of figures, representing Atheism, Selfishness, Annihilation, Crime, and Vice. These were formed out of combustible materials, and were to be set on fire as a sacrifice. The idea of a God was to reduce them to ashes. All the deputies, uniformly dressed in blue coats with red facings, each carrying a symbolical bouquet, slowly seated themselves on the steps. Robespierre appeared with the air of a master; imperial acclamations hailed him. The multitude was eager to hear him. Some expected an amnesty, others the organization of a powerful and merciful government. The minds of all were greatly agitated. Strangers embraced each other.

"Frenchmen, republicans!" said Robespierre; "at length the happy day has arrived, which the French people consecrate to the Supreme Being! Never did the world offer to its author a spectacle so worthy of his contemplation. He has seen tyranny, crime, imposture on the throne. He sees at this moment a whole nation fighting against all the oppressors of the human race, suspending the course of their heroic labors, to raise up their thoughts and vows to the Great Being who gave them this mission, and gave them the force to execute it!

"He did not create kings to oppress the human race; he did not create priests to yoke us like vile animals to the car of kings, and present an example of baseness, pride, perfidy, avarice, debauchery, and falsehood: but he created the universe to make known his power; he created men to aid and love each other, and to attain happiness by the path of virtue.

"It is He who places remorse in the bosom of the triumphant oppressor, and calm pride in the heart of oppressed innocence; it is He who forces the just man to hate the wicked, and the wicked man to respect the just; it is He who adorns with modesty the brow of beauty to embellish it the more; it is He who makes mothers' hearts to throb with tenderness and joy; it is He who bathes with delicious tears the eyes of the child pressed to its mother's bosom; it is He who makes sublime patriotism superior to the most energetic and tenderest passions; it is He who has covered nature with charms, wealth, and majesty. All that is good is His work—evil belongs to depraved man, who oppresses or allows his fellow-creatures to be oppressed.

"The Author of Nature had bound all mortals together by a vast chain of love and felicity: perish the tyrants who have dared to break it!

"Being of Beings! we address to thee no unjust prayers. Thou knowest the creatures sent forth from thy hands; their wants do not escape thine eyes, neither do their most secret thoughts. The hatred of hypocrisy and tyranny burns in our hearts with the love of justice and our country. Our blood flows for the cause of humanity! This is our prayer—this is our sacrifice—this the worship we offer unto thee!"

Strains of music then filled the air, and thousands of voices sang the hymn composed by Chénier.

THE LIFE OF ROBESPIERRE.

I.

THE MEN.

"Dieu puissant, d'un peuple intrépide,
C'est toi qui defends les remparts;
La victoire a, d'un vol rapide,
Accompagné nos étendards.
Les Alpes et les Pyrénées,
Des rois ont vu tomber l'orgueil;
Au nord nos champs sont le cerceuil
De leurs phalanges consternies.

Chorus.

Avant de déposer nos glaives triomphans,
Jurons d'anéantir le crime et les tyrans.

II.

THE WOMEN.

Entend les vierges et les mères,
Auteur de la fécondité!
Nos époux, nos enfans, nos frères
Combattent pour la liberté;
Et si quelque main criminelle
Terminait des destins si beaux,
Leurs fils viendront sur ses tombeaux
Venger la cendre paternelle.

Chorus.

Avant de déposer nos glaives triomphans,
Jurez d'anéantir le crime et les tyrans.

MEN AND WOMEN TOGETHER.

Guerriers, offrez votre courage;
Jeunes filles, offrez des fleurs;
Mères, viellards, pour votre hommage
Offrez vos fils triomphateurs;
Bénissez, dans ce jour de gloire,
Le fer consacré par leurs mains:
Sur ce fer, vengeur des humains,
L'Eternel grava la victoire.

Chorus.

Avant de déposer nos glaives triomphans,
Jurons ⎫
Jurez ⎭ d'anéantir le crime et les tyrans."

During this chorus, the women flung their flowers up into the air; the young men drew their swords, and swore to render their arms everywhere victorious; the old men placed their hands upon their heads, giving a paternal benediction.

Robespierre, descending from the tribune, set fire to the group of Atheism, amidst the acclamations of the multitude. Then the members of the Convention, following him at some distance, advanced in two columns, towards the Champ de Mars. Between these two columns were rustic cars, ploughs drawn by bullocks, and symbols of agriculture, the trades, and the arts. A group, of girls clothed in white, attached to each other by tri-colored ribbons, accompanied the Convention. Robespierre, with elated looks, on his lips an ineffable smile of security and enthusiasm, frequently turned round, in order to measure the distance left between himself and his colleagues; as if to accustom the people to separate him from them by respect, as he separated himself from them by distance. In the centre of the Champ de Mars, a symbolic eminence was raised on the spot of the ancient altar of the country. Robespierre, with Couthon, Saint Just, and Lebas, (all his friends,) were on the summit. The rest of the Convention were spread about at the sides.

From this elevation, amidst salvos of artillery, he proclaimed the Profession of Faith of the French People. The people were intoxicated, the Convention sullen. The enthusiasm of the people only rankled in the bosoms of the Convention. They saw Robespierre growing into the worst of dictators—a religious dictator. He noticed their sinister looks and menacing gestures, and overheard some of the significant phrases which escaped them. "There is but one step from the Capitol to the Tarpeian rock," exclaimed one. "Brutus still lives," murmured another. "Behold that man," said a third; "he wishes to accustom the people to adore

some one in order that they may learn to adore him by and by."
"He has invented a God because God is the supreme tyrant,"
said a fourth. "He wishes to be the high priest. Let him take
care he is not the victim!"

This day, indeed, so glorious for Robespierre, ruined him with
the Convention. He felt it, and returned pensive to his habitation.
He was there all day besieged by anonymous congratulations. Protracted shouts beneath his window thanked him for having "restored a soul to the people, and a god to the Republic." Several
notes contained only the word, "Dare!"

Such was the *Fête de l' Etre Suprême:* to France, a day of hope
and great rejoicing—a grand and imposing spectacle; to us, one
of the most colossal pieces of buffoonery written in the annals of
human folly. The idea of any man, or body of men, solemnly
decreeing the existence of a God, and that "consolatory idea" of
the immortality of the soul, is too much for our gravity. Yet it
was taken very seriously by the French, and the Journal of the
Mountain speaks of it in these terms:—"This fête, so imposing
in its object, was celebrated with a simple and majestic pomp,
truly worthy of the Eternal Author of Nature."

There can be no doubt of Robespierre's seriousness. There can
be no doubt of the people's seriousness. Even Charles Nodier,
writing many years afterwards, and writing from his recollections,
speaks of it as a most imposing solemnity. All one can say is,
that it was intensely French. For can we without a smile read a
plan of the fête, which was proposed by David, and decreed by
the Convention, in which the whole thing was laid out beforehand;
tears, enthusiasm, and shouts of joy included. "Whilst the infant presses its mother's breast, of which he is the most beautiful
ornament," says the prospective report, "the son with vigorous
arm seizes his sword; he will only receive the sword-belt from the
hands of his father. The old man, smiling with pleasure, his
eyes moist with tears of joy, feels his spirit become young again
in presenting the sword to the defender of liberty." And of
course the old man was obliged to fulfil this programme; he was
obliged to shed tears of joy. A command was laid upon his sen-

sibility; his patriotism was engaged for that performance. On the stage, actors sob with very dry eyes; a cambric handkerchief and two hands covering the countenance, suffice for the most heartbreaking distress. Let us hope, in this gigantic farce planned by the Convention, theatrical expedients were permitted, and that those who could not exhibit eyes moist with patriotic tears, were allowed to cover their eyes with patriotic hands!

In the same programme we see how the people are to fill the streets and public places, joy and fraternity inflaming their souls; and it is arranged, that the people, like a true chorus of opera-singers, "at certain intervals shall make the air resound with cries of joy; they shall embrace, and when they see Atheism in flames, tears of delight and gratitude shall flow from all their eyes." It is also arranged that there shall be numberless mothers with infants at the breast, in order that, at a given signal, they may press them more tenderly to those breasts, as a homage to the author of Nature. In this way is the fête arranged; in this theatrical way is it carried out: and yet, amidst all this buffoonery, this calculated sensibility, this well-rehearsed enthusiasm, there was a real seriousness, and an intense excitement pervading the whole ceremony. Such is the Frenchman's nature; he is theatrical when he is serious, and he is serious even in his theatricality.

Robespierre had gained the people; he had gained the dictatorship, if he had had the courage to take it. But he had also bitterly estranged from him the greater part of the Convention, who groaned over the approaching tyranny of a man who so obviously despised them; and Billaud Varennes, in his brutal way, said to Robespierre, "*Avec ton Être Suprême, tu commences à m'embêter:*—With your Supreme Being you begin infernally to bore me."

Saint Just endeavored to make Robespierre accept the dictatorship. Finding he could not prevail upon him, he tried to make the Committee of Public Safety decree it: but at the word Dictator every visage was overshadowed; no one dared dispute the genius and virtue of Robespierre, but the idea of a dictator made the Committee tremble. Of course, Saint Just's proposition was imputed to Robespierre as a crime. "These men," said Billaud, "do not beg the supreme power; they assume it. Let them seize it if they dare." On the day after the festival of the Supreme Being, the Convention, at the instigation of Robespierre and his adherents, passed a number of decrees imbued with the better spirit of the revolution. The people began to hope that they had at last obtained the true principle of democracy. The scaffold alone still threw its shadow over all their hopes; the scaffold still stood before them, darkening the bright future.

Robespierre secretly entertained hopes of abolishing it. Napoleon has told us that he had seen letters from Robespierre to his younger brother, in which his resolution was announced of abolishing terror, and commencing the reign of peace. Unhappily Robespierre had not courage, as I have said before, but only spasms of audacity. He could not calmly dare, he could only act spasmodically. He was terrible because he was weak, and his only notion of abolishing terror was by inspiring still greater terror!

Warned by the murmurs which he had heard around him at the Festival of the Supreme Being—warned by Saint Just and Lebas of the hatred of the committees, he resolved to astonish his rivals by his audacity, and outstrip them by his rapidity.

On the twenty-second Prairial, only two days after the festival, he suddenly proposed to the Convention a decree for the re-organization of the revolutionary tribunal. This terrible project had only been partly communicated to the Committee. It was a code of arbitrary power; its instrument was the guillotine; the dictatorship not of a man but of the scaffold.

He was wearied of the Terrorists. He had used them as his instruments to destroy obstacles on his path, and now wished to destroy them. Those who defend Robespierre should not overlook this. The man who had acted with the Terrorists and Anarchists, the man who had defended them, cannot be absolved from all participation in their acts. "Those who handle honey sometimes lick their fingers."* A man who lives with assassins cannot es-

---

* "Handelt einer mit Honig er leckt zuoveilen die Finger."
                                      Göthe: Reinecke Fuchs.

cape being stained with blood. Robespierre knew very well the characters with whom he associated, yet he defended Danton and condemned him. He defended General Rossignol, knowing very well what sort of a man he was. What his motives were is not so easy, perhaps, to ascertain. Men's motives form a delicate subject for the psychologist. In the hearts of all men there are dim *feelings* which never struggle into the clearness of *thoughts*. These feelings are motives which determine actions, but you are not to suppose, because *you* can drag them from their obscure recesses into the light of day, that therefore the men themselves saw them as clearly as you do. We should not forget this in judging of mankind. That which is, perhaps, a mystery to the man himself, we interpret; divesting it of all the sophisms with which he clouds his motives from his conscience, we make it very clear to us, and then attribute to him the same clear vision. Still it is impossible, even in the ferment of a revolution, that Robespierre should not, from time to time, have paused to ask himself, when he traveled on the same road with men he knew to be ruffians, whether the object of his journey was altogether pure. When he saw men using the same phrases as he used, performing the same acts, and professing the same opinions, why did he not ask himself whether there was not something unworthy of an honest man in such company, whether he was justified in using them even as instruments.

Enough for us, now, to know, that he was really heart-sick of this business, and that he wanted above all things to rid the nation of the Terrorists. Hence this famous law of the 22d Prairial; the first political crime, according to the Histoire Parlementaire, which he committed. The editors of that work think his conduct wholly pure and excusable before the presentation of that law, which they unhesitatingly condemn. "He wished," they say, "to create an instrument which would purify the Convention of those whose conduct stained the present, and menaced the future. In this sense he exaggerated revolutionary passions. He exaggerated even terror, in order to lull all suspicion, and to obtain an increase of authority. He made a compromise with evil, to acquire the power of doing some good."

What miserable weakness does such a plan reveal! A man

who can only rid himself of his enemies, and rid his country of its oppressors by such means, has clearly no vocation whatever to interfere in public affairs. The intention of Robespierre in this law was seen through. Among the decrees of the Convention, was one with which it had reserved to itself the exclusive right of ordering its members before the Revolutionary Tribunal, only allowing the Committee a power of arresting them. The law of the twenty-second Prairial reduced this procedure to a few points of form. The result was that the members of the Convention were placed under the immediate dependence of the Committee of Public Safety; they could be condemned as soon as designated. Obliged to explain himself on the drift of his law, Robespierre was forced to confess that he had no *arrière pensée*. He defended himself against such a thought, as unworthy of him, as a calumny imagined by those who wished to divide the Convention. Forced to break thus, with his own hands, the weapon which he had attempted to use, Robespierre ceased in point of fact to participate in the Government. He appeared no longer in the Committees, and turned all his efforts towards the Jacobins. There he labored to exalt the moral sentiments of the people, and to guide public opinion, in the hope of raising an insurrection against the corrupt portion of the Convention. Such a system could have but one issue. The law which Robespierre had proposed, to secure to himself a sure means of striking at the great culprits, became, in the hands of the Committees, by the use they made of it, the instrument of an atrocious despotism. Instead of decimating the Convention, it only increased the number of executions. It was then commenced the great *batches*, as they were called, when men were brought by fifties and sixties before the Revolutionary Tribunal, where they remained scarcely time enough to pronounce their names, and to hear their condemnation.

No sooner had Robespierre retired, than a commission was named by the Committee, to make a revision of the prisons. He exercised no sort of influence on the election of this commission, though all depended on its composition. It sent before the Tribunal all the names of the men it considered as culpable. The

Committee of Public Salvation transformed these lists into lists of accusation, and transmitted them to the public accuser. "It matters little," as the editors of the *Histoire Parlementaire* observes, "that Robespierre did not participate at all in this; it matters little that neither he, nor his friends knew of these lists; that the public accuser, Fouquier Tinville, declared at his trial, that Robespierre was always a stranger to these accusations, *and that he had never seen his signature;* Robespierre still stands before posterity, accused of having, by his decree, given the signal of these executions *en masse.*" On the evening previous to the day when Lacoste was to make his report on the conspiracy of Ladmiral, and Cecile Rénault, Vadier came to the Committee. "To-morrow," said he to Robespierre, "I shall make my report, and shall propose that the Sainte Amaranthe family be implicated in the accusation." "You will do nothing of the kind," replied Robespierre, imperatively. "I shall," was Vadier's rejoinder; "I have all the documents in my hand. They prove the conspiracy, and I will unfold the whole mystery." "*Proofs or no proofs, if you venture, I will attack you,*" retorted Robespierre. "You are the tyrant of the Committee," said Vadier. "Ah! I am the tyrant of the Committee," exclaimed Robespierre, with difficulty restraining tears of rage. "Well, then, I release you from my tyranny; I withdraw. Save my country without me, if you can. I am determined not to imitate Cromwell." And he withdrew.

Some regarded this as weakness, others as skilful policy. I confess I look upon it as weakness; as mere irritation and incompetency. Lamartine thinks that the courage which he had hitherto shown in the presence of his enemies, and which he afterwards exhibited in the presence of death, will not allow us to suppose that it was weakness which actuated him. But if I have presented his character truly, the reader will not hesitate as to the opinion to be formed respecting Robespierre's courage. It was in vain that, when he found he could not restrain the Committees, he separated himself from his colleagues, fancying that he acquitted himself of the responsibility of his law by his absence. He declared himself, indeed, in open opposition against the government, and as he meditated the overthrow of the Committee, he would not remain an accomplice of its acts. Not so would Cromwell, or Mirabeau, or Danton, or Buonaparte have acted. Indeed, when Robespierre said he would not imitate Cromwell, he should have said, I *cannot* imitate him.

It is certain that his absence caused even more blood to be shed. Terror became not only a passion, but a necessity. Whichever of the two parties should first relent was certain that instant to fall under the accusation of weakness, of moderation, or of complicity with the enemies of the Republic. The blood of innumerable victims was shed, to keep up this execrable hypocrisy of patriotism.

The struggle between Robespierre and his enemies was now daily growing fiercer. They had circulated a list of names which they attributed to him, and in which, by the side of men notoriously corrupt, they added the names of honest, honorable men. This tactic greatly heightened their force.

Robespierre's much ridiculed superstition, and "very preposterous belief in the existence of a God, and the immortality of the soul"—a piece of mental imbecility which the patriots could not tolerate—furnished the first pretext to strike at him. In a retired quarter of Paris there then lived a woman named Catherine Théot, or, as Barrère dexterously altered the name—Théos (*Theos* being the Greek name for God). This crazy old mystic called herself the Mother of God, and was a predecessor of our own Joanna Southcote. Believing, or pretending to believe herself endowed with supernatural power of prophecy, she declared Robespierre to be another Saul, and proclaimed him the Chosen of God. She displayed him to her disciples as the Saviour of Israel, the Regenerator of true religion, and the founder of perfect harmony upon earth.

Robespierre's rivals pounced upon this as a glorious opportunity for covering him with ridicule, and discrediting him with the public. Vadier was intrusted by the Committee with the duty of investigating the affair. His report was read, amidst shouts of laughter. It denounced a conspiracy of priests, turned fanatics into derision, but at the same time declared them worthy of death. A letter, addressed to Robespierre, purporting to be written by Catherine Théot, was found in her bed on the day of her arrest, in which she called him the Son of the Supreme Being, the *Word* of the Eternal, the Redeemer of the human race, and the Messiah designated by the prophets. This letter was a forgery, for the old woman was so uneducated as scarcely to be able to sign her name. It answered the purpose of Robespierre's enemies, however; for it not only placed in their hands the formidable weapon of ridicule, but also insinuated Robespierre's ambition to become the Mahomet of France. It was the reverse side of that medal, the brilliant face of which had been exhibited on the day of the Festival of the Supreme Being. It threw a doubt even on that very festival. It parodied and rendered it ridiculous. Robespierre, unable to deny the facts, was also unable, or too cowardly, to defend these fanatics. His position was truly pitiable. For while, on the one hand, his admirers sent him letters, in which he was styled the Envoy of God, the new Messiah; and children, all over the Republic, were named Maximilien, after him; on the other hand stood his enemies in the Committee, covering him with ridicule, and identifying him with the most stupid sect of fanatics. Although his house was jealously guarded by a body of Jacobins, and he never went out unaccompanied by his faithful band, who carried arms under their clothes, yet his name was execrated within closed walls; and on his table might be seen such letters as this:

" You yet live, assassin of your country! stained with the purest blood of France! I only wait the time when the people shall strike the hour of your fall. Should my hope prove vain, this hand, which now writes thy sentence; this hand, which thy bewildered eye seeks in vain; this hand, which presses thine with horror, shall pierce thee to the heart! Every day I am with thee; every hour my uplifted arm is ready to cut short thy life! Vilest of men! live yet a few days to be tortured with the fear of my vengeance! Sleep to dream of me! let my image, and thy fear, be the first prelude of thy punishment. This very night in seeing thee I shall enjoy thy terrors, but thy eye shall seek in vain for my avenging form."

A Mirabeau would have known very well what to do under such circumstances; a Danton would by mere rude force of audacity have carried himself triumphantly through; but Robespierre was terrified, hesitated, and was lost.

The language of Robespierre at the Jacobins, as Lamartine observes, was, during the next forty days, vague, obscure, and ambiguous. No one could comprehend whether he accused the Committee of cruelty or of indulgence. One moment he censured cruelty; at another he censured moderation.

About this period we must date the domestic squabbles, of which so slight a glimpse is given in the letters to follow, that no one will pronounce judgment thereon. Here is the letter of Robespierre's brother, found amongst the various papers seized on the arrest of the great demagogue:

"Our sister has not a single drop of blood which resembles our own. I have seen and learned so many things of her, that I must regard her as our greatest enemy. She takes advantage of our spotless reputation to bend us to her will, and to menace us that she will compromise us by some scandalous act. Something decisive must be determined on. We must send her to Arras, and thus free ourselves from a woman who will drive us to despair. She wishes to create for us the reputation of being bad brothers, and her calumnies will attain their end."

In connection apparently with this, is the following letter of Charlotte to Maximilien, also found among his papers:

"The 18th Messidor, L'an 2 de la République Française.

"Your aversion for me, brother, far from diminishing, as I had flattered myself, has been so implacable, that my very sight inspires you with horror, so that I dare not hope you will ever be calm enough to listen to me. That is why I write to you. Pressed down by the weight of my grief, incapable of connecting my ideas, I will not undertake an apology. It would, however, be easy for me to demonstrate that I have never in any way merited your anger. But I abandon my justification to time, which reveals all perfidies. Then, when the bandage which covers your eyes, shall have been torn off, if you can, in the disorder of your passions, distinguish the extent of your loss, if the cry of nature can make itself heard, then, casting aside the anger which was so fatal to me, fear not lest I should reproach you for having so long entertained it. I shall only occupy myself with the happiness of having found your heart again. Ah! if you could only read the bottom of mine, you would blush to outrage it in such a cruel manner. You would there see, with the proof of my innocence, that nothing can efface the tender attachment which binds me to you, and that it is the only sentiment which I entertain.

"If it were not for that, why should I care for your hatred? What would it matter to me to be hated by those who are indifferent to me, and whom I despise? Their recollection would never trouble me; but to be hated by my brothers—I who feel the want of loving them—is the only thing which can render me so unhappy as I now am.

"How horrible must be that passion of hatred, since it blinds you so far as to make you calumniate me amongst my friends! Do not hope, however, to make me lose the esteem of those few virtuous persons whom I now regard as the only good which remains to me. With a pure conscience, full of just confidence in my virtue, I can defy you to trouble that esteem, and I dare tell you that with those who know me, you will lose your reputation sooner than you can hurt mine.

"It is necessary then for your tranquillity that I should be removed from you! It is said to be necessary for public good that I should no longer live at Paris! I know not what I ought to do, but that which seems most urgent now, is to remove from your sight an odious object. Therefore, from to-morrow you may reenter your apartment without fearing to find me there. I shall quit it to-day, unless you formally oppose it. Let not my sojourn in Paris trouble you. I shall not associate my friends in my disgrace. The unhappiness which follows me is perhaps contagious, and your hatred for me is too blind not to extend itself to all those who would testify any interest in me; so that I have only need of a few days to calm myself, and to decide upon the place of my exile, for, in the stupor of my faculties, I am unable to make a decision. I leave, therefore, since you demand it; but in spite of your injustice, my friendship for you is so indestructible, that I shall preserve no resentment of your cruel treatment.

"When, sooner or later, disabused, you will feel for me the proper sentiments, do not let a false shame prevent your informing me that I have recovered your friendship, and in whatever place I may be, were it even beyond the seas, if I can be useful to you in anything let me know it, and I shall soon be by your side."

CHAPTER XXI.

Conspiracy of the Thermidorians—Robespierre's discourse against them—The struggle—His arrest—The closing scene—His execution.

MEANWHILE the conspiracy of the Thermidorians, as it is called, proceeded actively. The conspirators met at Clichy, in Barrère's house, and there plotted the destruction of the "tyrant."

Robespierre, aware of the impending danger, at last spoke, though vaguely, against the conspirators. "These wretches," he said, "devote every man to opprobrium whose austerity of manner and inflexible probity they fear. It would be better to return into the woods than to destroy the honor, renown, and wealth of the Republic. We can only found it by protective institutions; and these institutions themselves can only be based upon the downfall of the enemies of liberty and virtue. But these wretches shall not triumph! these conspirators shall renounce all their plots; or our lives shall fall a sacrifice."

Robespierre's friends urged him to name his enemies explicitly, and suggested an insurrection. They reprobated his temporizing scruples; but he persisted in refusing the dictatorship, although he believed the people were ready to rise at his voice to place power and vengeance in his hands.

But the idea of sedition struck him with horror. The shade of Catiline rose before him. The idea of obtaining power by force, and of seeing himself thus the violator of that national sovereignty which he had all his life professed, appeared too heinous a crime. He would not stain his republican virtue! He would rather, he said, be the victim, than the tyrant of his country! He desired power, but he desired it *granted*, not *usurped*.

So thinks Lamartine. To me this hesitation looks far more like want of nerve. Ambitious, he had not the courage of his ambition. Proud as he would have been to assume the reins of government, he had not the audacity to seize them. Robespierre, like many other timid men, bold enough on paper, or in the tribune, always wanted courage in action; and it seems to me profoundly significative of his character, that while his friends were urging him to act, while his situation imperiously demanded that he should act, he was slowly and elaborately preparing a discourse, in which he proposed to annihilate his enemies. This discourse was certainly a very remarkable effort, but it was an enormous mistake. He therein summed up every crime, every corruption, and every danger which degraded, stained, or threatened the Republic. By continued allusion, he cast the responsibility of all disasters upon the Government and the Committees. He drew portraits so striking, and so personal, that nothing was wanting but the names of his enemies. This discourse was divided into two parts, and occupied two sittings. The second he had reserved as a reply, if any one had the audacity to answer. Armed with such a weapon as this discourse, he awaited the struggle with something like confidence. He knew where his strength lay, and he thought it would avail him now. His adversaries began to mistrust themselves. They knew that the people remained faithful to him. Barrère insinuated the necessity of an accommodation.

"The negotiations," says Lamartine, "ended in an interview between Robespierre and the principal members of the two committees. They consented to meet in the Committee of Public Safety. Couthon, Saint Just, David, and Lebas, were with Robespierre. Countenances were reserved, eyes lowered, and mouths closed. It was felt that the two parties feared equally to allow their thoughts to transpire. Elie Lacoste gave vent to the committees. 'You form a *triumvirate*," said he to Saint Just, to Couthon, and to Robespierre. 'A triumvirate,' answered Couthon, 'is not formed by three ideas; triumvirs usurp power, and we leave it all to you.' 'It is precisely of that we accuse you,' exclaimed Collot D'Herbois; ' to withdraw from government, at such a time, a force such as yours, is to betray and deliver liberty to its enemies.' Then turning towards Robespierre, with a suppliant gesture, 'I conjure you, in the names of the country, and of your own glory,' said he to him, ' to allow yourself to be conquered by our frankness and abnegation; you are the first citizen of the Republic, we are in the second rank; we all respect your purity, your eloquence, and your genius;—return to us, let us understand each other, let us sacrifice the intriguers who divide us, and let us save liberty by our union.'

"Robespierre appeared moved by the protestations of Collot D'Herbois. He complained of the secret accusations which were disseminated of his pretended dictatorship; he affected a complete disinterestedness of power; he proposed even to renounce the direction of the police, over which they reproached him with domineering, and spoke vaguely of conspirators, whom it was necessary to crush in the Convention.

"Carnot and Saint Just had a bitter conversation on the subject of the 18,000 men, whom Carnot had detached from the army of the North, exposed to all the forces of Cobourg, and sent to invade maritime Flanders. 'You usurp everything,' exclaimed Carnot. ' You disconcert all my plans; you dismiss my generals; you cut short the campaigns. I leave the interior to you—leave me the field of battle; or if you wish to take it like the rest, take also the responsibility of the frontiers! What will become of liberty if you lose the country!'

"Saint Just defended himself with modesty, and declared himself full of deference for the military genius of Carnot. Barrère was caressing and conciliatory. Billaud alone was silent. His silence troubled Saint-Just. 'There are men,' said the young fanatic, ' who, from the sombre character of their physiognomy, and the paleness of their features, Lycurgus would have banished from Lacedemon.' 'There are men,' replied Billaud,' who conceal their ambition under their youth, and play Alcibiades to become Pisistratus!'

"At this name of Pisistratus, Robespierre thought himself designated. He rose to withdraw, but Robert Lindet interfered. Billaud relaxed his frowning countenance, and, stretching his hand to Robespierre, said, 'I reproach thee with nothing but perpetual suspicion; I lay aside willingly any suspicion I may have entertained towards thee. What have we to forgive each other? Have we not always thought alike upon all the great questions which have agitated the Republic?' 'That is true,' answered Robespierre: 'but you sacrifice indiscriminately the innocent and the guilty—aristocrats and patriots!' 'Why are you not with us to select them?' 'It is time,' answered Robespierre, to establish a tribunal of justice, which should not select, but should strike with the impartiality of the law, but not with the hazard or the prejudices of factions.' Discussion arose. Robespierre desiring to regulate and moderate terror, others declaring it more necessary than ever to exterminate and extirpate the conspirators. 'Why, then, have drawn up the law of the 22d Prairial?' said Billaud. 'Was it to let it sleep in the statute-book?' 'No,' replied Robespierre; 'it was to threaten the enemies of the revolution without exception, and myself, if ever my head rose above the laws!'

"It was agreed, it is said, to come to an understanding at their leisure respecting the few dangerous men who agitated the Convention, and to sacrifice them, if they were guilty, to the security of the Republic, and the concord of the government. It was agreed that Saint-Just should make a report upon the state of affairs, calculated to extinguish all appearance of dissension, and to demonstrate to the Republic that the most perfect harmony was re-established amongst them. They separated with every appearance of reconciliation."

The sesymptoms of reconciliation soon vanished. Once more Robespierre's friends told him that all reconciliation was only a snare. "They humble themselves because they tremble. Challenge them every day from the height of the tribune. If they refuse it, their cowardice dishonors and accuses them; if they accept it, the people are with you!" The Jacobins spoke loudly of an armed attack against the Convention. "If Robespierre will not be our chief," said they, "his name shall be our banner. We must disregard his disinterestedness, or the Republic will perish. Where is Danton? He would have saved the people. Why should virtue be more scrupulous than ambition? The disinterestedness which sacrifices liberty, is more culpable than the ambition which saves it. Would to God Robespierre possessed the ambition of which they accuse him! The Republic needs an ambitious man. Robespierre is only a wise man."

But Robespierre continued to shrink from an insurrection; he preferred relying on his discourse. As Lamartine says:

"Nothing around Robespierre announced a great design. With the exception of four or five men, carrying arms beneath their clothes, whom the

Jacobins had ordered, unknown to him, to follow and protect him, his appearance was that of the most humble citizen. He had never affected more simplicity and more humility in his habits. He isolated himself daily more and more. He appeared absorbed in the contemplation of the delights of nature; whether it were to consult, like Numa, the oracle in solitude, or to sweeten the last days of his uncertain life. He went no more to the Committees, seldom to the Convention, but occasionally to the Jacobins. His door was only opened to a few friends; he wrote no more. He read much. One would have said that he had placed himself in that state of philosophic repose in which, on the brink of a great catastrophe, men sometimes place themselves, to allow destiny to act undisturbed. An expression of discouragement softened his looks and features, generally too severe. The tone of his voice was sweetened by an accent of sorrow. He avoided meeting the daughters of Duplay; particularly her to whom he was to be united after the storm had passed. He discoursed no more of the prospect of a retired life. Too much blood lay shed between him and happiness. A terrible dictatorship or a scaffold were the only images upon which he could henceforth ponder. He sought to escape from these reflections during the early days of Thermidor, by long excursions in the neighborhood of Paris. He wandered entire days under the trees of Meudon, of St. Cloud, or of Viroflay. He usually carried a book under his coat. It was generally Rousseau, Raynal, Bernardin de St. Pierre, or some sentimental poet, such as Gesner and Young. He had the reveries and contemplations of a theosophist in the midst of the scenes of death and the proscriptions of a Marius."

He at last resolved to strike the blow. He bade adieu to his host in the morning with a disturbed countenance. Duplay and his daughters pressed round him and shed tears.

"You are about to encounter great danger to-day," said Duplay, "permit your friends to accompany you."

"No," he replied, "I am defended by my name. Besides the bulk of the Convention is pure. I have nothing to fear in the midst of the Assembly."

Dressed in the same costume which he had worn on the proclamation of the Supreme Being, he entered the Convention. The conspirators, surprised by his appearance, hastily descended from their places to warn their friends, dispersed about the gardens and halls, and to bring them back as quickly as possible to their benches.

A profound silence reigned. He unrolled his manuscript slowly, and began, with terrible calmness, his long deliberated attack, of which this is the substance:—

"Citizens," said he, "let others paint flattering pictures, I am about to utter useful truths. I come not here to repeat the ridiculous terrors spread abroad by perfidy, I come to stifle, if possible, discord by the force of truth. I come to defend your outraged authority; I shall also defend myself, nor will you be surprised at it, for you do not resemble the tyrants whom you combat.

"All friends of liberty seek to overthrow the power of tyrants by the force of truth. Tyrants seek to destroy the defenders of liberty by calumny. They even give the name of tyranny to the ascendency of truth. As long as this system prevailed liberty could not exist, for over men there can only exist two sorts of influence: the influence of tyranny, and the influence of reason. When reason is proscribed, as if it were a crime, tyranny reigns. When good citizens are condemned to silence, wretches alone can govern. Here let me open my heart. What is the foundation of this odious system of terror and calumny against me? Am I dreaded by patriots? I, who have destroyed the factions leagued against them, am I dreaded by the National Convention? What am I without it? Who, like me, has defended the Convention at the peril of his life? Who devoted himself for its preservation, when execrable factions conspired its ruin? Who devoted himself for its glory when the vile hirelings of tyranny preached atheism in its name, when so many others witnessed in silence the crimes of their accomplices, and seemed only awaiting the signal of bloodshed, to destroy the people's representative? And, for whom were destined the first blows of the conspirator? Who were the victims designated by Chaumette and Ronsin? Is there no poniard destined for us amongst those sent here from England? And what then are the acts of severity with which we are reproached? Who have been the victims? Hébert, Ronsin, Chabot, Danton, Lacroix, and their accomplices. Are we reproached with their punishment? No one dare defend them. No; we have not been too severe. I call that republic which now lives to attest it.

Let others note the absurdity of the charges brought against us, I see only their atrocity. You will render an account to public opinion—monsters that you are—for your frightful perseverance in prosecuting the people's friends. You, who endeavored to rob me of the esteem of the National Convention; that esteem which is the most glorious reward that man could reap from his labors, and which I have neither usurped nor surprised, but which I have been forced to conquer. To a sensitive mind there is no punishment equal to that of being regarded as an object of detestation by those whom he reveres and loves. To make him appear so is the greatest of crimes. It was pretended in the Convention that the Mountain was in danger because a few members believed themselves in danger, and, to interest the whole Convention in their cause, they revived the affair of the sixty-two imprisoned deputies; and to me these events were attributed, although I was absolutely a stranger to them. It was said that I wanted to destroy the other portion of the Convention, and while on one side I was depicted as the persecutor of the sixty-two deputies, on the other side I was accused of defending them.

"Ah! When, indeed, at the risk of outraging public opinion, I alone saved from a precipitate decision men whose opinions, had they triumphed, would have sent me to the scaffold; when, on other occasions, I stood out against the fury of a hypocritical faction, and demanded the strict principles of equity towards those who had judged me unfavorably, I little thought that I should one day be called to account for such conduct; but still less did I think that I should one day be accused of having been the persecutor of those towards whom I had fulfilled the first and indispensable duties of probity, and of being the enemy of that national representation which I had served with such fidelity.

"And yet this word *Dictatorship* has a magical effect; it kills liberty, it lowers the government, it destroys the Republic, it degrades all revolutionary institutions by presenting them as the work of a single man. What terrible use the enemies of the Republic have made of the name alone of a Roman magistracy! And if their erudition is so fatal to us, what are we to expect from their wealth and their intrigues?

"*They call me tyrant. If I were a tyrant they would grovel at my feet. I should cover them with gold, I should permit them to accomplish every crime, and they would be grateful.* If I were a tyrant, the kings whom we have vanquished, far from denouncing me, (what tender interest they take in our liberty!) would proffer me their guilty aid. I should league with them. By the aid of scoundrels we may attain power. Whither rush those who fight against them? To the tomb and to immortality. What tyrant protects me? To what faction do I belong? To yourselves! What faction is it which, since the beginning of the revolution, has crushed so many accredited traitors? You—the people!—principles! That is the faction to which I belong, and against which all the guilty are in league. What am I whom they accuse? The slave of liberty, the living martyr of the Republic, the victim no less than the enemy of crime. Every scoundrel outrages me; actions the most indifferent in others, in me are crimes; to know me is to be calumniated; others have their delinquencies pardoned, —in me, my very zeal is regarded as a crime. Were it not for my conscience, I should be the most miserable of men.

"In accusing me of aspiring to the dictatorship, they accuse me also of all their iniquities and of all the severities which the safety of the country rendered necessary. To the nobles they said, it is Robespierre alone who proscribes you. To the patriots they said, he wishes to save the nobles. To the priests they said, it is he alone who persecutes you; were it not for him, you would be at peace and triumphant. To the fanatics they said, it is he who destroys religion. To persecuted patriots they said, it is he alone who orders this or who will not prevent it. To others they said, your fate depends upon him alone. They took particular pains to show that the revolutionary tribunal was a tribunal of blood created by me alone, and which I ruled absolutely that I might crush both the well disposed and the guilty; for they wished to raise up against me enemies of all kinds. This cry filled the prisons.

"But who were the calumniators? I will tell you. In the

first place they were the Duke of York, Mr. Pitt, and all the tyrants armed against us. In the second place . . . . ah! I dare not name them at this moment and in this place. I cannot bring myself to tear aside the veil which covers this profound mystery of iniquity; but I can positively affirm that among the authors of this plot are the agents of that system of corruption and extravagance, the most powerful of all the means yet invented by foreigners for the destruction of the Republic, and that they are corrupt apostles of Atheism, and immorality of which it is the basis. What will be said of the authors if the plot to which I allude should be found amongst those who sent Danton, Fabre, and Desmoulins to the scaffold. The cowards! They wished to send me to the tomb covered with ignominy, leaving behind me nothing but the memory of a tyrant. With what perfidy they abused my good faith! How they seemed to adopt my principles! How naïve and caressing was their famed friendship! Suddenly their faces were overclouded. A ferocious joy shone in their eyes; they fancied my destruction was at hand. To-day they caress me again; their language is more affectionate than ever. Three days ago they were ready to denounce me as a Catiline. To-day they attribute to me the virtues of Cato. They want time to renew their plots. Their aim is atrocious, but how contemptible their means. You shall judge by a single trait. I was charged in the absence of my colleagues with the surveillance of a Bureau de Police Générale recently organized at the Committee of Public Safety. My brief administration was limited to the issue of thirty writs which were to set at liberty some persecuted patriots and to arrest some enemies of the revolution. Will it be believed that this single word *Police Générale* has sufficed to throw upon me the responsibility of all the acts of the Committtee of General Safety, all the errors of the constituted authorities, of the crimes of all my enemies? There has not, perhaps, been a single individual arrested who has not been told that I am the author of his misfortunes, and that he would be happy and free if I did not exist. It is enough for me to say that for the last six weeks, the force of calumny and my inability to effect good or to arrest evil has made me absolutely abandon my functions as a member of the Committee of Public Safety, and I swear that in doing so I have only consulted my reason and my country.

"Be that as it may, for six weeks my dictatorship has expired, for six weeks I have had no sort of influence over the government. Has patriotism been better protected? Has faction been less audacious? Has the country been happier? I hope so.

"But at all times my influence has been limited to pleading the cause of the country before its representatives, and to appeal to the tribunal of public opinion. I have combated the factions that menaced you, I have endeavored to uproot their system of corruption and of disorder, which I look upon as the sole obstacle to the establishment of the Republic. It has appeared to me that the Republic could only be established upon the eternal basis of morality. Factions are leagued against me and against all who hold the same principles. My life! oh, I abandon it to them without a sigh. I have known the past and I foresee the future. Wherefore should I survive when I can no longer serve my country or defend oppressed innocence? Wherefore should I remain in a society where intrigue eternally triumphs over truth; where justice is a lie; where the vilest passions and the absurdest terrors usurp the place of the sacred interests of humanity? Wherefore should I endure the agony of seeing a horrible succession of traitors, all more or less dexterous in concealing a hideous soul beneath the veil of virtue and of friendship, but who will all leave to posterity the difficulty of deciding who among the enemies of my country was the most cowardly and the most atrocious? In beholding the torrent of vices which the revolution has mingled with civic virtues, *I confess that I have sometimes feared lest I should be sullied in the eyes of posterity by the neighborhood of those corrupt men who mingle themselves among the sincere friends of humanity,* and I was pleased to see these Verreses and Catilines trace a profound line of demarkation by their fury between themselves and all the well-disposed. In history I have read how all the defenders of liberty were attacked by calumny. But their oppressors are also dead! The good and the wicked pass away from life, but under different conditions. Frenchmen, suffer not your enemies to degrade your souls and enervate your virtue by their desolating doctrine! No, Chaumette, death is not an eternal sleep! Citizens, efface from every tomb that maxim graven there by sacrilegious hands, which covers nature with a funereal crape, which takes away from oppressed innocence its courage, and which is an insult to death itself. No, rather engrave these words— *death is the commencement of immortality!* Some time ago, I promised to leave a testament formidable to all oppressors of the people. I will now publish it. I bequeath to them the terrible truth, and I bequeath them death!

"Wherefore do those who recently said that we were walking upon volcanoes believe that we to-day walk upon roses? Yesterday they believed in conspiracies—I declare that I believe in them still. *Those who tell you that the establishment of the Republic is so facile an enterprise deceive you. Where are the wise institutions, where is the plan of regeneration which can justify such ambitious language?* Have they even occupied themselves with this great object? What do I say? Did not they rather attempt to proscribe those who had prepared such plans? In four days we are told, every injustice will be repaired. Why, then, has it been for four months committed with impunity, and how is it possible in four days to punish and put to flight all the authors of our woes? Your victories are spoken of with an academic frivolity which would make one believe that they had cost our heroes neither blood nor toil. Recounted with less of pomp, they would appear greater. We shall not subdue Europe by rhetorical phrases, nor even by warlike exploits, but by the wisdom of our laws, by the majesty of our deliberations, and by the greatness of our characters. Liberty has no other guarantee than the strict observance of those principles of universal morality which you have proclaimed. What matters it to us to have vanquished kings, if we ourselves are vanquished by the vices which produce tyranny. As for me, whose existence seems to my enemies to be an obstacle to their odious projects, let them take it; willingly do I consent to the sacrifice, if their frightful reign is still to continue!

"People, remember that if in the Republic justice reigns not with absolute power, and if the name does not signify love of equality and patriotism, liberty is only an empty name! People, thou who art feared, who art flattered, and who are despised; thou, a recognized sovereign, always treated as a slave, remember that where justice reigns not, the passions of magistrates rule, and the people has changed its fetters but not its destiny.

"Know that every man who may arise to defend the cause of public morality will be overwhelmed by insults and proscribed by the base. Know that every friend of liberty will always stand between a duty and a calumny; that when he cannot be accused of treachery he will be accused of ambition, that the influence of his probity and his principles will be called tyranny; that thy confidence and thy esteem will bring down proscription upon all thy friends; that the cries of oppressed patriotism will be called the cries of sedition, and that, not daring to attack thee in a mass, they will do so in detail, by proscribing every good citizen until the ambitious have organized their tyranny.

"Thus the villains impose on us the necessity of betraying the people or of being styled dictator. Shall we subscribe to this necessity? No, let us defend the people even at the risk of being esteemed by them. Let our enemies reach the scaffold by the path of crime: we will seek it by the path of virtue!"

A long and awful pause followed this speech. The Convention knew not what attitude to adopt. One single voice broke silence.

It was that of Lecointre, who demanded that Robespierre's speech should be printed. The proposition was about to be voted, when Bourdon (de l'Oise), who read his own name under all the allusions of Robespierre, and who felt that further audacity could not endanger him more, resolved to stake his head upon the chance.

"I oppose," he said, "the printing of this discourse. It contains matters sufficiently weighty to be examined. It may contain errors no less than truths. It is but prudent in the Convention to return it to the examination of the two Committees of Public Safety and General Security."

"No explosion burst forth," says Lamartine, "against an objection which would have appeared on the preceding evening a blasphemy. The hearts of the conspirators rose. Robespierre was astonished at his fall. Barrère looked at him. Barrère voted for the printing of the discourse in terms which both parties could equally accept.

"Couthon, encouraged by the defection of Barrère, demanded its transmission to all the communes of the Republic. The printing of the discourse is voted triumphantly. The defeat of Robespierre's enemies is complete if they cannot rescind this vote. Vadier rises and devotes himself. Robespierre interrupts him. Vadier insists. 'I will speak,' says he, 'with the tranquillity which belongs to virtue.' He justified the report attacked by Robespierre, which he had made regarding Catherine Théos. In covert terms he insinuated that he knew of mysteries which his accusers themselves were implicated in. He defended the Committee of General Safety.

"'And I also enter the arena,' exclaims the austere and honest Cambon, 'although I have not sought to form a party around me. I do not come armed with long prepared speeches. All parties have found me intrepid in opposing to their ambition, the barrier of my patriotism. It is time, at length, to tell the truth. One single man paralyzes the National Convention, and that man is Robespierre!' At these words, which break out as the hitherto repressed thought of an upright man, Robespierre rises and denies having attacked Cambon's integrity.

"Billaud-Varennes demands that the two committees should submit their conduct to inspection. 'It is not the Committee I attack," replies Robespierre; 'but to avoid squabbles, I demand that I may explain myself more explicitly.' 'We all demand it!' exclaim two hundred members of La Montagne.

"Billaud-Varennes continues: 'Yes!' says he; 'Robespierre is right, the mask must be raised; and if it be true that we are no longer free, I would rather that my dead body should serve as a throne to an ambitious man, than that I should by my silence, become the accomplice of his ambition.'

"Panis, long the friend of, and afterwards proscribed by Robespierre in the Jacobins, reproaches him with domineering, and only proscribing those whom he himself suspected. ·'My heart is bursting,' exclaimed Panis; 'it is time I gave it utterance. They depict me as a wretch dripping with blood, and gorged with rapine, and yet I have not acquired, in the Revolution, even the means of buying a sabre for my son to march to the frontiers, and a garment for my daughters. Robespierre has drawn up a list, in which he inscribed my name, and devoted my head for the first condemnation *en masse!*'

"A torrent of indignation here poured forth against the tyrant. Robespierre met it with an imperturbable countenance. 'Throwing aside my buckler,' said he, 'I have presented myself uncovered to my enemies. I retract nothing; I flatter no one, I fear no one: I neither require the support nor the indulgence of any one. I do not seek to make a party for myself. I have done my duty, that is enough for me; let others do theirs. What!' continued he, 'I have had the courage to come and state, in the bosom of the Assembly, truths which I believe necessary to the safety of the country, and my accusation is to be submitted to the examination of those whom I accuse!'

"'When,' cried Charlier, 'a man boasts of having the courage of virtue, he should also have that of truth. Name those whom you accuse!' 'Yes—name—name!' repeated a group of Montagnards, rising, with looks of defiance. Robespierre was silent. Thirion declared that to send Robespierre's discourse into the provinces would be to condemn unheard those whom it accused. Barrère hesitated. Bréard asserted that the Convention ought to revoke the vote, and an immense majority voted with him.

"Robespierre, humiliated, but not vanquished, felt that the Convention was gone from his grasp. He left it, and hastened, accompanied with a body of friends, to the tribune of the Jacobins, where his party hailed him as a martyr. Carried into the tribune by the Jacobins, he read to them his discourse repudiated by the Convention, amidst furious cries, shouts of rage, and gestures of admiration. When these ceased, Robespierre, whose voice was exhausted, assuming a resigned attitude, said, 'Brothers, the discourse you have heard is my last will and testament!' 'No, no; you shall live, or we will all die,' shouted the tribunes. 'Yes, it is my last testament,' he repeated with prophetic solemnity—'my last testament. I have seen today that the league of villains is so strong that I cannot hope to escape. I yield without regret! I leave to you my memory; it will be dear to you, and you will defend it!'

"These last words, this adieu, which included at once reproach and resignation, affected the Jacobins even to tears. Coffinhal, Duplay, Payan, Buonarotti, Lebas, and David rose and called on Robespierre, conjuring him to defend his country and himself. Henriot exclaimed, that he had still sufficient artillery to overpower the Convention vote. Robespierre, roused by his enthusiasm, and carried away beyond his resolution, made signs that he was about to speak, and exclaimed—'Well, then!—yes!—separate the wicked from the weak! Free the Convention from the villains who oppress it! Restore it to liberty as you did on the 31st of May and the 2d of June! March, if necessary, and save the country. If in these generous efforts we fail, then, my friends, you shall see me drink hemlock calmly!' David, interrupting him at these words, said, with an antique gesture, 'Robespierre, if you drink hemlock, I will drink it with you!' 'all—all—

we will perish with you!' cried thousands of devoted voices. 'To perish with you is to perish with the people!'"

But this enthusiasm subsided, and Robespierre's scruples again resumed their empire. His friends irritated at his refusal, declared they would act without him; and the insurrection was planned.

Coffinhal secured the Faubourgs; Henriot the Commune; Payan the members of the municipality. Henriot, followed by his aides-de-camp, and already on horseback, in spite of the drunkenness of the previous night, galloped up and down the streets opposite the Hotel de Ville, and placed batteries of cannon on the bridges, and on the Place du Carrousel. The deputies betook themselves early to their post; the people were stirring in the streets, expecting some crisis. Robespierre appeared in the Convention, dressed with more than usual care. His step was slow, his countenance bold; success was in his glance.

"Saint Just made a vigorous attack.—"Robespierre," said he, "did not sufficiently explain himself yesterday. A plan was formed of usurping power, by the death of several members of the Committee. Billaud Varennes and Collot D'Herbois are guilty men. I do not content myself with naming them—I accuse them."

Tallien demanded to be heard.—"Saint Just has told you that he belongs to no faction. I tell you the same. But yesterday a member of the government separated himself from it, and made a speech in his own name. To-day another does the same. By this means the misfortunes of the country are aggravated. I demand that the veil be rent entirely asunder."

This was greeted with loud applause. Billaud Varennes rose, and in a voice tremulous with indignation, said:—"Yesterday the meeting of the Jacobins was filled with satellites, who openly avowed their intention of massacreing the Convention." A cry of horror interrupted him. Pointing towards the Mountain, he exclaimed, "I behold on the Mountain one of those who threatened the representatives of the people."

"Arrest him! arrest him!" was the cry; and the victim was dragged out of the chamber.

"The time is arrived to unveil the whole truth," continued Billaud. "The Assembly will not conceal from itself that it is threatened by two perils: if it be irresolute, all is lost." "No!" no!" exclaimed all the deputies, rising and waving their hats in the air, "*Vive le Comité!*" "You will shudder," continued Billaud, "when you hear the situation in which you are placed; when I tell you that the command of the armed force is intrusted to Henriot, who has been denounced as the accomplice of the conspirators. You will shudder when I tell you that there is a man here," and as he spoke he looked at Robespierre, "who, when it was proposed to send the representatives of the people into the departments, could not find twenty members of the Convention who were worthy of being intrusted with the mission (*murmurs of indignation.*) When Robespierre told you that he separated himself from the Committee because he was oppressed, he carefully disguised the truth from you. He did not tell you it was because, after having for six months domineered over the Committee, he met with resistance at the moment when he wished to pass the decree of the twenty-second Prairial; a decree, which, in the impure hands of the men he selected, might have been fatal to patriots." An outbreak of terror and indignation interrupted Billaud. "Death to the tyrants!" they exclaimed. "Men," said Billaud, "who, unceasingly talking of justice and virtue, are the first to trample them under foot. When I demanded the arrest of a secretary of the Committee of Public Safety, who had robbed the nation, Robespierre alone protected him. It is he who accuses us. What! men who belong to no party, who pass their days and nights at the Committee, who organize victory (here all eyes were turned towards the laborious Carnot), are conspirators? Those who abandoned Hébert, when it was no longer possible to support him, are virtuous citizens! When I denounced Danton for the first time, Robespierre rose in a fury, saying, I wished to destroy the best of patriots. But the gulf yawns at your feet! We must fill it with our bodies, or else precipitate the traitors into it."

Billaud left the tribune amidst tumultuous shouts. Robespierre entered it pale, and agitated, amidst loud cries of "Down with the Tyrant!" but Tallien, pushing him aside, said, "Just now I demanded that the veil should be rent. It is so at length. The conspirators are unmasked, they will perish, and liberty will triumph." "Yes, yes, it triumphs!" cried the Mountain. "I was present," continued Tallien, "at the Jacobins. I there heard plotted the formation of the army of this second Cromwell, and I armed myself with this dagger, with which to pierce his heart, if the National Convention had not the courage to order his arrest." Here Tallien drew a dagger from beneath his coat, and held it towards Robespierre, who receded.

Robespierre remained motionless at the tribune; his arms folded, his lips contracted, his features working with excitement, expressing alternate impatience and resignation, alternate indignation and contempt.

Vadier, president of the Committee of Safety, said, "Until the twenty-second Prairial, my eyes were not open to the real character of this astute villain, who has worn every mask, and who, when he could no longer shield his creatures, sent them to the guillotine. Every one knows he openly defended Bazire, Chabot, Camille Desmoulins, and Danton. The tyrant wanted to divide the two Committees. To hear him, one would fancy he was the single defender of liberty. He despairs of it; he will quit everything; his modesty is incomparable. . . . His eternal phrase is *I am oppressed . . . they will not let me speak*—and nobody speaks but he!"

"I recall the discussion," interrupted Tallien, "to the real question at issue . . ."

Robespierre in vain strove to obtain a hearing; Tallien was pitiless, the Mountain was incensed. He quitted the steps of the tribune and ascended among the benches of the Mountain, entreating his ancient supporters to hear him. They turned contemptuously aside. "Away from the benches," they exclaimed; "the shade of Danton, the shade of Camille repels you." "*Is it Danton you avenge?*" exclaimed Robespierre, with mingled astonishment and remorse. He descended amongst the benches of the Gironde. "Well, then," he said, "it is among you, upright men, I will seek for refuge;" and he seated himself. "Wretch," said the Girondins, "*that was Vergniaud's seat!*"

At this name he sprang up in terror and walked away. Thus baited on all sides, ancient allies joining ancient foes, the yells of a maddened assembly dinning in his ears, the fierce glances of ferocious assailants making his heart beat, he rushed in desperation to the tribune, and threatening the president with his upraised hand, he shrieked, in a voice cracked with rage, "President of Assassins! will you let me speak?"

"No! No! No!" His doom was sealed. They would not hear him. He who had been so pitiless to others, now found no mercy in his turn. He yelled, he supplicated, he threatened in vain. His cracked voice was indistinguishable amidst the howlings and hootings, the imprecations and menaces of the Convention. His eloquence was dumb-show. His voice grew hoarser and hoarser, till at last it failed him altogether. Seeing this, some one uttered this terrible phrase: "*The blood of Danton chokes you!*" All was over. Danton's prophecy, that his fall would drag down Robespierre, was fulfilled. The arrest of the tyrant was decreed.

The younger Robespierre now advanced and said, "I am as guilty as my brother; I have shared his opinions, I demand to share his fate." This extorted expressions of compassion from some present; but the mass accepted the sacrifice without a remark.

Robespierre tried to intercede for his brother, but no one would hear him. The decree of arrest was voted; and shouts of *Vive la République!* saluted it. Robespierre exclaimed, "The Republic is no more, for brigands triumph;" so saying, he folded his arms in contempt, and descended from the tribune.

The examination before the Committee of General Safety was brief; it ended in Robespierre being sent to the Prison of the Luxembourg, his brother to St. Lazare, St. Just to La Force, and Couthon to La Bourbe.

As soon as the Commune heard of Robespierre's arrest, it appointed a Committee of Twelve to organize an insurrection. They snatched the prisoners from their guard, and bore them in triumph to the Commune. The streets were glittering with bayonets, and Henriot had ordered out his artillery.

Robespierre reiterated his intention of not encouraging the insurrection. He was resolved to stand upon the law; by it to triumph or to perish. "The death of one man," he said, "is less hurtful to the Republic than the example of revolt against the National Convention."

Was this integrity? was it hypocrisy? The question is a delicate one. In favor of his integrity, one may adduce his firm resistance to the entreaties of his friends—a resistance he prolonged for three hours—and which was only finally overcome by Coffinhal dispersing the gens d'armes by force, and carrying off the scrupulous patriot. On the other side, we must recollect that Robespierre *had* frequently instigated insurrection, and that he felt assured the Convention would never dare to find him guilty.

The insurrection was organized, but the Convention was also on the alert, and assembled its forces. The situation was full of peril. Robespierre knew it, and refused to act. In vain Coffinhal, Henriot, and Payan urged him to present himself to the people—to allow his name to be a banner for the revolt. They wanted him to proclaim himself Dictator. He was resolute, and refused.

"Then," said Couthon, "Nothing remains for us but death." "You have said it," calmly replied Robespierre. "It is you who sacrifice us," exclaimed St. Just.

A paper had been drawn up calling upon the people to rise and defend the patriots against the Thermidorians. This proclamation Robespierre was entreated to sign. He took the pen, began the signature, then overcome by his scruples he flung aside the pen, and would not finish it. He would not countenance revolt.

About this time the troops of the Convention headed by Leonard Bourdon were silently marching along the Quays, and halted as they turned into the Place de Grève, where the shouts of "*Vive la Convention!*" saluted them. Henriot, sword in hand, galloped like a madman into the middle of the crowd and shouted "*Vive la Commune!*" but the contempt felt for him, his drunken, disordered appearance, the blocked up streets, the expected arrival of fresh troops, all combined to discourage the Sectionists. The cannoniers overwhelmed their general with hisses, and then turning the mouths of their cannon against the Hôtel de Ville, they cried "*Vive la Convention!*" and quickly dispersed.

A profound silence reigned at the Hôtel de Ville, and all at once the report of fire arms was heard within, and cries of horror followed. Dulac, a resolute agent of the Committee of General Safety, at the head of five-and-twenty sappers, and a party of grenadiers, crossed the square, and beating down the doors with hatchets, ascended the grand staircase.

Mute and motionless, around a table in the Salle d'Egalité, Robespierre and his companions listen to the sounds without; their eyes fixed on the door awaiting their fate. Robespierre is dressed in the sky blue coat, and nankeen trousers, which he had had made for the Festival of the Supreme Being. Lebas, armed with a brace of pistols, presents one to Robespierre, conjuring him to put an end to his existence; but Robespierre, although he always carried poison about him, refuses to commit suicide. Saint Just and Couthon side with him. And now the jingling noise of arms becomes frightfully distinct. Lebas places a pistol to his heart, and in another instant falls dead into the arms of Robespierre the younger, who leaps out of the window into the court, breaking a leg in the fall. Coffinhal makes the chambers and lobbies resound with his imprecations and hurried footsteps. He meets with Henriot, in a stupor of terror and wine, reproaches him for his cowardly conduct, then seizing him in his arms, hurls him out of the window on a dungheap, exclaiming, "Away, wretched drunkard, you are not worthy of a scaffold!"

Meanwhile Leonard Bourdon draws up his men in order of battle before the steps leading to the Hotel de Ville; ascends them himself, accompanied by five gens d'armes, and a detachment of soldiers. Dulac joins them; the whole party rushes eagerly towards the Salle de l'Egalité, where, with the butt-ends of their muskets, they drive in the doors, amidst cries of "Down with the tyrant!" The poor tyrant, pale and anxious, is sitting silent at the table. Leonard Bourdon dares not meet his look. With his right hand he seizes Meda's arm, and points with his left at Robespierre, exclaiming, "That's the man!" Meda levels his pistol, fires, and the head of the unhappy Robespierre drops on the table, staining with blood the *proclamation*, before mentioned.* The ball has entered the left side of his face, and carried away several of his teeth. Couthon endeavors to rise upon his withered limbs, but staggers under the table. Saint Just, the inexorable, imperturbable, and not unheroic fanatic, sits motionless at the table, now gazing mournfully at Robespierre, now with proud looks of defiance eyeing his enemies. In a few minutes all the prisoners are marched off in triumph to the Convention. The gray dawn gently stealing over the sky discovers Robespierre carried on a litter by four gens d'armes, his face covered with a handkerchief steeped in blood. At five o'clock, a column of soldiers enters the Tuileries, where the Convention is awaiting the termination of the affair. A loud murmur proclaims the approach of Barras and Fréron. Charlier is acting as President. "The coward Robespierre is there," he cries, pointing to the door. "Shall he come in?" "No! no!" exclaimed the members, some from horror, others from pity. "To bring before the Convention the body of so great a criminal, would be to rob this day of its glory. The corpse of a tyrant can only bring contagion with it. The only spot for Robespierre and his accomplices is the Place de la Revolution."

Meanwhile, Robespierre is laid upon a table in the adjoining ante-room. His head supported by the back of a chair; his sky-blue coat and nankeen trousers are stained with blood; his stockings are fallen down over his ankles. Crowds flock in, clamber on stools and benches, and look with strange curiosity and malicious triumph at this idol and ruler of the Republic now fallen so low! They shower on him expressions of contempt, invective, and abuse. The officers of the Convention point him out to the spec-

---

* This curious paper is extant, and in the possession of M. Saint Albin. The letters *Rob*—, of Robespierre's unfinished signature, are still legible on the blood-stained paper.

tators, as a tiger is pointed out in a menagerie. He closes his eyes and feigns death, to escape the insults and curses heaped upon him. "Search him," exclaims the crowd. He is searched. A brace of pistols, in a case, with the arms of France engraved upon them, is found in his pocket. "What a villain!" cry the bystanders. "Here is a proof of his aspiring to the throne. He uses the symbols of royalty."* There was also found upon him a pocket-book, containing bank-notes and bills to the amount of £400. There is no reason to suppose this money belonged to him. It was in all probability public money, and about to be applied to public use. All attempts to throw even a suspicion of pecuniary corruptibility upon him have signally failed. There were only a few francs found in his lodgings after his death.

His colleagues enter and insult him; some even spit in his face; while the clerks of the Bureau prick him with their penknives.† Legendre, entering the Salle, approaches the body, and in theatrical gesture apostrophizes it:—"So, then, tyrant! you, for whom only yesterday the Republic was not vast enough, occupy to-day about two feet wide of a little table!" What must have been Robespierre's scorn at the man who had so frequently followed

---

* These pistols, shut up in their case, still loaded prove that Robespierre did not shoot himself. Some accounts, and even the surgeon's testimony are cited to prove that he must have shot himself; but, although the evidence, with the exception of that cited above, is pretty equally balanced, yet that must be held as decisive. Besides, did he not refuse to commit suicide?

† This is very ignoble, very horrible, and yet very natural. Does not Homer makes his beloved Greeks thus insult the corpse of Hector, each wounding it with his spear:—

"ἄλλοι δὲ περίδραμον υἷες Ἀχαιῶν,
οἳ καὶ θηήσαντο φυὴν καὶ εἶδος ἀγητόν
Ἕκτορος· οὐδ᾽ ἄρα οἵ τις ἀνουτητί γε παρέστη."

Il. xxii. v. 370.

If the warlike Greeks could allow their enmity so far to overcome their sense of respect for the fallen foe, what wonder that the miserable mob of intriguers should glut their savage ire in insulting the fallen demagogue.

him with fulsome adulation, now triumphing over him in his last hour.

There he lies motionless and apparently unconscious. The blood which flowed from his wounds, has coagulated in his mouth. Regaining a little strength, he staunches this blood with the fur that covered the case of his pistols. His dim eye wanders vacantly among the crowd, there seeking some friendly countenance; there endeavoring to read justice or compassion. But in vain, in vain! Horror alone is imprinted on every face; the unhappy man shudders and closes his eyes. The heat of the chamber is intense. A burning fever glows on his cheeks, streams of perspiration pour from his brow. Not one hand is extended to assist him. Beside him, on the table, they have placed a cup of vinegar and a sponge. From time to time he moistens the sponge and applies it to his lips.

From the Salle he is taken to the Committee of General Safety, where Billaud, Collot, and Vadier go through the forms of examination. He replies only by his looks. He is then conveyed to the Hôtel Dieu, where his wounds are examined and dressed. The left jaw is broken, but the surgeon bandages it, and he is now, with his associates, taken away to the Conciergerie. They are all placed in the same dungeon. Beside them is the corpse of Lebas.

At three o'clock the prisoners are carried before the Revolutionary Tribunal. Fouquier Tinville—abashed for once in his life by the presence of a victim—dares not raise his eyes to Robespierre!

At five the carts came for the prisoners. Strange and ghastly burden did they bear that day! Not only were the prisoners men whose names had been venerated and execrated as names have seldom been, but Robespierre, his brother, Couthon, Lebas, and Henriot, were merely the mangled remains of men. These mangled remains were tied down to a cart, the jolting of which over the stones of the street extorted from them groans of pain. Through the most populous streets wended this hideous procession, and the windows, doors, and balconies, were crowded with spectators, especially with women dressed as for a fête. Strange sights had been seen from those balconies, strange processions had passed down those streets—a king, a queen, royal princes and princesses, orators, sycophants, traitors, men of high integrity, and noble genius, and men of foulest hearts and desperate lives—the youth, genius, beauty, and virtue of the Gironde, and the hideous obscurity and brutality of the Hébertists—but who could have expected to see the incorruptible Robespierre and the imperturbable St. Just following in that train which they had swelled with their victims? The fall of Danton stupefied the spectators, but what was Danton to Robespierre!

And women gaily attired clapped their hands for joy, exclaiming, "Death! Death! To the Guillotine!" The children and the friends of those who had fallen during the Terror now shrieked in triumph over the fall of the dictator.

And the people? What was the attitude of that people Robespierre had flattered, had served, and had roused to combat; that people for whom he had slaved and who almost worshiped his name? It was silent. It knew not what to think or what to do. It abandoned its idol, as it had abandoned Danton, Camille, and Hébert.

The procession moved on amidst curses; not one friendly voice relieved the weight of all the imprecations. The head of the unfortunate Robespierre was tied up in a blood-stained handkerchief, which, passing under his chin, left only the cheek, the forehead, and the eyes visible. He shrugged his shoulders as if in pity for the mob which insulted him. His aspect was calm and resigned. He made no attempt to speak. His thoughts were no longer of this world.

Once indeed he exhibited a touch of feeling. As the procession passed the house of Duplay, a lad carrying a pail of blood dipped a broom into it, and bespattered the walls. Robespierre closed his eyes; he could not bear that sight!

At length they reached la Place de la Revolution. Not a word did they address to the people. Their doom was inevitable, and they believed they died as martyrs. Robespierre mounted the ladder with a firm step. The executioners tore off the bandage which bound up his chin, in order to prevent it deadening the blow of the axe. Released from its support his lower jaw fell upon his breast; the piercing cry it extorted was heard on the opposite side of the Place de la Revolution. It was succeeded by a dead silence—the silence of the grave—broken by a dull, sullen noise. Down clanked the axe, and the head of Robespierre rolled into the basket. The crowd held their breath for some seconds, and then, as if an enormous load were rolled from their breasts, burst into a loud and unanimous cheer. The spectators shed tears of joy, and embraced each other in transport, crowding around the scaffold to behold the bloody remains of the tyrants. One man approaching said, " Yes, Robespierre, there is a God !"

And thus this strange mystery of a man passed away into eternity!

On that evening at the Opera, they performed Glück's "Armida," with the ballet of "Telemachus;" and the Opera Comique delighted its audience with "Melomanie!"

> "Frankreich's traurig Geschick, die Grossen mögen's bedenken;
> Aber bedenken, fürwahr, sollen es Kleine noch mehr.
> Grosse gingen zu Grunde; doch wer beschützte die Menge
> Gegen die Menge? Da war die Menge der Menge Tyrann."

CONCLUSION.

I HAVE now called up for the reader's judgment, the sad, strange, and somewhat fantastic career of a political Fanatic. All his acts, all his opinions, his feelings and his motives, such at least as researches have enabled me to discover, have been set down in the foregoing pages, with as much impartiality as it is given to erring man to employ in such a cause. Truly can I say, that I have "nothing extenuated"—naught have I "set down in malice." With the evidence before us, what is the judgment to be passed upon this man?

Cambacérès said, truly enough, to Napoleon, "*c'est un procès jugé mais non plaidé.*" Since that phrase escaped him there have not been wanting men to plead Robespierre's cause, with the passion of advocates and partisans. But that Robespierre was a great or good man, seems to me a conclusion little less preposterous, than that he was a blood-thirsty monster, altogether infamous. It is not difficult, however, to see the grounds for such diversity of judgment. All that is great and estimable in fanaticism—its sincerity, its singleness of purpose, its exalted aims, its vigorous consistency, its disdain of worldly temptations—all may be found in Robespierre; and those who only contemplate that aspect of the man, will venerate him. But there is another aspect of fanaticism—presenting narrow-mindedness, want of feeling, of consideration and of sympathy; unscrupulousness of means, pedantic wilfulness, and relentless ferocity; and whoso contemplates this aspect also, will look on Robespierre with strangely mingled feelings of admiration and abhorrence; and the abiding impression will be that of such disgust, that he will need perpetually to remind himself of the qualities which ought to mitigate his loathing.

We have had examples enough of fanaticism, to enable us to estimate it. Its frightful contradictions are no mystery to us. Religious fanaticism has reddened our annals, holding in its hand the gospel of peace and charity. Political fanaticism has decimated society in the name of universal benevolence. No doubt disturbs the serenity of the fanatic's soul. What is the agony of a few thousands, compared with the triumph of an opinion? Confident in the purity of his intentions, he is careless as to the consequences of his acts.

Is fanaticism a Virtue or a Vice? Is it the Love of Truth, or is it Pride?

It is Pride, assuming the majestic aspect of the Love of Truth. It is intense dogmatism coupled with a want of human sympathy, excusing the violence of its acts, by the supposed purity of its designs. That I should firmly maintain and unflinchingly promulgate what I believe to be the Truth, is manly and virtuous. That I should cast aside all doubts respecting human infallibility— that I should trample down all compassion, scorn tenderness as weakness, and stop at nothing which would make others either adopt my views, or send them to the scaffold; this is not virtuous, this is unpardonable. What is called the "courage of an opinion," is a readiness to suffer anything rather than renounce it; not to make others suffer because they refuse to accept it. To go to the block for an opinion, is heroism; to send others to the block because they differ from you, is fanaticism.

Robespierre, in his speeches and in his conduct, showed that he cared for the triumph of his opinions, but cared nothing for the welfare of individuals. Others may, if they please, credit his benevolence and philanthropy; I can believe in nothing but his intense vanity and dogmatism. They may avert their eyes from his conduct and only repeat his grand phrases; it is impossible for me to do so. I have studied his character with care, and have found nothing generous, nothing exalted in it. On the whole I greatly prefer Saint Just. He was perhaps more relentless, more systematic in his contempt for bloodshed, but his soul was not darkened as Robespierre's was, by envy and malignity. Robespierre had the greater intellect, but he was the weaker man.

Even Lamartine, who is so favorable to him, says, "He flattered the ignoble tendencies of the people. He exaggerated suspicion. He awoke envy. He sharpened anger. He envenomed vengeance. He opened the veins of the social body to cure its disease; but he allowed life to flow out, pure or impure, with perfect indifference, never once interfering between the axe and its victims. He did not desire evil, yet he accepted it."

He had qualities, it is true, which we must respect; he was honest, sincere, self-denying and consistent. But he was cowardly, relentless, pedantic, unloving, intensely vain and morbidly envious. Throughout his career I have met with no single generous action, with no example of warm feeling, with no expression which seemed to come from a high and noble heart. It is idle to set against this his honorable poverty, his political consistency, his sagacity, and his eloquence.

History will record of him that living in an epoch abounding in examples of heroism and greatness of all kinds, and wielding a power such as few have ever wielded, backed by an influence such as few have had to support them, he performed many acts, and delivered numberless orations, but he has not left the legacy to mankind of one grand thought, nor the example of one generous and exalted action.

THE END.

NEW BOOKS
RECENTLY PUBLISHED BY
CAREY & HART,
No. 126 Chestnut Street, Philadelphia.

STATE TRIALS OF THE UNITED STATES,
DURING THE
ADMINISTRATIONS OF WASHINGTON AND JOHN ADAMS,

WITH REFERENCES, HISTORICAL AND PROFESSIONAL, AND PRELIMINARY NOTES ON THE POLITICS OF THE TIMES.

BY FRANCIS WHARTON,
Author of "A Treatise on American Criminal Law," etc.

Complete in One Volume, Octavo, 727 Pages.

PRINTED ON CLEAR TYPE AND FINE WHITE PAPER.

" The subject needs no apology. The want of a correct history of those causes in which the Constitution was construed, and the powers accorded by it to the general government asserted, has long been felt; its importance will be acknowledged, if carried out in a fair and impartial spirit, untinctured by that party spirit which was so strongly exhibited in the trials. * * * * His style is bold and familiar, perhaps too much so were it intended merely as a report of adjudged cases; but as a work for the general reader, as well as the lawyer, its spirited and lively diction cannot fail to have an attraction which would be wanting were it more labored and formal."—*Legal Intelligencer*.

" The author has chosen a period, fruitful beyond all others in interesting incidents. The first workings of an experimental government in the hands of a people enfeebled by war, yet boldly venturing upon the hitherto perilous sea of republicanism, afford matter for a most interesting work. The early trials of our judicial tribunals, the exposition of constitutional points by judges, many of whom took part in the framing of that Constitution, and the legal opinions of the pure minded patriots of that day, possess an interest not, it is true, like that which gathers around the exciting struggles of the battle-field, but, to many minds, of equal importance.

" Mr. Wharton brings to the task he has undertaken, a degree of laborious investigation, such as gives us assurance that he will perform it thoroughly. As far as we have examined the proof sheets, we see evidence of the most thorough research. The politics and politicians of the time are sketched vigorously in the preliminary notes, many facts being stated, and incidents recalled that have escaped from the memory of most persons. To readers of all classes the work will be one of the highest interest."—*Evening Bulletin*.

" The preliminary notes of this volume are written with unusual spirit and freedom—a freedom, indeed, for which it would be difficult to find a parallel.

" The labors of Mr. Wharton manifests an enlarged knowledge of the history of our early administrations, and his annotations are full of interest."—*Daily News*.

" A work which cannot fail to be looked for anxiously and read with interest.

" But one must do Mr. Wharton the justice to say, that he has pursued his task not only with industry and ability, but with discrimination and boldness. Furnished with the proof sheets of the memoir of the administration of John Adams, we have been enabled, so far as a hasty perusal would allow us, to come to the conclusion that it is destined to rise into importance as a standard work as soon as its sterling merits are appreciated. We commend it as well to the politician as to the lawyer—to the statesman as well as to the mechanic."—*Pennsylvanian*.

A NARRATIVE OF THE
LATE EXPEDITION TO THE DEAD SEA,
FROM A DIARY BY ONE OF THE PARTY.

EDITED BY EDWARD P. MONTAGUE,

(ATTACHED TO THE U. S. EXPEDITION SHIP "SUPPLY".)

With Incidents of Travel from the time of the Sailing of the Expedition in 1847, till the Return of the same in 1848; accompanied by a Colored Map of the Holy Land.

In One Volume post octavo, 348 pages, cloth gilt, $1.

"The author of this interesting little volume accompanied Lieut. Lynch's exploring expedition in a private capacity, being prompted thereto by an enthusiastic desire to visit the localities to be explored. During the entire voyage he kept a diary, which forms the volume now before us. When the party made their observations upon the Dead Sea, our author was unfortunately absent, owing to a sickness, incurred during his attention to the principal officer while ill, but his diary was kindly written up by an intelligent friend, whose better fortune it was to be of the party at the critical and exciting juncture. Mr. Montague's narrative does not pretend to give the reader much scientific information. It is designed rather for general perusal, and relates in a pleasant and lively vein, the incidents of the expedition, with sufficient description of the Dead Sea, and the appearances of the region thereabout, to make the book worth more than the purchase money. It makes an excellent pioneer for Lieut. Lynch's forthcoming work, is more accessible to the people generally, being much less expensive, and will therefore diffuse valuable information, which otherwise might have very limited circulation. A good map—colored—accompanies the volume."—*N. Y. Com. Advertiser.*

"It is merely a spirited and graphic diary of the cruise, edited by Edward P. Montague. It gives an account of the personal adventures of the voyagers, and of what they saw and heard while engaged in this half romantic adventure. The volume contains a map of Palestine."—*American Saturday Courier.*

"This work does not lay claim to any peculiar scientific character. It is a personal narrative, kept during the time between the starting of the expedition in November, 1847, and its return in December, 1848. The Author describes in an easy, off-hand style, rather more carelessly than is desirable, some of the things he saw, and heard, and felt, during the expedition. Its everyday history is thus brought before us, perhaps much more vividly than in more elaborate journals. The writer was one of the party that descended the Jordan from the Lake of Tiberias to the Dead Sea. A part travelled by land, and the remainder in boats. There is a twofold interest connected with this trip on the river. As a mere narrative of travels, it is interesting. But more than this, it gives us an account of the whole length of the Jordan, and thus satisfies the mind of scientific inquirers, in what has been regarded as a singular phenomenon. It is well known that the level of the Dead Sea is 1000 feet below that of the Lake of Tiberias.

"The book will be found a very agreeable companion, opening at least some scenes that are new, and many that are full of interest. It is accompanied by a colored map of the Holy Land, with Jerusalem and its environs."
—*Christian Chronicle.*

"It is an interesting book, and from personal observation of many of the scenes described, we can vouch for its correctness, although the writer is evidently unacquainted with the customs of the Arabs. Those fond of narrations of an adventure, will find it much to their liking, and the scientific will do well to peruse it by way of creating a thirst for the more able work on the same subject, which we shall probably soon have."—*Boston Bee.*

"Messrs. Carey & Hart have just published a Narrative of the late Expedition to the Dead Sea, complied from the diary of one of the party. It is filled with the incidents and adventures, and is handsomely illustrated with maps, &c., and altogether one of the most interesting books we have lately come across."—*Pittsburgh Daily Despatch.*

"It occupies a volume of over three hundred pages, and is from a diary by one of the party. It is illustrated with a map of the Holy Land, handsomely colored, and furnishes interesting sketches of incidents and adventures, from the time of the sailing of the expedition in November, 1847, until the return of the same in December, 1848. This is one of the most entertaining publications of the day. It is printed in good style, and is handsomely bound."—*Phila. Inquirer and Courier.*

"This is a very agreeable and entertaining work, presenting life in new aspects, even where, as on ship-board, it has been already so much written about. The deeper interest of the narrative begins with the start, or rather the first attempt to start, over the mountains of Syria, for the great scene of the labors of the expedition of the Dead Sea. The voyage from Lake Tiberias, where the boats safely arrived by land carriage, down the rapid and winding Jordan, with the leaps over numerous falls; the spectacle of the thousands of pilgrims bathing in the Jordan, in the celebration of the baptism of Jesus; the explorations of the mysterious Dead Sea; all this is described in a rapid sketchy manner indeed, but furnishing a good outline of things."—*Christian Register.*

"It tells the incidents of the voyage, and of the explorations of the party, in an easy, gossiping style, and is altogether a most entertaining book. The writer seems to have settled in his own mind that the Dead Sea covers the site of Sodom and Gomorrah, and even believes that the pillar of salt is the true representation of Lot's wife. Whether he is right or wrong, it will trouble any one to prove that his opinions are incorrect."—*Evening Bulletin.*

"This is a very lively account of an undertaking that has been the subject of a great deal of remark, and which has furnished an immense number of paragraphs to the newspaper press. The author takes the reader as it were to the classical scenes he visited, and acts the part of an intelligent guide. The style of the book is agreeable and easy, and the facts which it contains will be found useful. The execution of the volume is good, and it has a handsome map of Palestine."—*Boston Daily Times.*

"Our readers have doubtless noticed several publications in relation to this volume, in which it is stated that the author did not accompany the expedition further than to Kaiffa, where the expedition embarked. If so, he has managed to prepare a very interesting volume upon the hearsay of others."—*Baltimore American.*

"The book is an interesting one, and among persons who take pleasure in the explorations of this Expedition, will meet with ready sale."—*The City Item.*

"Presents many things of interest that will not be found in the elaborate report of the Expedition."—*Worcester Palladium.*

"We have seen many favorable notices of this very amusing volume, and trust that it will find its way into the hands of all our readers."—*Burlington Gazette.*

"This Narrative interests by the incidents of travel on ship and shore growing out of the Expedition."—*Col. Herald.*

"It is an authentic journal, beyond doubt, of all the events which occurred in the Expedition—not as amplified, probably, as the official narrative will be, but still possessing interest as a personal narrative—commencing with the sailing of the vessel, and terminating on her return."—*Noah's Weekly Messenger.*

THE FAMILY ENCYCLOPEDIA
OF
USEFUL KNOWLEDGE
AND
GENERAL LITERATURE.

CONTAINING ABOUT

FOUR THOUSAND ARTICLES, UPON SCIENTIFIC AND POPULAR SUBJECTS, DESIGNED FOR INSTRUCTION AND AMUSEMENT.

WITH COLORED ENGRAVINGS.

BY REV. JOHN L. BLAKE, D. D.,

Author of a General Biographical Dictionary, and other works on Education and General Literature.

SEVENTH EDITION.

In One Volume, 8vo., full bound.

THE ART OF RHETORIC
OR THE
ELEMENTS OF ORATORY.

ADAPTED TO THE PRACTICE OF THE STUDENTS OF GREAT BRITAIN AND IRELAND.

METHODICALLY ARRANGED FROM THE ANCIENT AND MODERN RHETORICAL WRITERS, VIZ:

Aristotle, Cicero, Dionysius of Halicarnassus, Isocrates, Plato, Quintilian, Vossius, Petrus Ramus, Cyp. Soarius, Dugard, Blackwall, Blair, Burton, Butler, Farnaby, Lowe, Rollin, Smith, Walker, Archbishop of Cambray, Messrs. de Port Royal, etc. etc.

BY JOHN HOLMES,

Late Master of the Public Grammar School of Holt, Norfolk, (England.)

TO WHICH IS ADDED

QUINTILIAN'S COURSE OF AN ANCIENT ROMAN EDUCATION,

From the pupil's first elements, to his entrance into the school of oratory; a new and carefully corrected edition, in two books, entirely remodeled; for the use of schools, academies and colleges.

BY JOHN A. GETTY, A.M.

In One Volume, 12mo.

THE ENCYCLOPEDIA OF CHEMISTRY,
THEORETICAL AND PRACTICAL.

PRESENTING A COMPLETE AND EXTENDED VIEW OF THE PRESENT STATE OF

CHEMICAL SCIENCE.

BY JAMES C. BOOTH,

Member of the American Philosophical Society; Professor of Technical Chemistry in the Franklin Institute, etc. etc.

ASSISTED BY

CAMPBELL MORFIT,

Practical and Analytic Chemist; Author of "Applied Chemistry," "Chemical Manipulations," etc.

SHEEP HUSBANDRY IN THE SOUTH;

COMPRISING A TREATISE ON THE

ACCLIMATION OF SHEEP IN THE SOUTHERN STATES,

AND

AN ACCOUNT OF THE DIFFERENT BREEDS:

ALSO,

A COMPLETE MANUAL OF BREEDING, SUMMER AND WINTER MANAGEMENT, AND OF THE TREATMENT OF DISEASES.

With Portraits and other Illustrations.

IN A SERIES OF LETTERS FROM

HENRY S. RANDALL, Esq.,

OF COURTLAND VILLAGE, N. Y.,

TO

R. F. W. ALLSTON, Esq.,

OF SOUTH CAROLINA.

Complete in One Volume. 8vo.

THE DEERSTALKERS;

OR,

CIRCUMSTANTIAL EVIDENCE.

A TALE OF THE SOUTH-WESTERN COUNTIES,

BY FRANK FORESTER,

Author of "The Warwick Woodlands," "My Shooting Box," "Field Sports of America," &c.

ILLUSTRATED BY THE AUTHOR.

In One Volume, 12mo. Price Fifty Cents.

A MAN MADE OF MONEY.
A NOVEL.
BY DOUGLAS JERROLD,
Author of "Mrs. Caudle's Curtain Lectures," "Story of a Feather," &c. &c.
Complete in One Volume. Price 25 Cents.

"The very commencement of the volume testifies to having been written by the same hand that penned the "Caudle Lectures," of popular memory. Its accuracy as a daguerreotype of domestic happiness can be testified to by more than one husband who suffers his family to live beyond their means, that the wife and daughters may struggle up to a circle a little above their own."—*Saturday Post.*

VALERIE,
A TALE.
BY THE LATE CAPTAIN MARRYAT, R. N.,
Author of "Peter Simple," &c. &c.
COMPLETED BY A LITERARY GENTLEMAN.
In One Volume. Price 25 Cents.

"A new work by Capt. Marryat must always be attractive. This is his *last* work. He commenced it, but death, which came upon him whilst he was engaged in it, did not allow him to complete it. 'A Literary Gentleman' has taken it in charge and finished the story. There is an invention, a humor, and a vigor about all Capt. Marryat's writings which gave to them a particular charm, that at once takes hold of the reader and carries him to the end."—*Western Continent.*

STRAY SUBJECTS,
ARRESTED AND BOUND OVER;
BEING THE FUGITIVE OFFSPRING OF THE
"OLD 'UN," AND THE "YOUNG 'UN."
With Illustrations by Darley.

"The *two* wittiest sketch-writers in the country."

"We were only enabled to get through it short of fits, by bandaging—if persons read it without this precaution, we cannot answer for consequences, but shall expect every day to hear of a coroner's inquest—verdict, died a laughing."—*Jones' Advertiser.*

"A clever duodecimo volume, the sight of which will dispel the fogs from the brains of the most inveterate lovers of the dismal."—*Saturday Rambler.*

"It is a rare collection of wit, and warranted as a sure cure for the blues."—*Portland Argus.*

"Sketches which have had a wide circulation and popularity."—*N. Y. Sunday Atlas.*

"If any of our friends have the horrors, we recommend this book as a never failing remedy; it is running over with wit, humor and sarcasm."—*Newport News.*

THE FEMALE POETS OF AMERICA.
BY RUFUS W. GRISWOLD.

In One Volume, Octavo.

WITH SIX FINELY ENGRAVED ILLUSTRATIONS.

"Mr. Griswold has made greater and more important contributions towards preserving a record of the literature of America than any other man in the country, and we are happy to know that the public have shown a just appreciation of his efforts.

"In the present volume he has given selections from more than ninety of the poetesses of America, the writings and even the names of some of whom had almost been lost in the lapse of time and on the dusty shelves of old libraries. Accompanying these selections are ably and vigorously written biographical and critical notices of these authoresses and their poetry.

"The selection will be found a rare addition to our literature, and we have seen none so full, both as regards the specimens and the information contained in the remarks of the editor."—*Hunt's Merchant's Magazine.*

"A work which, after a careful examination, we venture to pronounce the best production which has yet come from the pen of Dr. Griswold, and the most valuable contribution which he has ever made to the literary celebrity of the country.

"His biographical narratives display a great deal of spirit and tact. His criticisms exhibit a thorough familiarity with the writings which he reviews, and are animated with sensibilities and perceptions kindred in their delicacy and ardor with that inspiration from which the verses themselves have flowed."—*N. Y. Tribune.*

"Dr. Griswold has performed the duties of his undertaking with a diligence, a taste, and a discrimination which we doubt whether any man in this country could have equaled."—*Home Journal.*

"Which cannot fail to please the intelligent reader."—*Baltimore American.*

"Like Shakspeare, it is not for a day, but for all time."—*N. Y. Mirror.*

"Anything from Mr. Griswold is welcomed as coming from an old and tried friend of the public.—*Newark Advertiser.*

RUDIMENTARY CHEMISTRY,
FOR THE USE OF BEGINNERS.

BY GEORGE FOWNES, F.R.S.,

Professor of Practical Chemistry in University College,
Author of "Elementary Chemistry, Theoretical and Practical."

IN ONE VOLUME.

Price 25 Cents.

"A valuable little book, written by an author of established reputation."

THE LIFE

OF

MAJ. GEN. PETER MUHLENBERG,

OF THE

REVOLUTIONARY ARMY.

BY HENRY A. MUHLENBERG.

IN ONE VOLUME, 12mo.

WITH A PORTRAIT.

"The perusal of this volume has proved a great treat to us."

"We rather devoured than read it, and, in two sittings, every syllable and word in the book came under our eye, and we regretted that the volume was not twice as large. It is the General's *military life* merely which is narrated; but this is exceedingly interesting, and in it many important Revolutionary incidents are detailed which have never before fallen under our notice. The author has executed his task with considerable ability; he is never tedious, always interesting and instructive, and the public will doubtless evince their high appreciation of the merits of the publication by buying up the first edition in a very short time."—*Lutheran Observer.*

"Mr. Muhlenberg's work is modestly and faithfully executed, and gives an interesting and valuable sketch of his relative's life and services."—*Boston Atlas.*

ELEMENTS OF AGRICULTURE;

FOR THE USE OF

PRIMARY AND SECONDARY SCHOOLS.

BY L. BENTZ, OF FRANCE,

Director of the Normal Primary School of the Muerthe, Member of Royal and Central, Societies of Nancy and Aurilliac,

AND

A. J. CRETIEN DE ROVILLE,

Professor of Rural Economy in the same School, Member of Agricultural Society of Nancy, &c. &c.

TRANSLATED AND ADAPTED TO THE USE OF THE RURAL PRIMARY SCHOOLS OF THE UNITED STATES,

BY F. G. SKINNER.

"The above work fully supplies all these deficiencies, and we endorse the remarks made by C. Mandel in his report to the Central Agricultural Society of the Muerthe in France, that the teacher may with confidence draw on its pages for all that seems to be of primary necessity for himself first, and then for the children or adults committed to his care. He might with equal justice have added, that it should be a text-book in every school in our country; that every agriculturist would, in studying its contents, derive pleasure from their perusal, and profit from their practical application."—*Baltimore American.*

Printed in Great Britain
by Amazon.co.uk, Ltd.,
Marston Gate.